This book poses incisive and provocative questions, providing critical insights to transitional justice literature. Its analysis of the various dynamics generated when dealing with the problem of enforced disappearances in different countries enriches this fascinating field by providing systematic comparisons and analytic sophistication.

Paloma Aguilar Fernández, *Departamento de Ciencia Política y de la Administración, Facultad de Ciencias Políticas y Sociología, UNED, Spain*

At a time when scholars and policymakers continue to grapple with the challenges of how best to deal with the troublesome legacies of past conflict, Iosif Kovras' exploration of the silences surrounding the missing people is particularly timely and welcome. Kovras systematically identifies the economic, legal, political and ideological factors contributing to support for, or opposition to, truth recovery. This book will be of immense value not only to scholars in the field, but to politicians, lawyers and policymakers and those who are interested or involved in transitional justice and peacemaking.

Professor Marie Breen-Smyth, *Associate Dean International FAHS, Professor of International Politics and Director of Research, University of Surrey, UK*

Truth Recovery and Transitional Justice

This book investigates why some societies defer transitional justice issues after successful democratic consolidation.

Despite democratization, the exhumation of mass graves containing the victims from the violence in Cyprus (1963–1974) and the Spanish Civil War (1936–1939) was delayed until the early 2000s, when both countries suddenly decided to revisit the past. Although this contradicts the actions of other countries such as South Africa, Bosnia and Guatemala where truth recovery for disappeared/missing persons was a central element of the transition to peace and democracy, Cyprus and Spain are not alone: this is an increasing trend among countries trying to come to terms with past violence.

Truth Recovery and Transitional Justice considers the case studies of Spain and Cyprus and explores three interrelated issues. First, the book examines which factors can explain prolonged silence on the issue of missing persons in transitional settings. It then goes on to explore the transformation of victims' groups from opponents of truth recovery to vocal pro-reconciliation pressure groups, and examines the circumstances in which it is better to tie victims' rights to an overall political settlement. Finally, the author goes on to compare Spain and Cyprus with Greece – a country that remains resistant to post-transitional justice norms.

This book will be of interest to students of transitional justice, human rights, peace and conflict studies and security studies in general.

Iosif Kovras is a Research Fellow at Queen's University, Belfast (Institute for the Study of Conflict Transformation and Social Justice).

Contemporary Security Studies
Series Editors: James Gow and Rachel Kerr
King's College London

This series focuses on new research across the spectrum of international peace and security, in an era where each year throws up multiple examples of conflicts that present new security challenges in the world around them.

NATO's Secret Armies
Operation Gladio and terrorism in Western Europe
Daniele Ganser

The US, NATO and Military Burden-sharing
Peter Kent Forster and Stephen J. Cimbala

Russian Governance in the Twenty-First Century
Geo-strategy, geopolitics and governance
Irina Isakova

The Foreign Office and Finland 1938–1940
Diplomatic sideshow
Craig Gerrard

Rethinking the Nature of War
Edited by Isabelle Duyvesteyn and Jan Angstrom

Perception and Reality in the Modern Yugoslav Conflict
Myth, falsehood and deceit 1991–1995
Brendan O'Shea

The Political Economy of Peacebuilding in Post-Dayton Bosnia
Tim Donais

The Distracted Eagle
The rift between America and Old Europe
Peter H. Merkl

The Iraq War
European perspectives on politics, strategy and operations
Edited by Jan Hallenberg and Håkan Karlsson

Strategic Contest
Weapons proliferation and war in the Greater Middle East
Richard L. Russell

Propaganda, the Press and Conflict
The Gulf War and Kosovo
David R. Willcox

Missile Defence
International, regional and national implications
Edited by Bertel Heurlin and Sten Rynning

Globalising Justice for Mass Atrocities
A revolution in accountability
Chandra Lekha Sriram

Ethnic Conflict and Terrorism
The origins and dynamics of civil wars
Joseph L. Soeters

Globalisation and the Future of Terrorism
Patterns and predictions
Brynjar Lia

Nuclear Weapons and Strategy
The evolution of American nuclear policy
Stephen J. Cimbala

Nasser and the Missile Age in the Middle East
Owen L. Sirrs

War as Risk Management
Strategy and conflict in an age of globalised risks
Yee-Kuang Heng

Military Nanotechnology
Potential applications and preventive arms control
Jurgen Altmann

NATO and Weapons of Mass Destruction
Regional alliance, global threats
Eric R. Terzuolo

Europeanisation of National Security Identity
The EU and the changing security identities of the Nordic states
Pernille Rieker

Conflict Prevention and Peacebuilding in Post-War Societies
Sustaining the peace
Edited by T. David Mason and James D. Meernik

Controlling the Weapons of War
Politics, persuasion, and the prohibition of inhumanity
Brian Rappert

Changing Transatlantic Security Relations
Do the US, the EU and Russia form a new strategic triangle?
Edited by Jan Hallenberg and Håkan Karlsson

Theoretical Roots of US Foreign Policy
Machiavelli and American unilateralism
Thomas M. Kane

Corporate Soldiers and International Security
The rise of private military companies
Christopher Kinsey

Transforming European Militaries
Coalition operations and the technology gap
Gordon Adams and Guy Ben-Ari

Globalization and Conflict
National security in a 'new' strategic era
Edited by Robert G. Patman

Military Forces in 21st Century Peace Operations
No job for a soldier?
James V. Arbuckle

The Political Road to War with Iraq
Bush, 9/11 and the drive to overthrow Saddam
Nick Ritchie and Paul Rogers

Bosnian Security after Dayton
New perspectives
Edited by Michael A. Innes

Kennedy, Johnson and NATO
Britain, America and the dynamics of alliance, 1962–68
Andrew Priest

Small Arms and Security
New emerging international norms
Denise Garcia

The United States and Europe
Beyond the neo-conservative divide?
Edited by John Baylis and Jon Roper

Russia, NATO and Cooperative Security
Bridging the gap
Lionel Ponsard

International Law and International Relations
Bridging theory and practice
Edited by Tom Bierstecker, Peter Spiro, Chandra Lekha Sriram and Veronica Raffo

Deterring International Terrorism and Rogue States
US national security policy after 9/11
James H. Lebovic

Vietnam in Iraq
Tactics, lessons, legacies and ghosts
Edited by John Dumbrell and David Ryan

Understanding Victory and Defeat in Contemporary War
Edited by Jan Angstrom and Isabelle Duyvesteyn

Propaganda and Information Warfare in the Twenty-First Century
Altered images and deception operations
Scot Macdonald

Governance in Post-Conflict Societies
Rebuilding fragile states
Edited by Derick W. Brinkerhoff

European Security in the Twenty-first Century
The challenge of multipolarity
Adrian Hyde-Price

Ethics, Technology and the American Way of War
Cruise missiles and US security policy
Reuben E. Brigety II

International Law and the Use of Armed Force
The UN charter and the major powers
Joel H. Westra

Disease and Security
Natural plagues and biological weapons in East Asia
Christian Enermark

Explaining War and Peace
Case studies and necessary condition counterfactuals
Jack Levy and Gary Goertz

War, Image and Legitimacy
Viewing contemporary conflict
James Gow and Milena Michalski

Information Strategy and Warfare
A guide to theory and practice
John Arquilla and Douglas A. Borer

Countering the Proliferation of Weapons of Mass Destruction
NATO and EU options in the Mediterranean and the Middle East
Thanos P. Dokos

Security and the War on Terror
Edited by Alex J. Bellamy, Roland Bleiker, Sara E. Davies, Richard Devetak

The European Union and Strategy
An emerging actor
Edited by Jan Hallenberg and Kjell Engelbrekt

Causes and Consequences of International Conflict
Data, methods and theory
Edited by Glenn Palmer

Russian Energy Policy and Military Power
Putin's quest for greatness
Pavel Baev

The Baltic Question during the Cold War
Edited by John Hiden, Vahur Made and David J. Smith

America, the EU and Strategic Culture
Renegotiating the transatlantic bargain
Asle Toje

Afghanistan, Arms and Conflict
Armed groups, disarmament and security in a post-war society
Michael Bhatia and Mark Sedra

Punishment, Justice and International Relations
Ethics and order after the Cold War
Anthony F. Lang, Jr.

Intra-State Conflict, Governments and Security
Dilemmas of deterrence and assurance
Edited by Stephen M. Saideman and Marie-Joëlle J. Zahar

Democracy and Security
Preferences, norms and policy-making
Edited by Matthew Evangelista, Harald Müller and Niklas Schörnig

The Homeland Security Dilemma
Fear, failure and the future of American security
Frank P. Harvey

Military Transformation and Strategy
Revolutions in military affairs and small states
Edited by Bernard Loo

Peace Operations and International Criminal Justice
Building peace after mass atrocities
Majbritt Lyck

NATO, Security and Risk Management
From Kosovo to Khandahar
M. J. Williams

Cyber Conflict and Global Politics
Edited by Athina Karatzogianni

Globalisation and Defence in the Asia-Pacific
Arms across Asia
Edited by Geoffrey Till, Emrys Chew and Joshua Ho

Security Strategies and American World Order
Lost power
Birthe Hansen, Peter Toft and Anders Wivel

War, Torture and Terrorism
Rethinking the rules of international security
Edited by Anthony F. Lang, Jr. and Amanda Russell Beattie

America and Iraq
Policy-making, intervention and regional politics
Edited by David Ryan and Patrick Kiely

European Security in a Global Context
Internal and external dynamics
Edited by Thierry Tardy

Women and Political Violence
Female combatants in ethno-national conflict
Miranda H. Alison

Justice, Intervention and Force in International Relations
Reassessing just war theory in the 21st century
Kimberley A. Hudson

Clinton's Foreign Policy
Between the Bushes, 1992–2000
John Dumbrell

Aggression, Crime and International Security
Moral, political and legal dimensions of international relations
Page Wilson

European Security Governance
The European Union in a Westphalian world
Charlotte Wagnsson, James Sperling and Jan Hallenberg

Private Security and the Reconstruction of Iraq
Christopher Kinsey

US Foreign Policy and Iran
American–Iranian relations since the Islamic revolution
Donette Murray

Legitimising the Use of Force in International Relations
Kosovo, Iraq and the ethics of intervention
Corneliu Bjola

The EU and European Security Order
Interfacing security actors
Rikard Bengtsson

US Counter-terrorism Strategy and al-Qaeda
Signalling and the terrorist world-view
Joshua Alexander Geltzer

Global Biosecurity
Threats and responses
Edited by Peter Katona, John P. Sullivan and Michael D. Intriligator

US Hegemony and International Legitimacy
Norms, power and followership in the wars on Iraq
Lavina Lee

Private Security Contractors and New Wars
Risk, law, and ethics
Kateri Carmola

Russia's Foreign Security Policy in the 21st Century
Putin, Medvedev and beyond
Marcel de Haas

Rethinking Security Governance
The problem of unintended consequences
Edited by Christopher Daase and Cornelius Friesendorf

Territory, War, and Peace
John A. Vasquez and Marie T. Henehan

Justifying America's Wars
The conduct and practice of US military intervention
Nicholas Kerton-Johnson

Legitimacy and the Use of Armed Force
Stability missions in the post-Cold War era
Chiyuki Aoi

Women, Peace and Security
Translating policy into practice
Edited by Funmi Olonisakin, Karen Barnes and Ekaette Ikpe

War, Ethics and Justice
New perspectives on a post-9/11 world
Edited by Annika Bergman-Rosamond and Mark Phythian

Transitional Justice, Peace and Accountability
Outreach and the role of international courts after conflict
Jessica Lincoln

International Law, Security and Ethics
Policy challenges in the post-9/11 world
Edited by Aidan Hehir, Matasha Kuhrt and Andrew Mumford

Multipolarity in the 21st Century
A new world order
Edited by David Brown and Donette Murray

European Homeland Security
A European strategy in the making?
Edited by Christian Kaunert, Sarah Léonard and Patryk Pawlak

Transatlantic Relations in the 21st Century
Europe, America and the rise of the rest
Erwan Lagadec

The EU, the UN and Collective Security
Making multilateralism effective
Edited by Joachim Krause and Natalino Ronzitti

Understanding Emerging Security Challenges
Threats and opportunities
Ashok Swain

Crime–Terror Alliances and the State
Ethnonationalist and Islamist challenges to regional security
Lyubov Grigorova Mincheva and Ted Robert Gurr

Understanding NATO in the 21st Century
Alliance strategies, security and global governance
Edited by Graeme P. Herd and John Kriendler

Ethics and the Laws of War
The moral justification of legal norms
Antony Lamb

Militancy and Violence in West Africa
Religion, politics and radicalisation
Edited by Ernst Dijxhoorn, James Gow and Funmi Olonisakin

Mechanistic Realism and US Foreign Policy
A new framework for analysis
Johannes Rø

Prosecuting War Crimes
Lessons and legacies of the International Criminal Tribunal for the Former Yugoslavia
Edited by James Gow, Rachel Kerr and Zoran Pajić

The NATO Intervention in Libya
Lessons learned from the campaign
Edited by Kjell Engelbrekt, Marcus Mohlin and Charlotte Wagnsson

Truth Recovery and Transitional Justice
Deferring human rights issues
Iosif Kovras

Truth Recovery and Transitional Justice
Deferring human rights issues

Iosif Kovras

LONDON AND NEW YORK

First published 2014
by Routledge
2 Park Square, Milton Park, Abingdon, Oxfordshire OX14 4RN
and by Routledge
711 Third Avenue, New York, NY 10017

First issued in paperback 2016

Routledge is an imprint of the Taylor & Francis Group, an informa business

© 2014 Iosif Kovras

The right of Iosif Kovras to be identified as author of this work has been asserted by him in accordance with sections 77 and 78 of the Copyright, Designs and Patents Act 1988.

All rights reserved. No part of this book may be reprinted or reproduced or utilized in any form or by any electronic, mechanical, or other means, now known or hereafter invented, including photocopying and recording, or in any information storage or retrieval system, without permission in writing from the publishers.

Trademark notice: Product or corporate names may be trademarks or registered trademarks, and are used only for identification and explanation without intent to infringe.

British Library Cataloguing in Publication Data
A catalogue record for this book is available from the British Library

Library of Congress Cataloging-in-Publication Data
Kovras, Iosif, 1983–
Truth recovery and transitional justice : deferring human rights issues / Iosif Kovras.
  pages cm. – (Contemporary security studies)
  Includes bibliographical references and index.
  1. Truth commissions–Case studies. 2. Human rights–Political aspects–Case studies. 3. Disappeared persons–Case studies. 4. Political violence–Cyprus–History–20th century. 5. Spain–History–Civil War, 1936–1939–Atrocities. I. Title.
  JC580.K68 2014
  323'.044–dc23   2013038674

ISBN 13: 978-1-138-65020-6 (pbk)
ISBN 13: 978-0-415-63883-8 (hbk)

Typeset in Times New Roman
by Wearset Ltd, Boldon, Tyne and Wear

To a wonderful family (Andromachi, Christos, Vasilis, Efpraxia, Simone and Manolia)

Contents

List of illustrations   xviii
Acknowledgements   xix
List of acronyms   xxi

1 Truth recovery for missing persons and the global diffusion of 'truth'   1
Transitional justice and truth recovery 3
The concept of truth and a critique of the literature 6
Research questions and hypotheses 10
The puzzles 12
Greece: resisting post-transitional justice 14
Central argument 14
Book outline 15

PART I
Prolonged silences   19

2 Spain: the persistence of the 'pact of silence'   21
The questions 24
Alternative explanations 25
Transition and hegemonic frames 26
Societal silence 33
Political institutions 36
PSOE: forgetting the past or pragmatic considerations? 39
Conclusion 41

3 The prevention of truth recovery for missing persons in Cyprus   43
Alternative explanations 47
Framing, transition and policy outcomes 49

xvi Contents

Missing frames 50
Three framing strategies to address the problem 52
Hegemonic belief 54
Political learning 55
Institutions and political culture 58
Institutionalized victims' associations 60
Conclusion 62

4 Cases compared: hegemonic silence and the 'linkage trap' 67
The rule of law and amnesties in transitions 70
'Revealing is healing'? 73
Hagiography of victims 74

PART II
Post-transitional justice 89

5 The crumbling of the pact of silence in Spain 81
The puzzles 83
Alternative explanations 84
Political opportunities 85
The volte face of Aznar 87
'Desaparecidos' and the split in the memory movement 90
Polarization and political opportunities 92
The 2004 election and the 'second transition' 96
The 'super judge' 99
Elite framing 100
Conclusion 104

6 The success story of the Cyprus problem 106
Linkage negotiations 108
The limitations of the 'linkage' strategy in the RoC 109
The first indications of delinkage at the Ministry of Foreign
  Affairs 111
The turning point 112
The 'missed chance' of 1997 113
The implementation of delinkage policy 114
Overcoming the debacle in the CMP 116
The volte face of Turkey under AKP 117
The ECtHR and Turkey's moderation 118
Ousting Denktaş 120
Delinking exhumations from truth recovery 121

Contents xvii

The emergence of a new vocal actor: relatives across the
  divide 122
Conclusion 124

7   **The Greek puzzle**   127
    Alternative explanations 131
    The Greek path to reconciliation 132
    Linkage of truth recovery to a sensitive national issue 137
    Party ideology: limited socialization to human rights norms 142
    Conclusion 145

8   **Cases compared: belated truth-seekers and post-transitional**
    justice   148
    Post-transitional justice: overcoming the 'linkage trap' 149
    Patterns of post-transitional justice 150
    Political learning 151
    Revised international normative framework 152
    Advancements in forensic science 154
    Resisting post-transitional justice 156
    Delinkage lessons for transitional justice 157

9   **Conclusion 'unearthing the truth'**   160
    Overview of findings 161
    Constructing and maintaining silence 162
    Delinkage and breaking prolonged silences 162
    The role of ideas in transitional justice 165
    Policy considerations 106
    The soft power of Europe 107
    Victims' groups: good intentions, positive outcomes? 107

    Da Capo   169

    Appendix: short timeline   170

    List of interviews   174
    Bibliography   176
    Index   203

Illustrations

Figures

3.1 The map of the distribution of Greek-Cypriot and Turkish-Cypriot missing. The Greek-Cypriot missing of the summer of 1974 are pictured in white and the Turkish-Cypriot of the 1963 to 1965 and the 1974 periods are in grey and black, respectively   44
3.2 The map of the Aghiou Konstantinou ke Elenis cemetery, Nicosia; 2β depicts the mass grave of the fallen during the coup of July 1974, while 3, 4, 5 and 6 depict the mass graves of the fallen during the Turkish invasion   46
4.1 Schematic presentation of the construction and maintenance of (hegemonic) silence   67
5.1 The map of exhumations in Spain in 2010   82
5.2 Self-positioning of the Spanish electorate   95
6.1 Evaluation of the CMP   106
7.1 Military cemetery in Florina   128
7.2 Field where the victims of the battle of Florina are buried   129
8.1 Schematic presentation of the emergence of the politics of exhumations   151

Tables

1.1 Summary presentation of Schools of Transitional Justice   4
5.1 Self-position of the Spanish electorate   95
5.2 Intention of voting PSOE   98

Acknowledgements

To a significant extent, this book is about learning from the past. When it comes to writing these lines of gratitude, authors necessarily screen the years preceding the completion of the book to identify those persons and institutions that contributed to their project. In my case, I feel that this influence was not limited to the level of the academic inquiry, but was a broader process of personal development. Over the course of this project, I learned a great deal from bright minds and from my own mistakes (both academic and personal).

This project originally started as a PhD thesis at Queen's University, Belfast, where I had the good fortune to work with three incredible supervisors, Adrian Guelke, Neophytos Loizides and Roberto Belloni, without whom it would have been impossible to complete this book. Adrian acted as a safe compass guiding my scattered ideas. I am particularly indebted to Neo, for being an excellent role model throughout my doctoral research. Working with him was one of the most fruitful experiences of my doctoral research. Although our collaboration with Roberto was brief, his contribution was equally useful in setting the foundations for a feasible project. I am also very grateful to the Political Studies Association of Ireland for awarding me the Basil Chubb Prize for best PhD thesis published in 2012.

Over the past few years, I have been privileged to work in vibrant academic environments in both Europe and the US, which greatly benefited the project. I am especially grateful to friends and colleagues at Queen's University, Belfast, for showing their interest in my research and supporting it in every possible way. Queen's also granted me a studentship, without which it would have been impossible to start working on this project. After completing my thesis, I spent a year at the University of Athens, where I worked with Dimitri Sotiropoulos, whose experienced guidance is very much appreciated. I am also grateful to the General Secretariat for Research and Technology, which funded my research in Greece.

Special thanks go to the Seeger Center for Hellenic Studies at Princeton University, where I completed this book. I am particularly indebted to its Director, Dimitri Gondicas, not only for providing ideal working conditions, but for encouraging and supporting me. I would also like to thank Marianne for spending a wonderful year together.

xx Acknowledgements

I would like to thank PIO, Cyprus, for its generous financial aid to conduct the second part of my fieldwork in Cyprus. During my fieldwork in Greece, Cyprus and Spain, I met a number of interesting people whose ideas helped me to shape the book. I feel particularly privileged to have established personal relations with Paloma Aguilar, Achilleas Antoniades, Giorgos Antoniou, Nancy Bermeo, Marie Breen-Smyth, Paul Sant Cassia, Bruce Clark, Costas Constantinou, Lisa Davis, Hastings Donnan, Paco Ferrándiz, Joseph Joseph, Stathis Kalyvas, Kostis Kornetis, Nikolas Kyriakou, Evan Liaras, Shaun McDaid, Kieran McEvoy, Louise Mallinder, Yiannis Papadakis, Nikos Philippou, Oliver Richmond, Nukhet Sandal and Nicos Trimikliniotis. All took a deep personal interest in my research.

PRIO, Cyprus and the Hellenic Studies Program at Yale receive thanks for inviting me to test some of my findings before a knowledgeable audience and get insightful feedback.

I am grateful to Elizabeth Thompson for her invaluable assistance in editing this book and Katerina Tsiligiri for her assistance in translating certain parliamentary debates in Spanish. I am particularly indebted to Sara Clavero, who put a great deal of personal effort into helping me improve my Spanish. Thanks go to the archivists as well, the 'gatekeepers of knowledge', in all three countries who facilitated my access to archival material. I am also grateful to the editorial and production team of Routledge for being so supportive.

Earlier versions of some of the chapters in this book were published in several articles, including: 'Explaining Prolonged Silences in Transitional Justice: The Disappeared in Cyprus and Spain', *Comparative Political Studies*, vol. 46 (2013), pp. 730–756; 'Delinkage Processes and Grassroots Movements in Transitional Justice', *Cooperation and Conflict*, vol. 47(1) (2012), pp. 88–105; 'Protracted Peace Processes: Policy (Un)learning and the Cyprus Debacle', *Ethnopolitics*, vol. 11(4) (2012), pp. 406–423 (with Neophytos Loizides); 'Delaying Truth Recovery for Missing Persons', *Nations and Nationalism*, vol. 17(3) (2011), pp. 520–540 (with Neophytos Loizides); 'Unearthing the Truth: The Politics of Exhumations in Cyprus and Spain', *History and Anthropology*, vol. 19(4) (2008), pp. 371–390; 'Non-Apologies and Prolonged Silences in Post-Conflict Settings', Special Issue on Memory and Historical Injustice, *Time and Society*, vol. 21(1) (2012), pp. 71–88 (with Kathleen Ireton). I am grateful to these journals for their permission to use part of the material in this book.

After five years of isolation from my closest friends, special thanks to Katia, Dimitris, Andreas and Yiannis, who have never stopped supporting, encouraging and believing in me. I am extremely lucky to have shared the happiest and most difficult moments of recent years with Dimitra, who never lost patience. I feel very privileged to be a member of a family that offers generous warmth and encouragement, so thanks to Christos for being a great father, Andromachi for her abundant love and Efpraxia, Simone and Manolia for cheering me up. Last, and certainly not least, I am grateful to my father Vasilis, whose life taught me the value of patience and determination in overcoming obstacles.

Acronyms

AAAS	American Association for the Advancement of Science
AKEL	Progressive Party for the Working People
AKP	Justice and Development Party
ARMH	Association for the Recovery of Historical Memory
CIS	Centre of Sociological Studies
CMP	Committee on Missing Persons
CONADEP	National Commission on Disappeared Persons
DIKO	Democratic Party
DISY	Democratic Rally
DSE	Democratic Army of Greece
EAAF	Argentine Forensic Anthropology Team
EAM	National Liberation Front
ECtHR	European Court of Human Rights
EDA	United Democratic Left
EOKA	National Organization of Cypriot Struggle
ERC	Republican Left of Catalonia
ETA	Basque Homeland and Freedom
EU	European Union
FYROM	Former Yugoslav Republic of Macedonia
ICMP	International Commission on Missing Persons
ICTR	International Criminal Tribunal for Rwanda
ICTY	International Criminal Tribunal for the Former Yugoslavia
IDEA	Institute for Democracy and Electoral Assistance
IU	United Left
KKE	Greek Communist Party
ND	New Democracy
PASOK	Panhellenic Socialist Movement
PCE	Spanish Communist Party
PP	Popular Party
PSOE	Spanish Socialist Workers' Party
RENAMO	Mozambican National Resistance
RoC	Republic of Cyprus

SYRIZA	Coalition of the Radical Left
TRNC	Turkish Republic of Northern Cyprus
UCD	Union of the Democratic Centre
WGEID	Working Group on Enforced and Involuntary Disappearances

1 Truth recovery for missing persons and the global diffusion of 'truth'

A few years before the beginning of the Spanish Civil War, Federico García Lorca said: 'In all countries death is an end. It comes, and the curtains are closed. Not in Spain. [...] In Spain the dead are more alive than in any other country in the world' (cited in Spicer 2006: 10). His words proved prophetic. Executed in the first month of the civil war (July 1936) and thrown into an unmarked grave in the region of Granada (Gibson 1979), this prominent poet and playwright is one of approximately 30,000 victims of the Spanish Civil War still lying in mass graves.[1] Today, his death continues to haunt Spain more than seven decades after his execution.

The recent wave of exhumations taking place throughout Spain has made tracing Lorca's burial site more feasible. However, this prospect instigated a heated debate between his family (who oppose exhumation and re-burial, because they want him to rest in peace) and leading intellectuals, who insist that the execution of the poet symbolizes a repressive era and, as such, his exhumation will not only symbolically expose this Francoist repression, but more importantly will detach the country from this legacy. In effect, Lorca encapsulates a central debate in contemporary Spanish society: should the country 'unearth' the truth and historical memory related to the civil war or is it better to continue to 'silence' the divisive past?

The impact of civil war on Spanish society was so traumatic that even 70 years after its conclusion people are reluctant to talk about it. Added to this, the death of General Franco was followed by a transition to democracy founded on the institutionalized pact of silence over past atrocities. Recently, however, this pact has been challenged. A wave of new social movements, the most visible of which is the Association for the Recovery of Historical Memory (ARMH),[2] have emerged since 2000 with two primary objectives. The first, and more fundamental, objective is to unearth the remains of those lying in unmarked mass graves and provide them with a decent burial. The second is to exert pressure on the promotion of policies of public acknowledgement of the suffering of (Republican) victims of the Spanish Civil War and, more generally, to recover historical memory. Both have achieved relative success: by the end of 2007, more than 3,000 victims had been exhumed and identified (Congram and Steadman 2009: 162); by the first quarter of 2010, more than 1,850 mass graves had been re-opened. In addition, in October 2007, the Socialist Government passed the Law of Historical Memory, which satisfies most of the demands of these associations: denouncing Franco's regime; banning public symbols that commemorate Franco or his allies; mandating local governments to finance exhumations of mass graves; declaring the summary military trials during the Spanish Civil War and Francoist dictatorship as 'illegitimate'; opening up military archives; and offering other measures of moral, symbolic and economic repair to all victims of the war.[3]

Spain is not the only Mediterranean country in the European Union (EU) currently dealing with its ghosts. During two waves of violence in Cyprus, the inter-communal violence (1963–1974) and the subsequent Turkish invasion (1974), approximately 2,000 Greek-Cypriots and Turkish-Cypriots went missing. Disappearances were political acts deployed at times by both communities to cleanse the island of the presence of the ethnic 'other' and fulfil official political objectives. In the 1960s, hundreds of Turkish-Cypriots were abducted, executed and buried in remote areas by Greek-Cypriot extremists in an effort to intimidate the Turkish-Cypriot community and promote the much-desired *enosis* (unification) with Greece (Patrick 1976). In the summer of 1974, it was the turn of the invading Turkish Army, with the collaboration of Turkish-Cypriot paramilitaries, to use this instrument to promote their own political objective of *Taksim* (partition).

The social representation of victim groups as 'moral beacons' and the subsequent instrumental exploitation of their suffering to construct 'cultures of victimhood' constitute central features of most societies emerging from communal violence (Breen-Smyth 2007: 76). Hence, after the cessation of hostilities (1974), the issue of the missing was again politicized, this time to legitimize official positions adopted by the two sides in negotiations for the reunification of the island. For the Greek-Cypriot community, these persons are still 'missing' (yet to be found), revealing their willingness to frame the problem in human rights terms in a bid to garner global support and attribute blame to Turkey for the ongoing suffering of Greek-Cypriots (Sant Cassia 2005: 22). By way of contrast, Turkish-Cypriot authorities perceived their own missing to be 'martyrs' (*şehitler*), who sacrificed their lives to protect the community from Greek-Cypriot repression. In short, the problem was deployed by both sides to symbolize the impossibility of peaceful coexistence and, ultimately, to legitimize the policy of partition (ibid.). Over the decades, for both societies, the problem of the missing has become a 'chosen trauma' (Volkan 1997: 49).

Even so, in 2004, a bi-communal agreement was reached to resume the activities of the Committee on Missing Persons (CMP) – a mechanism established in 1981, but never operationalized. Surprisingly, by 2012, it was probably the most successful bi-communal project on the island.[4] By February 2013, 1,012 bodies had been exhumed and 477 identified through its activities (CMP 2013).[5] However, the process has caused extensive political debate. On the one hand, the fruitful cooperation between Greek and Turkish-Cypriot scientists in the CMP,[6] along with the resolution of one of the most intractable issues of the Cyprus conflict, lends credence to the argument that these processes have the potential to act as building blocks of rapprochement and reconciliation. On the other hand, equally legitimate arguments are put forward by more sceptical observers, who say that if the only breakthrough is the exhumation of the missing, without even prosecuting those responsible, the prospects of reconciliation remain minimal.

Irrespective of the prospects for a political solution to the Cyprus problem, the CMP has provided many families with some form of closure in one of the prickliest issues of the Cyprus problem. The focus of this analysis is on why the two societies could not resolve these issues for decades and, more interestingly, why they recently changed their minds and re-opened this painful chapter. This phenomenon of delayed justice – also called 'post-transitional justice' – has gained ground over the past decade (Aguilar 2008; Collins 2010). For example, following Chile and El Salvador, Brazil and Turkey recently decided to set up fact-finding commissions, dealing with the problem of their disappeared and the traumatic past more broadly (Collins 2010; *The Economist* 2010).

Interestingly, despite similar background conditions, Greece remains resistant to this trend, challenging both theory and regional experience. One of the biggest unopened mass graves in Europe, containing approximately 700 to 800 victims of the Greek Civil War in 1940s, is in northern Greece. Despite similar or even more conducive conditions for truth recovery, including the 'ruptured' transition to democracy in 1974 and the early incorporation of political parties representing the defeated into mainstream politics, this grave remains closed, and issues related to past human rights violations have been neglected. Along with considering why some societies decide to act, the present work asks why others, such as Greece, resist post-transitional justice.

Transitional justice and truth recovery

Trials, truth commissions, policies of lustration, commemorations, revision of history textbooks and apologies have attracted the lion's share of academic attention in transitional justice literature as the most appropriate means to address a violent past.[7] The literature proposes the deployment of an appropriate combination of tools to achieve reconciliation and heal fractured relationships in societies emerging from conflict. Two broad clusters of theory have emerged from this overarching approach. The first, guided by a 'logic of appropriateness', argues for the need to re-evaluate past human rights abuses as a central prerequisite to reconciliation; this group is subdivided into scholars promoting a retributive/punitive approach in dealing with past human rights abuses and those supporting a more 'restorative' conceptualization of justice (Snyder and Vinjamuri 2003: 7).[8] The second has been guided by realpolitik considerations and subscribes to the view that it is not always possible or even necessary to tackle the past – at least in the period following the transition – to achieve reconciliation. Table 1.1 encapsulates the main differences of these approaches to transitional justice. As the table makes clear, while reconciliation is a common objective, the approaches differ considerably in their choice of instruments with which to promote

Table 1.1 Summary presentation of Schools of Transitional Justice

	Logic of appropriateness		Logic of consequences
	Retributive model	Restorative model	Realist model
Unit of Analysis	Individual(s)	Community	State
Means	Trials/Law	Truth	Amnesty laws
Objectives	(a) establish 'factual' truth; (b) punish perpetrators; reconciliation by individualizing guilt	(a) Restore broken relations; (b) reintegrate perpetrators in community; (c) establish common version of past	(a) Democratic consolidation; (b) stability; (c) reintegration of spoilers
Critique	(a) exclusion of victims' demands; (b) depoliticization of politics of memory; (c) risk of instability; (d) Western imposition	(a) Can truth (alone) heal a society?; (b) risk of instability	(a) Can democracy be established without human rights?; (b) limited trust to nascent institutions

reconciliation (trials, truth and amnesties), their units of analysis (individual, community and state) and their conceptualization of reconciliation per se.

The common thread linking scholars subscribing to the 'logic of appropriateness' is the belief that tackling the past in the aftermath of a conflict or an authoritarian regime constitutes a moral imperative. Following this line of argument, the undeserved suffering of the victims (and/or their relatives) should be acknowledged (Biggar 2003). Within this 'idealist' body of literature, there are both *retributive* and *restorative* strands.

One the one hand, it has been argued that in societies emerging from mass human rights abuses 'justice should be done'. Retributive justice constitutes a universally acceptable model of acknowledgement (Orentlicher 1991), whose legitimizing moment is the post-World War II Nuremberg trials. In this view, societies that acknowledge (factual) truth about the violent past have better prospects of strengthening the rule of law and respect for human rights and, more generally, of educating citizens in democratic practices (Elster 2004; Kaminski et al. 2006; Long and Brecke 2003; Popkin and Roht-Arriaza 1995). Efforts to compromise justice by using other forms of acknowledgement – such as amnesties or even truth commissions – are eschewed (Méndez 2001: 32). Proponents say punitive approaches that individualize guilt onto specific perpetrators prevent societies from attributing responsibility to whole communities – a significant cause of political violence. Finally, truth-seeking through retributive measures produces an authoritative version of the past – based on 'uncontested' evidence – which prevents deployment of the past for political purposes (Orentlicher 1991).

Equally important is the 'deterring function' of justice in post-conflict settings: preventing potential spoilers from engaging in similar heinous activities in the future. Recent research shows that states are increasingly deploying policies of accountability to deal with past violence, not only for strategic reasons, but also because they domesticate international accountability norms (Kim and Sikkink 2010; Sikkink 2011). The wider diffusion of these accountability norms has the potential to realize the Kantian/liberal peace thesis, whereby ultimately all democratic societies will not go to war with each other, setting the stage for global reconciliation. And in this respect, it is true that over the past few decades, a growing number of post-conflict societies have adopted retributive models of justice, leading to a 'justice cascade' (Sikkink 2011).

Scholars subscribing to this logic of appropriateness frequently adopt restorative arguments to justify the acknowledgment of past human rights abuses, such as enforced disappearances. In essence, truth recovery is seen as both a moral imperative and the most effective seed with which to yield a harvest of peace, stability and reconciliation (Feher 1999; Kiss 2001). As Michael Ignatieff puts it, the objective of truth recovery is 'to reduce the number of lies that can be circulated unchallenged in public discourse' (1998: 173). Truth recovery has the potential to uproot long-standing myths that serve as the founding tenets of collective (national) identities that bolster cultures of victimhood (Galanter 2002; Gibson 2006; Hayner 1996, 2002; Norval 1998; Rosenblum 2002). Establishing an official version of truth not only 'breaks the cycle of hatred' (Minow 2002), but under certain circumstances could contribute to forgiveness (Philpott 2006; Torrance 2006), while revised collective identities could set the stage for intergroup reconciliation (Kelman 1999).

The healing power of truth is central in restorative approaches, precisely because the unit of analysis is the community (relations). In restorative forms of justice, trading truth for amnesties is not perceived as handing out immunity; rather, the healing function of truth recovery is deemed a prerequisite of reconciliation and, therefore, a superior form of justice (Asmal *et al.* 1996; Boraine 2000). If Nuremberg is the legitimizing myth for scholars subscribing to retributive justice, then the South African Truth and Reconciliation Commission is the standard for restorative approaches.

Not surprisingly, scholars subscribing to the 'logic of consequences' (Snyder and Vinjamuri 2003: 7) often disagree with the idealists. They argue that because (negotiated) transitions/peace agreements are particularly fragile processes (Higley and Burton 1989; Hesse and Post 1999; Licklider 1995), any effort to comprehensively address the past may upset certain people who perceive any truth recovery initiative as blatant scapegoating, causing them to become spoilers and endangering the transition or implementation of a peace settlement (Newman 2002; Vinjamuri and Snyder 2004: 355). It is true that an official acknowledgement of the past constitutes a legitimate goal, but the overarching objective of any transition/peace settlement is the consolidation of democratic institutions and the rule of law. As realist scholars consider the state as the main unit of analysis, in principle, this is the only possible form of reconciliation.

If this requires the sacrifice of a comprehensive screening of past human rights abuses, then societies should be ready to adopt amnesties that could contribute to peace. As Snyder and Vinjamuri say: 'Justice does not lead; it follows' (2003: 6).

In essence, the decision to address the past or to avoid it depends on the balance of power between the former enemies during the transition. Samuel Huntington's findings in *The Third Wave*, where he scrutinizes countries experiencing transition during the so-called 'third wave' of democratization, indicate that 'in actual practice what happened was little affected by moral and legal considerations. It was shaped almost exclusively by politics, by the nature of the democratization process, and by the distribution of political power during and after the transition' (1991: 212). Therefore, scrutinizing the past is not a normative decision but a political one and, as such, any measure that might contribute to the stability and consolidation of the regime can be legitimately used, even if this requires the adoption of amnesties, impunity or forgetting (Mallinder 2007; Meister 1999).

Truth recovery is to be expected only in cases where, during transition, the violators of human rights are weak and lack sufficient power to negotiate amnesties (Snyder and Vinjamuri 2006). Scholars in this camp underscore successful reconciliation in several societies that deployed amnesties during the third wave of democratization, such as Spain.[9]

All in all, the three strands of the literature refer to the same objective, reconciliation, but adopt rather different conceptualizations of reconciliation, focus on different levels of analysis and prioritize different tools. It is not mere coincidence that all three are dominated by scholars coming from different disciplines. Broadly speaking, legal scholars dominate and promote retributive approaches, theologians and psychologists support a restorative justice, while political scientists adopt a state-centric approach, guided by realpolitik considerations. The important point is that all support a different type of truth regarding missing persons, so it is worth taking a close look at the conception of truth in the literature.

The concept of truth and a critique of the literature

Truth, transitional justice and reconciliation are relatively new concepts that emerged concurrently with a wider normative turn in the early 1990s. The emergence of truth recovery as a central tool in transitional justice is a stark illustration of the wider *volte face*. In the 1980s, truth commissions were established in Latin American countries as a 'second-best' alternative, given the impossibility of trying those responsible for the disappearances and other heinous human rights breaches. Since the 1990s, however, the functions of truth have been considerably broadened. In the aftermath of the South African Truth and Reconciliation Commission (TRC), truth came to be valued as a universally acceptable model of peace-building, based on the argument that revealing is healing (Hirsch 2007). In fact, truth is now a central tool in the transitional justice toolbox of the most prestigious international organizations, including the United Nations (UN) (UN 2004). Nevertheless, it remains questionable whether this 'one-size-fits-all' approach reflects the demands of local communities (Richmond 2005a; Richmond and Franks 2009) or whether these concepts have become tools used by domestic elites to promote their own political agendas, leading to the phenomenon of 'hijacked' transitional justice (Subotic 2009).

Even central working concepts in the study of transitional justice, though, such as truth recovery and reconciliation, remain vague, since there is no single agreed-upon definition. To begin with, although defining 'truth' has been a central philosophical debate for centuries, it seems that transitional justice literature has evaded the necessity to acknowledge its complex nature. Undoubtedly, forensic evidence from mass graves can establish some elements of 'factual truth' that cannot be contested. Still, even the most celebrated venues of 'acknowledging the truth' in the literature, such as trials or truth commissions, analyse individual narratives through a kaleidoscopic view of the past that seeks to establish a new mental framework to make sense of complex and confusing past events (Wilson 2003: 370). Therefore, verdicts of trials and final reports of truth commissions frequently exclude, obscure or marginalize other accounts that contravene this framework (De Brito *et al.* 2001: 25; Leebaw 2011). A fundamental question is to what extent truth is even retrievable in such complex political contexts as post-conflict settings, especially as individuals/victims who have suffered extremely violent experiences frequently develop resistance mechanisms to cope with trauma, as a result of which their memory changes retrospectively.

Although the concept of truth recovery in transitional settings has gained currency, it has been used to refer to a wide range of different – even contradictory – phenomena. It remains contested whether truth recovery constitutes a means to a higher end (i.e. reconciliation) or an end/value in itself. It is equally undetermined if truth refers to a process (i.e. truth-telling) or an outcome (i.e. report of a truth commission). Nor have scholars determined whether the scope of truth is individual (micro-truth) or social (macro-truth). Taking all these into consideration, truth in transitional justice literature is an overstretched concept, used to describe different societal processes by different scholars, often leading to a dialogue of the deaf.

In essence, the literature fails to address a number of ontological, epistemological and political problems. To avoid this problem, this book adopts a bifurcated view of truth recovery. The analysis acknowledges the multifaceted nature of truth, while it adopts a critical stance to the (purported) functions of truth recovery presented by the literature.

On the one hand, *narrow truth recovery* is used to refer to a minimalist conception of truth – more precisely, to forensic evidence relating to the whereabouts of disappeared/missing persons. Since the early 1990s, forensic exhumations have become a conventional tool of international institutions in addressing the individual and narrow demand for truth (Stover *et al.* 2003: 663–664). On the other hand, *wider truth recovery* indicates the official and unofficial efforts of societies emerging from conflict or authoritarian regimes to 'democratize' the process of dealing with the past (Breen-Smyth 2007), by broadening accessibility to the public discourse of previously excluded voices. These range from truth commissions to tribunals, traditional justice, community storytelling initiatives and official apologies. Needless to say, these conceptions of truth frequently overlap. Truth recovery for missing persons illustrates this effort to acknowledge/'unearth' a truth hitherto buried: political exhumations as truth recovery disrupt hegemonic schemes and legitimize previously unacceptable versions of the truth.

A stark limitation of the literature is the lack of rich empirical evidence to delimit the credibility of the proffered arguments. In fact, the still nascent body of literature is guided by principles, causing certain scholars to call it a 'faith-based' discipline (Thoms *et al.* 2008). Frequently, the primary objective of the literature is to convince readers of the need for a comprehensive screening of the past, often based on normative assumptions, rather than empirically rich analyses (Mendeloff 2004). This is also reflected in the descriptive nature of the majority of analyses, which focus on the strengths and limitations of specific transitional justice tools or on explaining why certain societies have adopted specific tools (Backer 2009: 50).

Another significant limitation deriving from the descriptive and normatively coloured literature is the *absence of long-term evaluations of transitional justice measures*. Its status as a nascent field, established only in the mid-1990s, may explain why scholars have tended to describe events, rather than establishing cause and effect relationships. As the literature focuses almost exclusively on specific debates (i.e. peace versus justice and truth versus justice) (Hayner 2002; Kritz 1997; Minow 1998; Roht-Arriaza and Mariezcurrena 2006; Rotberg and Thompson 2000), other fundamental questions remain under-studied, such as the reasons why some societies silence certain aspects of their past and defer truth recovery.

Even realist scholars who have been analytically quite coherent in explaining the (non-)solution of human rights issues have failed to comprehensively address this question. Although societies during transition may decide to defer solving human rights issues, this does not necessarily mean that a demand to acknowledge this reality will not emerge in the future. By focusing explicitly on the period of transition or the period immediately following it, the literature has failed to address two analytically central issues. First, even when societies decide to silence their past, *how is this silence being constructed and perpetuated*? Second, *why* and *when* do the same societies decide to *break the silence and revisit their past*?

The literature of transitional justice has reserved its main attention for a small number of well-known cases where transitional justice measures have been applied, such as South Africa, Yugoslavia and Rwanda, frequently with a relative degree of success (Brahm 2007; Wiebelhaus-Brahm 2010; Thoms *et al.* 2008). Little notice has been taken of cases where transitional justice is absent, such as Cyprus and Spain. The absence of comparative analysis or comparisons of specific tools, such as the implementation of truth commissions in two different post-conflict settings, have inhibited efforts to establish causal patterns and an analytically sound theoretical framework based on rich empirical evidence.

Moreover, the *raison d'être* of transitional justice is the restoration of broken social relationships, and the major novelty of this approach is that for the first time the demands of victims are at the centre of academic and policymaking agendas. Still, the literature has not explored who should be considered victims, what victims demand, why different victims' groups demand different forms of acknowledgment or why these groups use their moral/symbolic capital to bolster nationalism and 'cultures of victimhood' (Breen-Smyth 2007: 77). Instead, all victims are uncritically treated as a homogeneous unit, thus limiting the explanatory value of this approach.

Finally, the literature has been dominated by a narrow 'peace versus justice' debate, which has left little space for thinking outside this analytical framework (Rotberg and Thompson 2000; Vinjamuri and Snyder 2004). Little attention has been paid to the complex relationship between the management of specific human rights problems – most notably, the missing – and the prospect of reconciliation. Even those scholars who have tackled the issue see a negative relationship between enforced disappearances and the prospect of reconciliation in post-conflict settings, both at individual and political levels (Clark 2010). It has been argued that at the individual level, unresolved trauma prevents closure (Cretoll and La Rosa 2006: 355–362; Robins 2013). As long as relatives are distressed by the unknown fate of their loved ones, any reconciliation initiative is doomed to fail, because open wounds tend to 'fester' (Kiss 2001: 71). Nor can families bury their relatives according to culturally embedded rituals that facilitate the mourning process (Robins 2013). In essence, the relatives of missing persons live in a parallel 'trauma time' that inhibits any effort to restore broken relations (Edkins 2003: xiv). It has also been argued that the perpetuation of this situation prevents victims from being able to 'accept and acknowledge the suffering of others' (Clark 2010: 432). As long as empathy constitutes a precondition of reconciliation, pending human rights issues – especially relating to the missing – prevent reconciliation (Blaaw and Lähteenmäki 2002).

The literature has argued that the issue of the missing impedes reconciliation at the political level, too. Following the predominant view in the transitional justice literature cited above that revealing is healing (Hirsch 2007; IDEA 2003), in the absence of truth recovery on the fate of the missing, it is impossible to convince members of society that there has been a clean break with the past – a prerequisite of national reconciliation. The approach of social psychology to conflict resolution constructs an image of victims' groups as 'moral beacons', who justify inflicting harm on opponents seen as responsible for the crimes (Breen-Smyth 2007: 76). Alternatively put, because missing persons and dead bodies have significant symbolic capital, the problem is often hijacked for nationalistic purposes. The institutionalization of this culture of victimhood, which turns missing persons into symbols of the ongoing suffering of society, often blocks a comprehensive debate about the violent past reconciliation (Kovras and Loizides 2011).

Even so, in certain cases and against all odds, positive transformation is achieved. Consider, for example, the instructive story of the Cypriot CMP mentioned above and the ensuing grassroots mobilization. A main weakness of the literature is its temporal and analytical focus reserved exclusively for policies implemented during or immediately after the transition. The majority of analyses merely describe the strengths and limitations of specific transitional justice tools or explain why certain societies adopt certain tools (i.e. truth commissions versus trials) (Backer 2009: 50). It is no coincidence that the lion's share of critical attention has been reserved for a small number of cases where transitional justice is implemented with a relative degree of success. Little notice has been taken of cases where transitional justice is absent, such as in Cyprus or Spain (Kovras 2013). The descriptive nature of the literature is reflected in its static picture of missing persons and its failure to account for positive transformations, leaving out or ignoring how positive transformation frequently occurs in the absence of an official transitional justice policy. Nor can this picture explain the clash between the humanitarian demands of relatives and the 'evidentiary' needs of official transitional justice mechanisms, such as international tribunals (Stover and Shigekane 2002: 846).

By studying the occasional and admittedly puzzling transformation of sensitive and intractable human rights problems into building blocks of reconciliation, as in Cyprus, academic and policymakers may discover innovative ways to reconcile tensions. Resolving sensitive human rights issues that carry enormous symbolic capital can pave the way for meaningful reconciliation in frozen conflicts, as in Abkhazia, Nagorno-Karabakh, Kashmir and Lebanon.

Research questions and hypotheses

This book aspires to contribute to the limited knowledge on truth recovery related to human rights issues, with specific emphasis on the problem of enforced disappearances/the missing[10] as a result of political violence in societies emerging from conflict or authoritarianism. More precisely, it focuses on four overlapping questions. First, why do some post-conflict societies defer the recovery of those who forcibly disappeared as a result of political violence, even after a fully-fledged democratic regime is consolidated? Although there is an implicit agreement that silence is consolidated during transitional periods, it is important to shed analytical light on how (if at all) transitional justice settlements persist over time. Second, why and under what circumstances do the same societies decide after several decades to resolve these human rights issues and break the silence, leading to the novel phenomenon of *post-transitional justice*? This is an important contribution of the book, as a growing number of democracies, such as Brazil, Turkey and Spain, have started to adopt post-transitional justice policies. Third, the book highlights the neglected role of victims' groups in post-conflict settings, as well as their struggle to recover the truth. To this end, a central question is to determine which processes can address the occasional and puzzling transformation of victims' groups from opponents of truth recovery to vocal pro-reconciliation pressure groups. Fourth and finally, the book draws on conflict resolution literature to enhance the understanding of dealing with protracted human rights problems during transitions. Under which conditions, is it better to tie victims' rights to an overall political settlement? Alternatively, is it better to treat human rights issues separately?

The analysis tests several theoretically grounded hypotheses treating human rights problems as both dependent and independent variables. To begin, it explores the role of ideas (Lustick 1993) and the process of deployment of human rights issues in constructing hegemonic beliefs. The book also investigates security threats posed by a truth recovery initiative to the nascent regime. Furthermore, drawing on the literature of conflict resolution, it considers alternative negotiating strategies, such as 'linking' (or 'delinking') human rights issues to a political settlement (Lohman 1997). It considers the extent to which different actors, such as civil society groups, political parties and bureaucracies, influence outcomes, especially in the recovery of truth. Alternative hypotheses on the activities of victims' associations and bureaucrats are explored, such as political opportunities (Tarrow 1998), elite socialization (Risse and Sikkink 1999), political learning (Bermeo 1992) and strategic adaptation (Moravcsik 2000).

After selecting its cases, the book carefully traces the causal mechanisms and the outcomes that are not convincingly explained by the literature (George and Bennett 2005: 215). Its tracing of the construction of silence and truth recovery is based on data collected during fieldwork in Spain, Cyprus and Greece. More than 80 interviews were conducted with relatives' associations, policymakers, political elites, academics and members of NGOs actively engaging with historical memory in all three countries.[11] I have carried out wide-ranging archival work, including analysis of parliamentary debates to trace the construction of elite discourse(s) on the issue. In addition, I had limited access to classified documents from the Cypriot House of Representatives, as well as memos prepared for the Ministry of Foreign Affairs of the Republic of Cyprus (henceforth, RoC). I took a close look at a number of party documents, such as electoral programmes and party memoranda, to scrutinize the development of political discourse on the topic. My interviews with political elites shed light on the timing of change in the two countries, along with their deployment of specific measures – in this case, exhumations. Finally, I have utilized interviews with individuals with privileged information, such as top bureaucrats and policymakers, to 'triangulate' hypotheses (Tansey 2007).

The book deploys an innovative, multi-method approach to the study of framing and social movements, including 'elite framing' (Benford and Snow 2000; Gamson 1992; Goffman 1974; Loizides 2009), drawing on an extensive and comprehensive study of parliamentary speeches over the last three decades. Framing is 'to select some aspects of a perceived reality and make them more salient in a communicating text, in such a way as to promote a particular problem, definition, causal interpretation, moral evaluation, and/or treatment recommendations' (Entman 1993: 52). It should be mentioned that framing is not an epiphenomenon. It is not a reflection of reality, but a simplification of a 'perceived reality'. In essence, framing is the deliberate effort of different social actors to produce, guide and maintain meanings for their constituents; as such, it is important to examine how specific political problems are framed (Benford and Snow 2000: 613). More importantly, by examining framing strategies, we can establish cause and effect relationships.

To examine elite framing of the *desaparecidos* in Spain and the 'missing' in Cyprus, the analysis draws on the two countries' parliamentary debates since the mid-1970s, as well as looking at the Greek Parliament since 1974 to establish the framing of the memory of the Greek Civil War. Parliamentary debates are extremely useful in the study of elite framing, as they depict framing at a very specific point in time, without the actors being able to retrospectively change their positions to suit temporal changes in context. They also facilitate process-tracing, since an examination of debates illuminates the construction, maintenance and, in certain circumstances, revision of elite framing. Finally, in addition to the debates, I gained privileged access to certain classified documents of the Cypriot Parliament and memos prepared for the Ministry of Foreign Affairs of the RoC; these filled important gaps in the activities of the CMP.

The puzzles

As Edward Newman has rightly pointed out, there is an intrinsic paradox in societies emerging from conflict/authoritarian regimes: '[S]ome sense of justice is necessary to move forward; it is integral to the peace and democratization process. But stability, inclusion and support for all actors make the search for truth and justice difficult' (2002: 33). This is a pressing dilemma that all societies emerging from authoritarianism or conflict have at some point faced. As mentioned, the central objective of this book is to explain why certain societies decide to 'silence', or selectively silence, some aspects of their past related to human rights violations and how this silence is constructed, maintained and perpetuated. Similarly, why and in what circumstances do the same societies decide, even after several decades have passed, to resolve these human rights issues, leading to the emergence of the phenomenon of post-transitional justice?

Cyprus, Spain and Greece are well-suited to test certain arguments of the literature. The transition (Spain and Greece) or the cessation of hostilities (Cyprus) in all three societies took place well before the normative turn in the 1990s, and all have abstained from implementing any transitional justice measures. Although Greece was one of the first countries to implement transitional justice policy to deal with human rights abuses carried out by the military junta (1967–1974), no similar measures were taken with regard to the civil war – the focal point of this analysis. Hence, three societies where impunity and minimal demand for truth reigned for decades are used to comprehensively test the central arguments of transitional justice literature – namely, that early truth recovery strengthens the rule of law, educates citizenry into human rights practices and assists democratic consolidation.

The time-lag permits us to draw safer conclusions, test alternative hypotheses and examine causal patterns of silence/non-silence about human rights abuses than would be possible in more recent cases. In fact, because these human rights issues emerged well before the normative turn in international politics, at a time when foreign intervention for human rights was minimal, the countries provide instructive examples of how societies used to manage humanitarian problems in the absence of the 'international factor'.

The book addresses several puzzles. The first is that Cyprus remains the only divided country where despite the absence of an overall political settlement and the prevalence of nationalist discourses in both communities, a remarkable breakthrough has been achieved as regards one of the prickliest and most sensitive issues – that is, the problem of missing persons. How can one explain the remarkable transformation of a mechanism that had been inoperative for almost 25 years into a successful bi-communal project? The literature suggests that these issues have better chances of being solved during or immediately after transition when popular support is high (Elster 2004: 77; O'Donnell and Schmitter 1986). But Cyprus proves the literature wrong. What lessons can be exported from the study of the Cypriot 'success story' on the issue of the disappeared? How is positive transformation achieved in intractable human rights problems, *even in the absence of a political settlement*? Why do societies decide to change their decades-long policies and promote truth? Which actors facilitate or impede these processes?

A second major puzzle derives from the study of Spain. The vast majority of the disappeared went missing during the Spanish Civil War (1936–1939), hence it would have been incongruous to expect these issues to be resolved during the Francoist regime (1939–1975). During the transition to democracy (1975), as expected by the realist school of thought, Spanish society and political elites decided to establish a pact of silence and literally bury these complex issues. Although this development is predicted by the literature, it is puzzling that Spain, 70 years after the conclusion of the civil war and almost 30 years after the consolidation of democracy, decided to make an impressive *volte face* and start digging into its past. Moreover, it is odd that the Spanish Socialist Party, *Partido Socialista Obrero Española* (henceforth, PSOE), heir to the Republican tradition and the defeated side in the civil war, did nothing to address and redress truth recovery for 12 consecutive years (1982–1996) following its election to government.

Finally, it is illogical that although other societies with less advanced legal and institutional tools in their power mobilized earlier and more effectively to address the demand for truth and acknowledgment for the disappeared, this did not happen in Cyprus and Spain earlier, even though they were members of prestigious international organisations. One would expect that societies with more advanced legal instruments would be more proactive and effective in resolving humanitarian issues, but, paradoxically, this is not the case for the countries under scrutiny.

Greece: resisting post-transitional justice

The book probes the generalizability of the two main case studies by using Greece as a control case. Greece took an entirely different trajectory; here, silence was prolonged, despite similar or even more conducive background conditions. Absolute numbers are missing, but the most reliable sources say that more than 2,000 combatants remain unaccounted for since the civil war in the 1940s, and neither the Greek state nor the actors representing the defeated have mobilized to address this issue. Added to this, the region of Florina has one of the biggest unopened mass graves in Europe, with the remains of combatants of the Democratic Army of Greece (henceforth, DSE).

The Greek case becomes even odder if we take into account that its process of democratic consolidation was not bound by a pacted transition, as in Spain; in fact, Greece was one of the first countries to adopt policies of accountability for the military leaders of the junta (Sotiropoulos 2010). Therefore, in theory at least, Greek victims of the civil war had better prospects than the Spanish to address their demands. Similarly, the ruptured transition and the complete delegitimization of the military junta provided space for political parties of the left representing the defeated victims of the Greek Civil War to introduce their demands in mainstream politics. But the Greek Socialist Party, *Panhellenic Socialist Movement* (henceforth, PASOK), took only minimal steps to address the legacy of the civil war, despite consecutive terms in government in the 1980s, 1990s and 2000s. Finally, the Greek experience challenges a trend in the region, whereby a growing number of neighbouring countries in the Balkans and south-eastern Europe have started to deal with the past, despite a significant delay.

For all these reasons, the Greek experience can shed analytical light on why norms that resonate in certain regions remain feeble elsewhere.

Central argument

Contradicting the emphasis of the literature of transitional justice on mechanisms for a prompt and comprehensive screening of past human rights' abuses as a prerequisite for achieving democratic consolidation and reconciliation (Biggar 2003; De Brito *et al.* 2001), the study of Cyprus and Spain reveals a different (even reverse) story: in this version, a certain minimum level of democratic consolidation and development of democratic institutions provides the necessary tools for potential truth-seekers, promoting truth recovery and acknowledgement of past atrocities, albeit in the long term.

Although victims' groups or their political representatives have significant incentives to promote an alternative version of the truth, these actors are often silenced, either because of the fragile political balance of power or because a comprehensive truth recovery would shed light on notorious aspects of previously admired groups, thereby having the potential to delegitimize the predominant discourse. As time passes, a 'linkage trap' is constructed. Frequently, during the transition to democracy/peace, a subtle agreement is reached between parties previously in conflict to link non-use of the bitter past in the political arena with commitment to the new (democratic) political regime. In this way, silence or selective memories become ingrained in political discourse, either to establish a culture of victimhood (Cyprus) or to achieve other political objectives, such as democratic consolidation (Spain) and political consensus on critical national issues (Greece). In the long term, such elite framing becomes institutionalized and eventually acquires hegemonic status. This linkage often constitutes the most efficient path to peace, stability and democratic consolidation. In Greece, Cyprus and Spain, the decision *not* to unearth the past early on did not prevent the culmination of full-blown democratic regimes. Despite the realities imposed by the de facto partition of the island, the RoC has become a member of the EU – an indication of its democratic credentials.

Paradoxically, this decision (i.e. to remain silent) in the long term provides the institutional tools that allow domestic truth-seekers to carry out a comprehensive truth recovery. In essence, a minimum threshold of democratic consolidation provides the necessary institutional tools to these actors whenever they decide to initiate the process, not the reverse. However, a comparative analysis of the experience of the three countries shows that the most important tool is the deployment of human rights discourse, making socialization of international human rights norms by domestic actors a *necessary* condition of post-transitional justice.

The process of dealing with the past and the shaping of collective memory of traumatic events are inevitably politicized struggles that do not take place in a political vacuum (Leebaw 2011). To understand how and when excluded voices enter into and shape public debates, it is necessary to examine how domestic groups, such as relatives' associations, acquire agency and overcome obstacles, win legal and social battles, form effective alliances and become influential political agents. Hence, to a significant extent, this book is about the relentless struggles of excluded voices to acquire agency and democratize discourse about the past – this is the essence of truth recovery.

Book outline

The book is divided into three parts. The first investigates why civil societies and state elites in Cyprus and Spain remained silent for decades on the issue of the disappeared. It also probes the nature of historical memory. More specifically, Chapter 2 explores the prolonged silence in Spain in the aftermath of the transition to democracy, focusing on the pact of silence that became the central political tenet of its political institutions. Political learning from the painful experiences of the Spanish Civil War contributed to the adoption of this specific framing, which subsequently became institutionalized and silenced dissenting voices. The chapter explores the reasons why several initiatives of relatives attempting to unearth the remains of their family members put forward in the immediate aftermath of the transition were blocked. Chapter 3 unwraps the prevention of truth recovery for missing persons in Cyprus. It highlights the construction of an early elite pact on the issue of the missing by the Greek-Cypriot community and traces the process through which this gradually attained a hegemonic position, preventing an early solution. Equally, the chapter focuses on political learning from previous experiences of intra-communal violence; this was a founding tenet of the elite pact that guided post-1974 politics on the island. It also identifies the causal mechanisms through which this hegemonic belief became institutionalized. Chapter 4 is a comparative chapter; it identifies a causal pattern in the construction of silence and discusses the implications for the study of transitions.

Chapter 5 opens the second part of the book, which investigates the reasons for the recent change and the emergence of the politics of exhumations in Spain. It unveils the new Law of Historical Memory, which tackles the issue of the disappeared and the proactive involvement of civil society in these processes. Chapter 6 follows the transformation of the Cypriot CMP from a defunct body into a successful bi-communal project. It explores the reasons for the *volte face* of the major Cypriot actors (the two communities and Turkey) and the emergence of a bi-communal grassroots group that promotes comprehensive screening of the past. Chapter 7 deploys the experience of the Greek Civil War as a control case to examine the generalizability of the proffered arguments.

Chapter 8, the first chapter of the third part, comparatively explores the experiences of Cyprus, Spain and Greece and investigates the emergence of the phenomenon of post-transitional justice in consolidated democracies. It draws significant theoretical and policy-relevant conclusions from the comparative study of the three countries. Chapter 9, the concluding chapter, summarizes the book's primary findings and contributions. It notes the growing tendency in post-traumatic societies to revise pacts of silence, even after a considerable delay – a trend that reflects the broader normative turn in international politics. Finally, it sums up and explains post-transitional justice.

Notes

1 The estimated number of remains still lying in unmarked mass graves ranges from 30,000 to 100,000 (Ferrándiz 2009).
2 An equally visible group is *Foro Por La Memoria* (Forum for Memory), which has strong affiliations with the Spanish Communist Party.
3 Law 52/2007, 'por la que se reconocen y amplían derechos y se establecen medidas en favor de quienes padecieron per secución o violencia durante la guerra civil y la dictadura' (26 December 2007).
4 The resumption of the activities of the CMP and the exhumations of hundreds of bodies does not mean that it is a clear-cut 'success story'. As will be shown, the restricted mandate of the CMP, precluding wider truth recovery or punitive justice, has disappointed many families. Still, it has managed to provide some elementary form of closure to thousands of families on the island, overcoming important obstacles thrown up by the de facto partition of the island.
5 Of the 477 identified victims, 358 are Greek-Cypriots and 119 are Turkish-Cypriots.
6 The entire project is carried out by bi-communal teams of Greek-Cypriot and Turkish-Cypriot scientists (geneticists, forensic anthropologists and archaeologists).

7 Transitional justice is defined as 'the array of processes designed to address systematic or widespread human rights violations committed during periods of state repression or armed conflict, where human rights violations are defined as extrajudicial killings, disappearances, torture, and arbitrary arrest and imprisonment' (Olsen *et al.* 2010: 805).
8 I draw on the conceptualization of Jack Snyder and Leslie Vinjamuri (2003), who distinguish among 'the logic of consequences', the 'logic of appropriateness' and the 'logic of emotions'. For the purposes of this book, I have slightly changed this categorization, as the most important question with respect to the missing is whether it is important to address this issue during transition (either through punitive or restorative models) or not, thereby implying that amnesty laws may be a legitimate policy with which to deal with the problem. Besides, as the book deploys a bifurcated view of truth recovery, the central question is whether exhumations (i.e. 'narrow truth recovery') alone could be a legitimate policy. The common thread linking retributive and restorative approaches is that exhumations, when decoupled from a 'broader' process of truth recovery, whether trials or a truth commission, inhibit reconciliation; instead, realist scholars suggest that exhumations could be a useful tool to provide closure without destabilizing democracy and the prospects of reconciliation.
9 Critical theorists, such as Bronwyn Leebaw, have shed analytical light on the unproblematic and, at times, superficial depoliticization of the type of memory that both restorative and retributive forms of justice seek to produce (2011).
10 Although 'missing persons' and 'disappeared' refer to distinct legal categories, for the purposes of this book the two terms will be used interchangeably. The book explores the efforts of different societies to deal with tensions and dilemmas arising from their efforts to deal with the problem of the missing/disappeared during transitions. More precisely, according to Article 2 of the International Convention for the Protection of All Persons from Enforced Disappearances, disappearance

> is considered to be the arrest, detention, abduction or any other form of deprivation of liberty by agents of the state or by persons or group of persons acting with the authorization, support or acquiescence of the State, followed by a refusal to acknowledge he deprivation of liberty or by concealment of the fate or whereabouts of the disappeared persons, which place such a person outside the protection of the law.

The definition of a missing person is 'people unaccounted for as a result of international or non-international armed conflict or internal violence' (Crettol and La Rosa 2006: 355).
11 I used 'snowball' sampling, because it facilitates the process tracing approach (Tansey 2007: 770). The full list of interviews can be found in the Appendix.

Part I
Prolonged silences

2 Spain
The persistence of the 'pact of silence'

The Spanish Civil War (1936–1939) took an exceptionally heavy toll on Spanish society. Approximately 95,000 persons were killed by the Nationalist Forces, the 'white terror', and 38,000 individuals died at the hands of the Republicans, the 'red terror' (Juliá 1999; Ruiz 2007).[1] By 1939, approximately 470,000 persons had fled to neighbouring France to escape the Francoist violence, and 15,000 defeated Spaniards were transferred to Mauthausen concentration camp in the aftermath of the conflict (Moreno 1999). Tactics ranged from systematic torture and mass executions to the imprisonment of hundreds of thousands.[2]

In recent decades, Spanish historians have deployed innovative historiographic tools, including oral history and extensive archival research of judicial bodies and public records, to shed light on the violence of the civil war (Graham 2004). Perhaps the most significant finding of this growing body of research is the institutionalized use of violence as a means of instilling terror and legitimizing the foundations of the new regime. To be sure, both sides committed heinous atrocities. Those in the zones controlled by those loyal to the Republicans were carried out as part of a Jacobin-inspired revolution that targeted the 'oppressors', predominantly the wealthy and the clergy (Casanova 2010: 181). The execution of more than 6,000 priests and monks is attributed to segments of the Republican camp (De la Cueva 1998: 355; Frazer 1994: 164–166; Jackson 1965: 285; Maddox 1995; Payne 1990). However, the recourse to extreme levels of violence by the 'rebels'/Nationalists was a calculated process of purifying (*limpieza*) the country of 'anti-Spanish elements', such as Communists, Jews and freemasons (Cazorla-Sánchez 2005; Salvado 2005). The instructions of General Mola are revealing: 'It is necessary to spread an atmosphere of terror. We have to create the impression of mastery [...]. Anyone who is overtly or secretly a supporter of the Popular Front must be shot' (Thomas 1977: 260).

While both parties engaged in a total war, for the Nationalist camp it was not merely a conflict to be won but a crusade, and extreme violence became a constitutive element of the tactics deployed. This explains the disproportionally high levels of casualties away from the front lines (Juliá 1999). Notably, the number of executions was significantly higher in areas that fell immediately into the hands of the Nationalists than in the areas of resistance (Preston 1990). In fact, in the first two months of the war, the number of executions accounted for approximately 50 per cent of all victims during the civil war (Solé i Sabaté and Villaroya 1999: 64). A common form of violence employed by the Nationalist camp was the *paseo*.[3] Victims were detained as 'enemies of Spain'; they were taken for a 'stroll', executed and buried in unmarked graves (ibid.). According to some figures, approximately 38,000 executions were carried out in the zones under Republican control and 100,000 in the Nationalist zone (Juliá 1999; Ruiz 2005).

The Nationalist violence ('white terror') did not decrease with the end of the Spanish Civil War in April 1939. Rather, it became institutionalized and more meticulously designed, passing from 'warm terror' (*terror caliente*) to 'legal terror' (Ruiz 2005; Solé i Sabaté y Vilaroya 1999). It is estimated that 'no less than 50,000 persons died in the first ten years following the official end of the war' (Casanova 2002: 8).[4] The new Francoist state institutionalized repression by employing a wide range of tools, such as imprisonment, internment in concentration camps of approximately half a million Republicans, recruitment of the defeated as forced labour and the institutionalization of the executions of the defeated through judicial measures (Casanova 2002; Cenarro 2003).[5] A renowned illustration of forced labour was the construction of a major Francoist symbol, the *Valle de los Caídos* (Valley of the Fallen). The 'Valley' contains the grave of Franco, along with approximately 40,000 victims of the civil war – mostly Nationalists. Construction of the monument took almost two decades, and it is still the subject of ongoing debate, because it was built by 20,000 Republican prisoners used as forced labour.

In this period of institutionalized repression – under the direction of the military tribunals (*Consejos de Guerra*) – the number of arbitrary executions rooted in vengeance decreased. Probably the most violent period of the post-war repression was from 1947 to 1949, the so-called *triennio del terror*. This period is linked to the efforts of the regime to cleanse the last sources of resistance – organized by the resistance groups (*maquis*) in remote mountain areas. The Francoist regime directed its repressive apparatus at the relatives or neighbours of suspected guerrillas to extract information (Moreno 1999). Ten years after the conclusion of the war, the resumption of executions and *paseos* again increased the number of casualties (ibid.). At the same time, approximately half-a-million people went into exile to escape repression.

This texture of violence explains the creation of the problem of *desaparecidos* (disappeared). During the war, a disproportionate number of casualties included civilians executed in areas far removed from the battlefield (Juliá 1999; Richards 2002). And in the first months of the war, the majority of those executed were buried in unmarked mass graves. According to Solé i Sabaté and Villaroyo:

> Thousands of persons were not registered, while others appeared to be man or woman without being identified.... [T]he dead were not transferred to the cemeteries, so enormous common graves were opened, as in Lardero, a village close to Logrono where they were executed and buried approximately 400 persons.
>
> (1999: 66)

In Tenerife, it is estimated that during the period of civil war and post-war repression, approximately 1,600 persons 'disappeared' in this way (Moreno 1999: 336). This, in combination with the institutionalization of the executions in the post-war repression and the silence/terror instilled in the relatives of the executed, made the recording of the executions difficult, if not impossible. Richards indicates that

> many bodies, to the authorities counted for little in life and were not counted in death.... [A]n explicit order was given that no death certificates be issued even to those family members brave enough to identify the bodies of the executed.
>
> (Richards 1998: 30)

In any event, thousands of Spaniards went missing or were buried in unmarked mass graves without having their deaths recorded.

The problem of disappearances as a result of political violence is a modern phenomenon, most commonly understood to occur in the authoritarian regimes of Latin America in the 1970s and 1980s. In traditional warfare, soldiers are the primary casualties, yet disappearances have become a central feature of the 'new wars'. The Spanish Civil War has features of a 'modern' war, since the texture of violence employed by the Nationalists made the issue of political disappearances and executions (*paseos* and *sacas*) a 'sophisticated instrument of terror [...] intended to bury the social memory of violence and thus to strengthen the fear-based regime of the perpetrators' (Ferrándiz 2006: 7).

Although my present emphasis is on *desaparecidos*, it is crucial to remember the nature of the violence that wounded so many segments of Spanish society. Consider, for example, the children who were taken away from their defeated families for adoption (*niños de la Guerra*) or sent to other countries (*niños del exilio*),[6] the forced labour and the expatriated (*exiliados*), to mention only a few of those affected. In short, the civil war had a lasting impact on Spanish society and politics. It is estimated that in the 1980s, approximately 25 per cent of Spaniards had a relative killed during the war, and two out of three had a relative who fought in the war (Preston 1990: 40).

The end of the civil war and the victory of the Nationalist camp led to a prolonged period of dictatorship (1939–1975) under General Francisco Franco. Unlike other Mediterranean countries belonging to the so-called 'third wave' of democratization, such as Greece and Portugal, where the transition to democracy came as a result of the demise of a dictatorial regime, in Spain, Franco died as state leader. Even so, democratic consolidation has been relatively successful, taking into consideration that the first change in government – serving as a central indication of consolidation, according to the literature – took place in 1982 with the landslide victory of the Spanish Socialist Party (Gunther and Montero 2009). The success of democratic consolidation in Spain can largely be attributed to the 'pacted' nature of the transition, one of the most significant provisions of which was the non-instrumental use of the past as a political tool in public discourse (Blakeley 2008). Until recently, the defeated of the civil war did not demand the restitution of their narrative through inclusion in the public discourse. While victims' groups on the Nationalist side were granted benefits after the civil war and throughout the Francoist 'reign', the vanquished were not compensated, either morally or materially.

The recent wave of exhumations and identification of the remains of those disappeared during the civil war or the post-war repression (Elkin 2006) that began in the early 2000s opened up all sorts of questions about the past, including the official acknowledgement of the illegitimacy of the Francoist regime, free access to the military archives of the civil war, the annulment of the military tribunals' decisions and the implementation of an official policy towards recovering/identifying the bodies of the disappeared (Aguilar 2009). The activities of civil associations resumed (Gálvez-Biesca 2006), leading to the establishment of the Law of Historical Memory (2007) (Crawford 2007). There was also a wave of publications, activities, documentaries and artistic exhibitions on the defeated (Camino 2007; Richards 2002).

The questions

Despite the remarkable success in democratic consolidation, the issue of (narrow) truth recovery for *desaparecidos*, in particular, and (wider) truth recovery of human rights abuses, in general, was not raised until very recently. Undoubtedly, any attempt to recover the truth during the dictatorial regime of Franco was not feasible. However, an interesting question remains: why such a demand did not – or could not – emerge immediately following the restoration of democracy in the late 1970s. An even more puzzling question naturally follows: why the Spanish Socialist Party, PSOE, heir to the Republican tradition and the most significant political group of the Second Republic, did nothing to address and redress the issue of truth recovery or historical memory, even though the party was in government for 14 consecutive years (1982–1996) and its reluctance dissatisfied many constituents.

Despite official recalcitrance, in the early years of the transition to democracy, a number of unofficial exhumations were carried out by families of *desaparecidos* seeking to provide their relatives with a decent burial (Silva and Macias 2009). Furthermore, an archival search of popular magazines of the time reveals a wider demand for truth recovery, with publications covering a range of issues related to the civil war, from the repressive educational system under the Francoist regime to exhumations and the civil war, personal testimonies of ex-prisoners and the student protests of the late 1950s. However, these were not followed by a mass societal mobilization towards recovering the fate of relatives or a wider recovery of truth, as happened in several Latin American societies. This, then, leads to a final pressing question: why did this grassroots wave of truth recovery die?

The first part of this chapter focuses on several possible answers to the above questions. It goes on to note specific features of the transition in Spain, emphasizing the concept of 'partial political learning' from past painful experiences. The chapter analyses the rich empirical evidence to highlight the elite framing of the issue of the *desaparecidos* as found in parliamentary debates, the electoral programmes of the most significant political parties and personal interviews with members of the designated parliamentary committee for drafting the Law of Historical Memory. It also contains comments gleaned from interviews with politicians, activists, academics and journalists familiar with the topic. The chapter shows that one of the founding tenets of the Spanish transition to democracy – namely, not to allow the past to become a political instrument – obtained a hegemonic position, becoming institutionalized and preventing any truth-seeking initiative. It also examines the idea of 'frozen democracy' to shed light on the limited societal demand for truth-seeking. Finally, it discusses PSOE's reluctance to tackle this issue.

Alternative explanations

A popular explanation of the prevention of truth recovery for such an extended period of time in Spain mentions a 'pact of oblivion' (*pacto de olvido*) during the transition to democracy. According to this, the lack of any provision for addressing the past during the transition, epitomized in the blanket amnesty of 1977, coupled with the will of the Spanish people to let bygones be bygones, set the stage for widespread oblivion (Rigby 2000).

As will be illustrated in the following pages, this explanation contains certain analytical insights, but falls short of explaining several questions. For one thing, during the first period of the transition, exhumations of common graves were carried out in several Spanish provinces by relatives of the executed, indicating that, at least for one segment of society, the past was definitely not forgotten (Silva and Macias 2009). Furthermore, as the archival research for this study illustrates (and as noted above), throughout the transition, extensive media attention was brought to bear on the executions and other crimes committed during the civil war (Interviú 1978c: 60–64), the personal testimonies of former prisoners narrating their experiences (Interviú 1978b: 59–61), the repressive educational system (Interviú 1980b: 38–41) and the students' resistance movement of the late 1950s. Finally, the voluminous number of books and films about the civil war contradict this argument of societal forgetting (Aguilar 2008; Edles 1998: 45; Ledesma 2006: 101).[7] Rather, as Santos Juliá has argued, the pacted transition refers to a subtle agreement among political elites *not to let the past become a political instrument* in the nascent democratic life (Juliá 1999). To be sure, as will be shown, the nature of the transition affected and prevented truth recovery, but the 'pact' involved primarily the political elite.

Another popular explanation notes a 'generational aspect'. For certain scholars, the generation of the political leaders who carried out the transition in the late 1970s (the children of the war) did not have first-hand experience of the fratricidal violence; therefore, they were free of the unpleasant heritage of the past (Iguarta and Paez 1997). This generation hypothesis is also used to explain the recent process of the recovery of historical memory; such arguments point to the disengagement of the contemporary generation of leaders (grandchildren of the war) from the legacy of transition and its commitments. While this is an interesting standpoint and offers analytical insight, taken alone it is insufficient to explain why certain societal groups demanded the truth early during the transition (i.e. 1970s) or why they were silenced. It is also difficult to refer to generational groups as a homogeneous unit of analysis, since there are variations even within these groups. Clearly, the passage of time constitutes an important factor in creating new opportunities for truth-seekers, but this is not necessarily related to generational groups. In essence, the temporal aspect, although sometimes important, cannot be a causal determinant.

One might argue that the absence of scientific knowledge, such as DNA testing, previously precluded this kind of effort. If a scientific way of unearthing the truth is missing, post-traumatic societies may prefer to keep the contentious book of the past closed. But to explain truth recovery and the absence of an official acknowledgement, it is necessary to go beyond the technical details of forensic science to consider political resolution, focusing not merely on exhumations, but also on other aspects of the civil war. Why was early interest (i.e. unofficial exhumations) not followed by official policy?

Transition and hegemonic frames

Frames constitute simplified mental representations of reality that elites deploy to interpret social events, enabling them to choose among alternative courses of action (Tetlock 1998: 876). As such, framing is a useful tool for analysing symbolic aspects of a conflict, such as the issue of missing persons. Ervin Goffman defines frames as 'schemata of interpretation' that allow the audience/public 'to locate, perceive, identify and label occurrences within their life space and the world at large' (1974: 21). The chief function of frames is to 'organize experience and guide action' (Snow *et al.* 1986: 464); thus, a core element of the framing process is the degree of instrumentalization in the definition of an issue at hand (Loizides 2009). The framing process determines 'reality' because of its ability to highlight certain aspects and ignore others (Benford 1997; Benford and Snow 2000; Brewer *et al.* 2003). As Entman aptly notes: 'The frame determines whether most people notice and how they understand and remember a problem, as well as how they evaluate and choose to act upon it' (1993: 54). According to Marc Howard Ross:

> [Frames] are normative accounts with heroes and villains and lessons about how life should be lived. They offer in-group versions of the past, including the origin and development of the group; they invoke past threats and conflict and enemies; and they laud group survival. In some cases there is a conscious effort to develop a narrative with an eye toward future political goals.
>
> (Ross 2007: 33)

Before turning to the framing in the Spanish Congress of Deputies, I should note that framing has two analytical components. First, 'diagnostic framing' refers to the identification of the source of the problematic situation at hand and the ascription of blame to the responsible agent(s) (Benford and Snow 2000). In essence, diagnostic framing presupposes a sense of injustice triggered by the action/inaction of another agent and, therefore, feelings of moral indignation and grievances are prevalent in this process (Gamson 1992; Kaufman 2008; Klandermans 1997). The second component, 'prognostic framing', refers to the strategy and the tactics pursued to rectify the unjust situation (Benford and Snow 2000).

My central argument is that an early and tacit elite consensus to silence the past – at the elite level – gradually acquired a hegemonic status that precluded a truth-seeking initiative. The causal mechanisms of this transformation will be highlighted in the remaining sections, with special emphasis on 'elite framing'. The sections will explore the institutionalization of this elite frame into political institutions and political culture and discuss in what ways this demobilized the civil society.

For the purposes of this study, I searched the parliamentary debates, questions and laws related to the issue of *desaparecidos*, and truth recovery more generally,[8] as presented in the Spanish *Congreso de los Diputados* (Lower House).[9] This is coupled with interviews with several members of the designated Parliamentary Committee on Historical Memory and extensive research into the electoral programmes of the major nationwide political parties since the restoration of democracy and the first elections in 1977.[10]

The first remarkable observation from the study of the parliamentary debates and the electoral programmes is that the issue of the recovery of *desaparecidos* was not raised until the early 2000s.[11] As will be shown, this silence constitutes a central strategy of the elite framing on truth recovery, and, as such, it is an indicator of hegemonic belief. One might argue that this merely reflects a societal lack of interest in the issue. However, the publications of the time (Interviú 1978h, 1980a), coupled with the efforts of individual relatives to exhume their loved ones, tell a different story: certain people and groups were not indifferent about truth recovery.

Still, this silence poses a methodological problem in the elaboration of the elite framing. To overcome this methodological problem, I pursue two complementary paths. On the one hand, I analyse the debates treating other victims' groups of the civil war and post-war repression: those mutilated in the civil war; pensions and social security offered to widows and children; compensation for the imprisoned; the restoration of confiscated properties. I explain the difference between the treatment of these groups' demands and the silence over the issue of *desaparecidos* and show how this is related to the prevention of truth recovery. On the other hand, the debates on the amnesty law (1977) – perceived to be the founding tenet of the transition – provide an equally insightful way to sketch the elite framing on the issues related to the past. The two sets of analyses, together with the interviews of members of the designated parliamentary commission and the study of electoral programmes, are sufficient to overcome this methodological concern.

Contrary to other cases, in Spain, amnesty became the most important demand by the *defeated*. During negotiations between the moderate segments of the Francoist regime and the exiled leaders of the defeated in the period preceding transition, amnesty was the priority in the demands of the defeated. As Juliá aptly remarks, 'amnesty became the synonym of freedom' for the defeated (2008). The first partial amnesty law was granted by King Juan Carlos on 30 July 1976 and freed approximately 410 prisoners. Its intention was to symbolically link his coronation with national reconciliation (Aguilar 2002). A more comprehensive law came into effect in October 1977, which covered 'politically motivated' crimes. Its primary provisions were to free political prisoners and to provide immunity from prosecution for Francoists (Aguilar 2008; Juliá 2006). For many Spaniards, the amnesty law was simultaneously a *sine qua non* precondition for democratic consolidation and an insurmountable obstacle to a comprehensive screening of past human rights abuses. For all these reasons, the debates on the amnesty law of 1977 are an invaluable analytical resource for the study of elite framing on the topic.

It is interesting that 'diagnostic framing' is implied from the study of 'prognostic framing', since any reference to the causes of the problematic situation (i.e. the civil war and post-war repression) would contradict the prognostic framing, which – as will be shown below – emphasizes the need to overcome the past and achieve national reconciliation by burying the past. The debate on the amnesty law of 1977 is revealing. The civil war is presented as a period of 'collective madness', where both sides committed heinous crimes; the attribution of responsibility is strictly avoided, since there is no 'rational' actor to blame for such an immense tragedy. An illustrative example of this diagnostic framing is presented by the spokesperson of the governing party, *Unión de Centro Democrático* (henceforth, UCD), in 1978 in a reference to the debated law on pensions for widows and orphans:

> Those widows and orphans that today we talk about … are not merely widows or orphans of the communists, of the socialists, or anarchists, but widows and orphans of the tragic Spain [...] we can provide different explanations about what happened between 1936 and 1939, but in any case, it was a national tragedy.
> (Diario De Sesiones del Pleno (Congreso) 1978b: 5576–5578)

According to this widely shared reading, the problematic situation is rooted in the 'tragic' period of civil war. This diagnostic framing complies with the unofficial version of the past formulated before and during the transition: the civil war was a period of 'collective madness' (*locura colectiva*) that is better forgotten. This diagnostic reading transcends the ideological inclination of the speakers. As another MP argued: 'We have to accept our past, but we have to forget its errors' (Diario De Sesiones del Pleno (Congreso) 1977b: 961–963).

When we proceed to the analysis of the prognostic framing, the diagnostic component becomes clearer. Two central courses of action to address the problematic situation are identified: to establish a wide political consensus, so as to bury the divisive past and achieve reconciliation – seen as a *sine qua non* precondition for democratic consolidation; and to define an instrumental rationale for redressing victims groups' material needs, so as to achieve closure.

The element of learning (Bermeo 1992) from past experiences is evident in the speeches covering the amnesty law. In a significant illustration of political learning, it is framed as the *symbolic closure* of a prolonged period of divisions and the beginning of a new and democratic era. A member of the Socialist Party insists: 'Today is the date, in which finally, the civil war is buried' (Diario De Sesiones del Pleno (Congreso) 1977c: 965–968). Similarly, the spokesperson of the governing party (UCD) argues:

> Amnesty is the political-ethical precondition of democracy, of that democracy that we aspire, that, being authentic does not look back, but fervently wants to get over and transcend the divisions that separated us and brought us into conflict in the past.
> (Diario De Sesiones del Pleno (Congreso) 1977f: 972–973)

The parties from the autonomous regions seem to subscribe to this reading as well, emphasizing the need for a 'mutual forgetting. At this moment we cannot allege facts of bloodshed because there has been bloodshed by both sides ... and some of them really sad' (Diario De Sesiones del Pleno (Congreso) 1977d: 968–970).

An example of the consensus to forget the past as a precondition for democratic consolidation comes from the Spanish Communist Party, *Partido Comunista Española* (hencefore, PCE). In the debate on the amnesty law, a communist MP says:

> Today we do not want to remember that past [...] we have buried out dead and our grudges, and for this reason, today, apart from speaking of that past, the communist minority is very pleased by the consensus [...] and we would also have wished that this was an act of national unanimity.
> (Diario De Sesiones del Pleno (Congreso) 1977a: 959–961)[12]

It is remarkable that every reference of the Communist Party to issues related to the amnesty law or to any form of reparation to the victims of the civil war is accompanied by underlining the party's leading role in this 'national reconciliation'. In fact, PCE's official policy since 1956 was the replacement of Franco by non-violent means (Edles 1998: 49). Referring to amnesty, the Socialist Party subscribes to the rhetoric of symbolic closure:

> [This] holds the uncontested value of being an amnesty on which almost all political forces of this room have the will to bury a sad past for the History

of Spain and to construct a different one on different assumptions, getting over the division that the Spanish people have suffered for the last 40 years.
(Diario De Sesiones del Pleno (Congreso) 1977c: 965–968)

Even certain segments of the Basque representatives agreed that 'forgetting is necessary, in order to cease the dialogue of the deaf and the mutual accusations' (Diario De Sesiones del Pleno (Congreso) 1977c: 82–84).

Burying the past stems from the implicit learning derived from past experiences, both the civil war and the dramatic instability that characterized the start of the Second Republic (1931–1936). Throughout the parliamentary records, the need to bury the hatchet is seen as the distilled experience of painful lessons: 'We have behind us a past that is very ambiguous, that in political terms, committed huge mistakes' (Diario De Sesiones del Pleno (Congreso) 1977d: 85–94). This is equally obvious in the position of a Socialist Party parliamentarian, who admonishes other MPs: 'We should think maturely of the fragility that had always accompanied the democratic life in our country' (Diario De Sesiones del Pleno (Congreso) July 1977a: 66–72). Also important is the following statement made by the leader of the Communist Party, Santiago Carillo:

> The will to overcome the passionate and ideological remains of the civil war and the consolidation of democracy are born today [...] for the communists the essential question today is not Monarchy or Republic; it is democracy or dictatorship, and we are ready, this moment, to overcome our preferences for the political form of governance in order to achieve the most wide consensus for the consolidation of democracy.
> (Diario De Sesiones del Pleno (Congreso) 1977b: 73–76)

Consider, too, the intervention of the communist representative during the amnesty debate: 'We considered that the principal part of this reconciliation policy had to be an amnesty. How could we reconcile, those of us who had been killing each other, if we did not delete the past once and for all?' (Diario De Sesiones del Pleno (Congreso) 1977a: 959–961) Even more striking, in the interviews I conducted with members of the designated parliamentary committee for the Law of Historical Memory, almost all interviewees subscribed to this prognostic framing, saying that an agreement to bury the past was mandatory at the time (Interview nos 37 and 39).[13]

So, too, an examination of the framing of the treatment of victims' groups reveals an instrumental rationale. More specifically, reparations are granted to certain groups not as an acknowledgement of the suffering of the victims or of their contribution to a noble cause, *but as a necessary measure to comfort the disaffected*. In part, these measures constitute acts of benevolence – not justice. They are perceived as solving problems not covered by the amnesty law; therefore, they are treated as humanitarian solutions that will enable closure (*punto final*) and accelerate national reconciliation and democratic consolidation. This is further illustrated by the fact that reparations are not framed in terms of moral acknowledgement, but are limited to economic or social measures, while symbolic acts of acknowledgement are rare. To link the diagnostic framing, the victims are not perceived to be *luchadores* (fighters) for a value (the protection of the Republic), but as persons who experienced a 'tragic' period of Spanish history; as such, they deserve material support, but not moral acknowledgement.

Hence, the civil war is recruited instrumentally to accommodate the material needs of certain victims' groups in order to accelerate the process of transition, while any references to the origins of the war or the ensuing repression are downplayed to avoid provoking the military (Ryan 2009). In the framing, the army retains its status as trustee of the Francoist legacy. This is not surprising, as even after the transition, the army remained powerful and very cautious of the transition process. Therefore, all parties had to be careful not to initiate processes that would infuriate segments of the army and derailed democratic consolidation. In fact, in 1981, there was a short, failed coup.

The Republican veterans of the civil war were excluded from the amnesty law of 1977, largely because the military establishment found it hard to accept any measure that would have delegitimized its own version of the past, such as the reintegration of the Republicans into the corps (Aguilar 1999: 101). This is obvious even in the amnesty debate, where a Socialist Party MP stated:

> The amnesty is a result of a compromise [...] we clearly know that with this law proposal we do not satisfy nor do we do justice to some sectors [...] but the conditions that the actual powers have seemingly established have prevented us and make us suspect that we have left flags that can be collected and brandished in the future.
> (Diario De Sesiones del Pleno (Congreso) 1977a: 959–961)

This instrumental rationale for granting benefits to victims is clear in many speeches. The constitutional obligation of the state to equal treatment among Spaniards – following the novel constitution (1978) – is also deployed as an argument to bend potential resistance from rightists to legislate these benefits. This was called 'constitutional reconciliation'. However, the communist representative argued that with respect to the provision of pensions to the widows and orphans of the civil war, '[r]econciliation would not be possible, will not be effective while equality in every respect among the Spaniards and the families of those that fought in one or another band in the civil war is missing, is not achieved' (Diario De Sesiones del Pleno (Congreso) 1978a: 5575–5576).

The link between granting benefits and building reconciliation is evident in the following preamble to the 1978 Law (6/1978) that regulates the situation of the military personnel taking part in the civil war: 'The government and His Majesty, in their willingness to continue the policy designed by the Crown to overcome the consequences deriving from the past conflict [...] considers necessary to designate a rule that harmonizes the overcoming of the past' (Royal Decree 6/1978).

Even though the consensus acquired hegemonic status, the representative of the Basque *Euskadiko Ezquerra* (during the debate on the amnesty law) inserted a radically different perspective into the debate, whereby

> amnesty is not a shameful pardon to people still considered common delinquents. On the contrary, it is the recognition of the right of a people to use all measures in their reach in order to defend themselves from the aggression of the dictatorship.
> (Diario De Sesiones del Pleno (Congreso) 1977e: 970–971)

This is the only framing that rejects the instrumental approach and makes a deontological argument – namely, that these victims should be seen as fighters for liberty. Of course, this reading should be linked to the Basque nationalism, which was severely persecuted during the Francoist regime and not merely during the civil war. In fact, some scholars explain the emergence of ETA as a reaction to this repression. Hence, for a limited – but visible – segment of the Basque population, transition could not be successful if it did not morally acknowledge the suffering of the Basque people in an ongoing Spanish repression (Aguilar 1999). This reading explains the continuing violence between 1975 and 1982, where ETA caused more violence in the Basque Country than in any other part of Spain (Muro 2009: 665).

This instrumental approach adopted in compensating victims' groups is clearly reflected in the debates on compensating as divergent groups as the widows and orphans (Law 5/1977; Royal Decree 8/1980; Diario De Sesiones del Pleno (Congreso) 1978c: 4199–4201) and the military personnel of the Republican Army (Law 34/1984); and the compensation of those imprisoned through recognizing their years in prison as valid for social security (Law 18/1984). The possibility of declaring the indictments of trials during the Francoist regime as illegitimate was discussed, but finally a decision was reached to abstain from addressing this issue, also explained by the prevalence of pragmatist considerations.[14]

The issue of the disappeared appears for the first time – and then only marginally – in 1978 in a proposal of a law to provide pensions to widows and orphans of the civil war. This provision appears in the final law; Article 1(a) asserts the eligibility of the relatives of *desaparecidos* to apply for those benefits. However, this was limited to material support for the families; it did not constitute a more comprehensive policy of exhumations or tracing the whereabouts of the victims.

As this analysis has indicated, in the elite framing, victims' groups were not shown as fighters for liberty or as a group whose struggles should be morally acknowledged. The material benefits granted to certain victims' groups constitute concessions to fill the gaps not covered by the amnesty law, which was supposed to have been a 'full stop' (Aguilar 2008: 420). The perception of these benefits as a means to an end (national reconciliation and democratic consolidation) blocked any alternative discourse that might have opened the issue of responsibilities. In this framing, any reference to the disappeared or to political violence would have led to all sorts of inconvenient questions, seriously delegitimizing the process of national reconciliation and democratic consolidation. Why were the Nationalist victims exhumed and transferred to their relatives with the expenses covered by the state when the Republican victims were not?[15] Who was responsible for the war? Who had been responsible for the suffering of hundreds of thousands of Spaniards for several decades? In other words, political exhumations would have raised the issue of *responsibility*: asking and answering the question 'who did what to whom'? This had the potential to derail the democratic consolidation. Therefore, any truth-seeking initiative was out of the question.

Any society ready to face its past must be ready to ascribe moral responsibility for the suffering inflicted in human rights abuses. In fact, truth recovery is a complex issue, because it combines the past (human rights abuses), the present (the type of transition) and the future (the projected path to democracy) (Pridham 2000). In Spain, any reference to the *desaparecidos* would have destabilized and delegitimized the fragile transition. This explains why, although other less contentious victims' groups were compensated, issues directly related to political violence were never raised.

However, the elite consensus to bury the past and achieve national reconciliation alone cannot explain the lack of truth recovery. As will be shown in the following section, this consensus was entrenched in the political institutions of the nascent regime. This, coupled with the inherently weak civil society (usually the main source of truth-seeking), provides a more comprehensive explanation of the delay.

Societal silence

One could insist that societal 'silence' in Spain was a deliberate (indeed, the best available) strategy of disengagement from a prolonged dictatorship. In fact, several indications point to this argument. For one thing, the public response in key instances was remarkably moderate. For example, the referendum for political reform and the constitution were widely perceived as symbols of reconciliation and closure, and the voting on these triggered a massive response (Ortega 1985). Equally, according to an opinion poll in 1983, most Spaniards perceived the civil war as a shameful period and a collective tragedy (Preston 1990: 40). By the mid-1980s, the moderation of the citizens was so pronounced that no party from the extreme left or right could get more than 3 per cent in general elections (Preston 1990). This should also be linked to the findings of opinion polls during the transition, showing that the most valued concepts were peace, order and stability – not liberty or democracy (Aguilar 2002). Finally, the complicity of ordinary Spaniards may have been a motivation for the collective forgetfulness of a period of extreme violence and moral disintegration (Aguilar and Humlebaek 2002; Graham 2004). So long as this was a period of collective madness and could not be explained in rational terms, it should remain buried, acting only as an instructive lesson for the present and the future.

34 Prolonged silences

Although this argument has some explanatory value, truth recovery processes do not necessarily mean a widespread societal movement. Indeed, the demand for truth originates from minor social forces – most frequently, relatives and activists – challenging a dominant version of truth. Hence, a simplistic explanation that focuses merely on the societal exercise of 'oblivion' fails to take into account more complicated societal processes during the first period of the transition. More importantly, they do not provide a comprehensive explanation of why, although a demand was expressed, it eventually died away.

My archival research shows that from 1977 and throughout this first step towards democracy, exhumations took place throughout the country.[16] In fact, a popular magazine of the time, *Interviú*,[17] featured detailed coverage of the efforts of the relatives of *desaparecidos* to exhume the graves and provide their loved ones with a decent burial (Interviú 1978h, 1980a). These exhumations took place throughout Spain, including La Rioja (Interviú 1977d), Casas de don Pedro (Badajoz) (Barrero 2007; Interviú 1978e),[18] Granada (Interviú 1977c), Navarra (Interviú 1978f, 1978g) and Galicia (Interviú 1979). A 1979 documentary records the experiences of the relatives in the exhumations in the region of La Rioja.[19] But as a noted scholar who has carried out research on the topic, Francisco Ferrándiz, says: '[We] still do not know the extent of these exhumations. Every week we become aware of a new incident in 1970s. Most of these (exhumations) had a very low-profile and they were not even reported' (Personal Interview no. 45). Although loose and disorganized initiatives – to be expected after almost 40 years of dictatorship – these processes indicate the demand for narrow truth, at least in some segments of society.

Published commentary was not limited to the *desaparecidos*. As noted previously, one can find other articles related to the 'repressive past': the personal testimonies of prisoners or forced labourers (Interviú 1978b); the analysis of the repressive educational system (Interviú 1978e); the role of Catholic Church (Interviú July 1977b); and the comprehensive coverage of the student protests in the 1960s (Interviú 1980a) (Juliá 2006). Clearly, some people wanted to recover the truth. Why, then, did these early and loose processes die away? Why were they not inserted into the public debate and political agenda?

In theoretical terms, although indications of resistance (Scott 1987) to the early elite consensus to bury the past were evident, these lost momentum and succumbed to the overriding predominant discourse. How did this become possible and through which causal mechanisms? I argue that the early elite consensus and the urgent priority to bury the divisive past in order to achieve the twin end-goals of national reconciliation and democratic consolidation (prognostic framing) were entrenched in the new democratic institutions and the demobilization of civil society. Certain issues were excluded from the public discourse because of the hegemonic frame.

First, a (*legal*) *expression* of this hegemonic discourse is the legal and societal persecution of those who carried out exhumations. Ryan (2009: 123) states:

> [In] August 1979, the excavation of a cemetery in Torravieja (Badajoz) revealed the remains of 35 republicans shot in the war. Later, however, the

mayor of this town was reprimanded by a fine for having carried out a supposedly illegal exhumation. Likewise, in the villages of Alfaroy Calahorra, the residents had to mount a campaign to ensure that their loved ones received a dignified burial.

The legal expression of this hegemonic belief is still obvious in the contemporary wave of exhumations. On 8 November 2008, Spain's top criminal court (*Audenica Nacional*) stopped the exhumations ordered by Judge Baltázar Garzón in Granada (BBC 2008). This legal battle and the recruitment of legal instruments in the recovery of historical memory will be further analysed in Chapter 5.

Democratization literature shows that transitions through elite pacts seem to freeze the nascent democracy by disproportionally empowering the political elites, who subsequently monopolize public discourse (Encarnación 2003). This, in combination with a second side-effect of pacted transitions – namely, the prevention of the emergence of a full-blown civil society – inhibits the development of a strong democratic regime (Diamond 1999; Encarnación 2003; Licklider 1995: 685; Linz and Stepan 1996: 56). Therefore, although pacted transitions usually provide the necessary stability for the consolidation of democracy, this is achieved at the expense of the quality of the emerging regime (Burton *et al.* 1992: 13).

A noteworthy feature of the Spanish transition was the absence of a visible societal movement demanding truth and an acknowledgement of past human rights abuses – a situation quite unlike the vocal social movements in Latin American societies, which proliferated concurrently with the transition to democracy. Although the level of societal mobilization was high, taking into consideration the impressive strikes and the terrorist attacks of ETA (Bermeo 1999; Maravall 1982), the absence of a similar demand for truth in Spain is striking. Spain's experience seems to affirm the theoretical argument that pacted transitions prevent the formation of a strong civil society. Although the prolonged Francoist indoctrination – promoting apathy – can explain the disengagement of the older generation from politics (Aguilar 2009), the groundbreaking social and political transformations that Spanish society experienced after the civil war fail to explain the durability of certain features of the political culture, including: low levels of interest in politics; low exposure to political communication; and cynicism towards political life and political parties (Encarnación 2001; Gunther and Montero 2009: 175). The most vivid expression of this 'civic anemia', as Omar Encarnación aptly puts it, is the meagre participation in voluntary associations (2001: 63). More than 20 years after the consolidation of democracy, only one in three Spaniards belong to any voluntary association; levels similar to the post-communist regimes of Eastern Europe (ibid.). Another explanation for the non-existence of a strong civil society movement that would challenge the predominant discourse is the close link between political parties and civic associations. An endemic feature of Spanish political culture is the penetration/control of all sorts of civic associations by political parties, primarily through financial control (Encarnación 2003), which indicates that, to some extent, the parties shaped the agenda of the associations.

In any event, the absence of a strong civil society movement that would have supported the demand for narrow truth explains why these early efforts to unearth the past were doomed to fail. Of course, it could be argued that the shock of the unsuccessful *coup d'état* on 23 February 1981 had a restraining effect on the discussion of any contentious issue that could have provoked the wrath of the military. Even when democracy was fully consolidated, and the conditions were propitious under the Socialist Government, 'silence' prevailed, because the army was still a powerful actor.

To be sure, the pacted transition and the absence of a strong civil society alone do not explain the prevention of truth recovery. A causal mechanism transformed this elite framing into a widely shared hegemonic belief; the examination of the post-transition political institutions may reveal this mechanism.

Political institutions

During the transition to democracy, the central tenets of the political culture of a new regime are shaped, including: the political elites, the political institutions and the general political culture (Manning 2007a). Political institutions serve the fundamental demand to resolve societal conflicts in a legitimate and widely acceptable way (Huntington 1968), and they incorporate the historical, political and social realities of the period during their inception. As Omar Encarnación says: 'Institutions and their historical legacies matter to politics *by structuring preferences, interests and values in society* (2001: 55 [emphasis added]). As such, the consensual nature of the transition in Spain had a catalytic impact on the formation of political institutions, since consensus and 'learning' are two elements that are well-entrenched in the new institutions.

However, an inherent problem of pacts is that 'the short term security concerns of the bargaining parties may be at odds with the long-term institution-building needs of the society' (Rothschild 2002: 118). Hence, the institutional design reflected the realities of the Spanish transition (learning from the past; threat of extremists, etc.). According to Field and Hamann, in Spain, certain 'informal institutions', such as

> reaching supermajority consensus on issues of the state, the 'pact to forget' and centripetal alliance strategies were efficient ways to consolidate democracy, but at the same time, they delimited interparty competition and limited the representation of distinct societal interest and kept certain issues off the political agenda.
>
> (2008b: 210)

What is equally interesting is that in their study, Field and Hamann find that 'where consensus meant the resolution of key institutional issues, we are more likely to find earlier and stronger institutionalization' (2008a: 2). In fact, institutionalization took considerably longer on issues where elite consensus dictated the deferral of resolution to a point in the future, such as the issue of autonomies (ibid.). This substantiates the argument that an early elite consensus on the issue of past human rights abuses (i.e. rejection of any transitional justice measure) was a founding tenet of the pacted transition and was transformed into a hegemonic and institutionalized belief.

Until very recently, several political institutions in the Spanish democracy safeguarded and reproduced the consensual nature of transition and prevented truth-seeking. The constitution, the role of political parties, the electoral system, as well as the parliament and the educational system (Boyd 2006), to name only a few, blocked any source that could have challenged the resolution of the political elites to bury the past.

First and foremost, the *electoral system* adopted during the transition illustrates the institutionalization of the elite consensus. Two notable features of the Second Republic (1931–1936) were governmental instability and ideological polarization. In each of the three elections (1931, 1933 and 1936) preceding the civil war, over 20 parties had parliamentary representation, while the governing party never had more than 24 per cent of the seats (Gunther and Montero 2009: 21). It is estimated that the average duration of Cabinet during the short-lived Second Republic was 101 days (Magone 2004: 12). This reality polarized the political cleavages, since a change in government was usually accompanied by the annulment of the policies carried out by former governments. The electoral system accentuated polarization and governmental instability and was perceived to be a factor that paved the way to civil war. Therefore, the electoral system became a key issue of negotiations during transition.

Although all parties agreed on the necessity to establish strong and stable governments, they had divergent preferences. The right supported a majoritarian system with single-member constituencies (first-past-the-post), since at that time they enjoyed the support of small to medium provinces. The parties of the left encouraged a proportional system (Kohler 1982). A final compromise established a bicameral system with a simple majority in the Upper House (Senate) and a modified proportional representation in the Lower House (Congress). Finally, a 3 per cent threshold was inserted to prevent the fragmentation of the system (Heywood 1995). The single most important feature of the electoral system is the high degree of political stability, which was 'certainly influenced by the negative experience of former electoral systems up to the civil war' (Gunther 1992; Magone 2004: 79). By 2009, the average Cabinet durability of the Spanish Government since the transition was 107 months (Gunther and Montero 2009: 56).

This is important for truth recovery processes, since the priority to establish a stable political system is often achieved at the expense of party competition and political representation. The two largest nationwide political parties have always received a greater share of seats than their percentage of the total popular vote (ibid.). What is even more critical to the study of truth-seeking is the process of coalition-building in minority governments; this forces major parties aspiring to form the government to adopt moderate but flexible agendas to build bridges and create a coalition with another minority or regional party. In essence, a big party has a greater chance of building a coalition with a moderate and flexible agenda than with a contentious one.[20] It should be mentioned, though, that a coalition does not imply perfect alignment in all aspects of the declared policies, only in certain specific areas that the two – or more – parties agree upon. In areas outside the agreement, the government may pursue a policy that contravenes the ideological principles of the coalition party (Field and Hamann 2008a). Still, it would be reckless for a mainstream party to adopt a policy that challenges a central informal institution upon which the political regime is based. Even the Socialist Government with consecutive majority governments in 1980s did not challenge this tacit pact of silence at the political level.

Furthermore, the stability of the Spanish political system is achieved by the *disproportionately powerful role of the executive branch in comparison to the parliament*. More precisely, the 1978 Constitution assigns a privileged position to the prime minister (Chari and Heywood 2008).[21] The strength of the Spanish Prime Minister is so pronounced that scholars call it the 'presidentialization' of the government (Biezen and Hopkin 2005). In any event, the prime minister is the most important person in the executive, with the ability to control the process of policymaking.

This should be linked with the overall functioning of the political party system and the weak role of parliament. Strict party discipline is a central component of the functioning of the political party system in Spain. Party discipline is safeguarded by the closed lists system of voting (Esteban and Guerra 1985: 60; Gunther and Montero 2009; Heywood 1995). The higher the place of the candidate on the list, the more likely it is that he or she will be (re-)elected. Voters *cannot* express their personal preferences for individual candidates, but must express their party preference (Field 2005; Gibbons 1999; Gunther and Montero 2009). This measure is important: it strengthens the role of the party leader; it reduces the ability of the voter/citizen to follow a different line than that pursued by the leadership of the party; and potential candidates with agendas deviating from the formal party line are castigated by party leadership by being placed low on the list of candidates. In other words, the party system – also shaped by the negotiated nature of the transition – prevents activities that may challenge the party's priorities, including truth-seeking.

Of course, it would be a tautology to explain the absence of a certain policy by referring to the institutional design of the executive. In order to draw such a conclusion, it is essential to illustrate that party preferences prevent the adoption of a specific policy. In this case, the study of the electoral programmes of the major nationwide parties reveals that the issue of truth recovery or the acknowledgement of the suffering of the victims of the civil war was never a priority of past governments. Of course, the Popular Party, *Partido Popular*[22] (henceforth, PP), with several party members having strong affiliations to the Francoist past, had limited incentives to promote such a policy. However, the Socialist Party's lack of interest is intriguing. A study of all electoral programmes from the restoration of democracy in 1977 to the general elections in 2008 reveals that PSOE never touched on the issue of the recovery of historical memory or any other measure to address the past. None of the electoral programmes refers to this topic, except in 2008 when the Law of Historical Memory was already enacted (Aguilar 2008; PSOE 2004).

Finally, the specific nature of the transition, with its emphasis on moderation, consensus and negotiation, contributed to the formation of an institutionally feeble parliament (Heywood 1995). Contrary to the auditing function of the parliament in a democratic regime, in Spain, the consensual transition 'paradoxically weakened parliament because of the difficulty of the compromises the parties had to make, and the need to ensure the acquiescence of extra-parliamentary forces the real action took place behind the scenes' (Biezen and Hopkin 2005: 107). Parliament merely follows the policy pursued by the government, with negative effects on the level of political representation. The seminal analysis of Bonnie Field indicates that the pacted nature of the transition in Spain decreased the level of inter-party competition (Field 2005). The analysis of deputy votes in the Spanish Congress between 1977 and 2004 shows that, until very recently, the level of collaboration was extremely high – a pattern that only began to wane in the mid-1990s.[23] Hence, the central political institutions converted the elite pact of transition into concrete political outcomes, preventing truth recovery.

The analysis now turns to the final question – namely, why the PSOE did not put forward a policy of addressing the past, even though it governed for 14 consecutive years (1982–1996).

PSOE: forgetting the past or pragmatic considerations?

In the period preceding the death of Franco and throughout the transition, a visible fraction of the PSOE demanded a 'break with the past', once democracy was consolidated (Maravall 1985: 136). However, pragmatic electoral considerations prevailed during transition, changing a 'clean break' to a 'negotiated' settlement.

In fact, the transition – and especially the period preceding the first elections of 1977 – constituted a particularly fluid period for the electoral strategies of all parties, since almost 40 years of dictatorship made accurate speculations as to the preferences of the electorate extremely difficult. Furthermore, parties had the multifaceted task of party-building, maximizing their votes without being fully aware of the electorate's priorities and, most importantly, consolidating democracy (Gunther et al. 1988; Gunther and Hopkin 2002: 194). Therefore, most parties chose 'risk aversion' to survive in an unknown political climate (Aguilar 2002: 94). All parties, even the PCE, had no alternative but to take a moderate position (Carillo 2009).

After its impressive results in constitutive elections (1977), PSOE changed its electoral strategy, abandoning any affiliation to Marxism or any other radical reference that could alienate centrist voters and wholeheartedly dedicating itself to the consolidation of democracy (Heywood 1995). The general election of 1982 was pivotal for PSOE for two reasons. First, the party achieved a landslide victory and formed an absolute-majority government. Second, and equally importantly, the then governing party of the UCD collapsed, leaving a significant pool of centrist voters available for PSOE. The collapse of the UCD had an instructive and moderating effect on PSOE, since a central reason for UCD's failure was the electorate's disapproval of the party's inability to protect the process of democratic consolidation, especially after the shock of the attempted *coup d'état* in 1981 (Gunther and Hopkin 2002: 191).[24] Equally, the low success rate of the right-wing AP Party (predecessor of the Popular Party) in the first elections made PSOE the only candidate to dominate the centre. At any rate, PSOE willingly made a slight centrist move to support the immense body of voters dissatisfied with the UCD Government. The transformation of PSOE into a 'catch-all' party signified the exclusion of radical policies that would have frightened the centrist electorate. After this transformation, however, tackling issues that contravened and challenged the central tenets of the transitional/democratic consensus, such as the elite determination to bury the past, became unimaginable.

Added to this, PSOE's parliamentary win of 1982 signified the political victory of the 'defeated' in the civil war and the symbolic closure of a traumatic 50-year period, beginning with the civil war. There was no need to look back: the civil war was 'history' (Juliá 2006). Besides, according to survey data, the ideological self-positioning of the majority of the electorate between 1976 and 1990 was on the centre–left (Heywood 1995: 179), and this projected a favourable electoral future for PSOE. PSOE had no incentive to play the card of the past: it had politically crushed its political and historical adversaries, and, until 1993, it received comfortable governmental majorities.

Of course, this does not necessarily mean that the past was 'forgotten'. It has been argued that politics is the art of playing out symbols. PSOE was simply portraying its electoral victories as the victory of democracy against the Francoist legacy; at the same time, though, it was careful not to be too provocative and alienate the centrist electorate. A similar rationale informed the Greek Socialist Party in its landmark victory in 1982; national reconciliation was symbolically achieved, without any comprehensive screening of the past. In fact, as neither Socialist Party had any political incentive to look back, the only compensatory policies for the 'defeated' were economic ones or pragmatic benefits to the victims. In the 1980s, PASOK granted citizenship to a significant group of political refugees who left the country in the aftermath of the Greek Civil War (1946–1949). A massive wave of repatriation – especially from countries allied to the Soviet Union – was observed in the 1980s, and this was seen as working towards symbolic closure and reconciliation. A similar strategy of controlled polarization, while staying loyal to the founding tenets of transition, was followed by the AKEL Party in Cyprus, at times highlighting the legacy of resistance to coupists and loyalty to the Republic, but avoiding ascribing moral and legal responsibility to its political opponents.

In short, it seems that pragmatic considerations dictated PSOE's decision to avoid addressing the past. However, this pragmatism was defined in the context of the pacted transition and the hegemonic discourse about the past; PSOE had to protect this discourse to achieve its electoral objectives.

Conclusion

To sum up, the pacted nature of the transition to democracy had a catalytic effect on the formation of the political institutions of the nascent Spanish democracy. The early elite consensus to bury the past at the political elite level served as a founding tenet and subsequently achieved a hegemonic position. The ensuing hegemonic discourse was incorporated into the political institutions, making it difficult for any political party to challenge one of the most important tenets of the transition. Druliolle sketches this hegemonic position as

> consubstantial to the foundation of Spanish democracy, and its power can be seen in the fact that projects which challenge the representation of the transition institutionalized as the legitimate framework for the construction of society, have been criticized for threatening to undermine the regime.
> (2008: 77)

The only potential challenge to this hegemonic discourse could come from civil society. However, the weakness of civil society – usually the main source of truth-seeking – explains the long-term prevention of truth recovery.

Notes

1 One of the most credible lines of research on this topic is a study conducted by Santos Juliá (ed.) (1999). The above-mentioned figures include only 25 provinces; the total number of casualties is likely considerably higher.
2 Interestingly, in the literature of the Spanish Civil War, the 'insurgent group' (*los rebeldes – bando sublevado*) refers to the Nationalist group, headed by General Francisco Franco, that revolted against the legitimate regime of the Second Republic on 18 July 1936.
3 Literally, the walk, the stroll.
4 In only 33 regions investigated by Casanova, 35,000 executions were carried out in the post-war period (2002: 20).
5 The most significant 'legal' tools established by the Francoist state were the Law of Political Responsibilities (9 February 1939); *Ley de Represion de la Masoneria y el Comunismo* (2 March 1940); *Ley de Seguridad del Estado* (April 1941); *Ley de Funga* (i.e. deaths registered as 'fallen in their attempt to escape'); and the *Ley del Bandidaje y Terrorismo* (1947) (Fontana 2003).
6 It is estimated that during this 'salvation campaign' no fewer than 37,487 children were sent to other countries, and only half returned to Spain at the end of the war (Moreno 1999: 286).
7 It is estimated that approximately 15,000 to 20,000 titles of books are dedicated to the study of the Spanish Civil War.
8 I used an electronic search engine in my examination of the parliamentary archives, focusing on 'disappearances' and 'exhumations', but including wider victims' groups during the civil war.
9 The parliamentary system in Spain is bi-cameral: the Upper House (Senate) and the

42 *Prolonged silences*

Lower House (Congress) (Heywood 1995). The bulk of the legislative work is done in Congress; therefore, here I focus on debates in Congress.

10 An Inter-ministerial Commission was established in 2004 to study the situation of the victims of the civil war and Francoism.
11 There are minor scattered references in the 1970s and 1980s, which have nothing to do with the recovery of the remains or the tracing of the whereabouts; instead, they are limited to the economic reparations of the relatives.
12 This refers to the abstention of *Alianza Popular* (the predecessor of the Popular Party*)* from the voting of the amnesty law.
13 It should be mentioned that for the representative of *Izquierda Unida* (United Left – the party that evolved from the coalition of the Spanish Communist Party with other leftist factions), silence was not a mandatory policy deriving from the amnesty law (Interview no. 49).
14 Question by Rodolfo Guerra i Fontana (parliamentary group: Socialists of Cataluña), no. 3.363-I, 5 June 1982.
15 The first exhumations took place immediately following the civil war. The Francoist regime legislated laws that safeguarded the places where those had fallen for 'the God and Spain' and ensured proper reburial according to the religious rituals (El País 1 March 2009; BOE 1936: 154; BOE 1937; BOE 1940: 1015–1016).
16 I am grateful to Professor Santos Juliá for bringing this source of information to my attention.
17 In this and similar publications, the voices of certain victims' groups appear; these subscribe to a completely different narrative of the past.
18 Interviú, 'El Pueblo Desentierra a sus Muertos. Casas de Don Pedro, 39 Años Después de la Matanza', *Interviú*, no. 19 (15 June 1978), pp. 86–88.
19 The title is 'the recovery of a prohibited past', and a portion of it can be found at: www.youtube.com/watch?v=3YmCxrHBCw4&feature=player_embedded# (accessed 9 January 2014).
20 As shown in Chapter 5, the necessity of the Socialist Party to form a government coalition with radical left parties was one of the major reasons for the adoption of an agenda conducive to the recovery of historical memory.
21 The central role of the prime minister is shown in the fact that the confidence of parliament is given to the prime minister, not to the entire Cabinet, which is formed after the nomination of the prime minister (Heywood 1995: 88).
22 Originally, the party was called Popular Alliance (*Alianza Popular*); in the late 1980s, it was renamed the Popular Party.
23 As will be shown in Chapter 5, the period of breaking this elite collaboration coincides with the popular demand for the recovery of historical memory.
24 For a vivid account of the attempted coup, see Cercas (2009).

3 The prevention of truth recovery for missing persons in Cyprus

In February 2009, while in the office of the assistant to the Greek-Cypriot member of the Committee on Missing Persons (CMP) for an interview, I witnessed a touching scene. Our interview was paused because the relatives of a recently exhumed and identified Greek-Cypriot missing person arrived to collect the coffin with his remains. The flags of the Republic of Cyprus and Greece were draped over the small coffin, and it was given a military escort to the cemetery. It was definitely not a typical funeral – especially as it had been delayed for three decades – but I felt awkward, as I was intruding at a very personal moment. Still, the expressions on the faces of the family members did not show grief; rather, they seemed both confused and relieved. As the assistant to the Greek-Cypriot member of the CMP explained, although all individuals are granted birth and death certificates to prove their passing from the human community, missing persons constitute a novel category; they are neither members of the human community, nor the imagined community of the dead. Hence, after 35 years of uncertainty, this family was 'fortunate' enough to retrieve the remains, bury their relative and bring about some closure.

That being said, the CMP is established on the premise that after identification of the remains, the cause of death will neither be revealed nor even examined. Thus, although families like this one achieve some form of closure, they are not told the conditions under which their relative died, who was responsible or why it took so long to identify him. And even as I write this, thousands of families, on both sides of the divide, are still waiting for their relatives who went missing during the turbulent decades of the 1960s and 1970s.

Both major Greek-Cypriot and Turkish-Cypriot communities in Cyprus have missing persons from the two main periods of conflict: the inter-communal violence of 1963–1967; and, more significantly, the violence during the later Turkish invasion (1974). During these periods, approximately 2,000 Cypriots from both communities went missing.[1] Taking into consideration the relatively small population of the island (792,600), the issue of missing persons clearly affects a considerable number of families from both communities.

Figure 3.1 provides a comprehensive picture of the problem of the missing in Cyprus. It shows the period and the place of disappearance of the Greek- and Turkish-Cypriot missing, according to the lists of missing submitted to the CMP in

44 Prolonged silences

2004. As the map shows, a substantial number of Turkish-Cypriots went missing in territories currently under the control of the so-called 'TRNC',[2] making the prospect of tracing and exhuming the remains a plausible scenario. Why did this not happen? There are both practical and political reasons. For one thing, a closer look at the map reveals that the vast majority of the Turkish-Cypriots falling into this category went missing in the period of inter-communal violence (1963–1964). Hence, at the time of their disappearance, most of these areas were under the control of the RoC, and this status changed with the Turkish invasion in 1974. However, after the passage of a decade and the absence of personal testimonies of the Greek-Cypriot perpetrators, due to the de facto partition of the island, even if political will were present, it would have been particularly difficult to trace the location of the grave. A second overlapping political explanation may better account for this apparent paradox. Drawing on Paul Sant Cassia's seminal analysis, I argue that since late 1974 the Turkish-Cypriot leadership deployed a specific political discourse framing the missing as *şehitler* (martyrs), therefore as dead, not missing (Sant Cassia 2006a: 116). This reading of the problem is part and parcel of the official discourse of the Turkish-Cypriot leadership on the Cyprus problem, emphasizing the impossibility of the peaceful coexistence of the two communities and, subsequently, subtly legitimizing the island's uneasy status quo. As a result, for several decades, and definitely until very recently, for the Turkish-Cypriot leadership there was no issue of missing persons.[3]

Puzzling questions emerge from the study of the Greek-Cypriot missing, though. It is obvious from the map that all persons who went missing in the

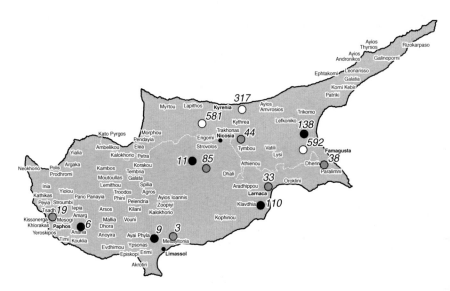

Figure 3.1 The map of the distribution of Greek-Cypriot and Turkish-Cypriot missing. The Greek-Cypriot missing of the summer of 1974 are pictured in white and the Turkish-Cypriot of the 1963 to 1965 and the 1974 periods are in grey and black, respectively (source: lists of missing submitted to the CMP).

summer of 1974[4] were in areas not under the control of the RoC; apparently, then, the Greek-Cypriot leadership could do little. In fact, the Greek-Cypriot official line emphasized (until recently) the number 1,619, denoting the number of persons still missing, the vast majority of whom disappeared during the 1974 Turkish invasion. Their official status is αγνοούμενοι/missing, thus symbolizing ongoing suffering and the constant search for their fate (Sant Cassia 2005).[5] The discourse on the problem of the missing reflects the official negotiating line of the RoC on the Cyprus issue – namely, that the issue remains to be solved, due to lack of cooperation by Turkey.

A paradox appears in the summer of 1999, when the RoC carried out unilateral exhumations in two cemeteries within its jurisdiction. The exhumations revealed that several Greek-Cypriot persons considered missing were buried in these common graves (see Figure 3.2). More precisely, in the aftermath of the Turkish invasion, several persons who died in the battle were hurriedly buried in the cemeteries of the RoC (Hadjikiriakou 1999; Paroutis 1999; Theodoulou 2009). However, some were officially declared missing, and their relatives considered them to be missing until very recently, when the Ministry of Foreign Affairs carried out exhumations in Greek-Cypriot cemeteries and discovered the reality.[6] This discovery was followed by a remarkable public apology by the Minister of Foreign Affairs for unnecessarily perpetuating the suffering of the relatives (Anastasiou 2008; Alitheia 1999).

This raises a set of perplexing questions: why did the authorities of the RoC, despite possessing valid information that several missing persons were buried in cemeteries within its control/jurisdiction,[7] do nothing to address this problem and bring closure to the relatives of the missing who had been looking for them for more than 30 years? Why Greek-Cypriots did not opt for unilateral exhumations earlier is paradoxical, especially as the recovery of the missing was both a public and political priority for several decades.

There are other puzzling questions. To address the problem of missing persons in Cyprus, a bi-communal agreement was reached under the auspices of the United Nations (UN) General Assembly in 1981, establishing the Committee on Missing Persons (henceforth, CMP) (UN 1981). Its primary objective was to trace the whereabouts of the missing persons from both communities; to this end, the trilateral committee was composed of one member of each community, with an independent chair appointed directly by the UN Secretary General. Oddly, despite the rigorous international involvement and in spite of massive public support for the recovery of the missing, not to mention the declarations of both communities that the problem of the missing was purely humanitarian and therefore independent of the wider Cyprus problem, until recently, no coordinated action was taken to solve the problem. In fact, from its inception until 2004, the CMP remained inoperative, not managing to ascertain the fate of a single person or exhume any graves.[8]

Immediately following the abortive Annan referendums in 2004 (rejected by the Greek-Cypriot community), at a time when the bi-communal trust reached rock bottom, a bi-communal agreement between the two leaders, Tassos

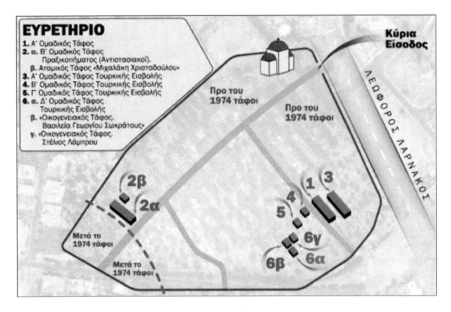

Figure 3.2 The map of the Aghiou Konstantinou ke Elenis cemetery, Nicosia; 2β depicts the mass grave of the fallen during the coup of July 1974, while 3, 4, 5 and 6 depict the mass graves of the fallen during the Turkish invasion (source: Politis 3 September 2010: 82).

Papadopoulos and Mehmet Ali Talat, to revitalize the CMP was reached in August 2004. At the time of writing, the CMP has become the most successful bi-communal project in Cyprus, having exhumed 1,012 bodies: 477 individuals have been identified and returned to their relatives, including 358 Greek-Cypriots and 119 Turkish-Cypriots (CMP 2013).[9] This leads to another question: why, despite the declared political intention of both communities to resolve the issue and the long-term engagement of the international community, was a solution not achieved earlier?

This points to several unaddressed questions in the study of transitional justice. For example, although Latin American societies had limited access to legal and institutional tools to address the problem of their disappeared, they mobilized earlier and more effectively to address the demand for truth than the Republic of Cyprus, even though the latter was a member of influential international organizations. Also, the enduring silence in Cyprus makes the Cypriot experience an interesting case study, first, in explaining why some states in the aftermath of negotiated transitions opt for a policy of silence and, second, in highlighting why and how transitional settlements (i.e. silence) endure over time. Why were potential domestic truth-seeking actors, such as relatives' associations and other civil society groups, so inefficient compared to similar grassroots organizations in other societies? Why did the actors representing the victims not challenge this silence over the course of several decades? Briefly stated, the study of the prolonged silences in Cyprus sheds analytical insight into the study of grassroots associations and political parties and the endurance of transitional settlements.

The chapter provides an array of alternative answers to the questions posed above. It analyses the basic tenets of framing and its use as an analytical tool in this context. Finally, it focuses on empirical evidence gathered during fieldwork in Cyprus to explain the conundrum. Based on rich empirical material extracted from the classified and ordinary parliamentary sessions in the House of Representatives, as well as personal interviews conducted with politicians, it argues that an early elite consensus was set immediately after the Turkish invasion in 1974. This circumscribed the issue, identifying Turkey as the only agent responsible for the debacle in resolving the problem of the missing. The analysis highlights the transformation of this elite framing into a hegemonic belief and the causal mechanisms by which it inhibited the scope and prospect of truth recovery, even when this became the official state policy.

Alternative explanations

Perhaps the most significant reason for the delay of the recovery of the missing was the de facto partition of the island and the obstacles it created. As Figure 3.1 reveals, the vast majority of disappearances for every community – and most probably the burial sites of the missing – took place in areas now under jurisdiction/occupation of the 'other' community. This mitigates the effectiveness of unilateral steps, without the cooperation of the 'other' side. Even more significantly, the physical division of the island considerably decreased the possibility of establishing and sustaining contacts across the divide. Subsequently, this inhibited the development of a strong grassroots movement that could have acted in a contentious manner, demanding the truth, following the example of countries with similar experiences of disappeared persons, such as the Abuelas (grandmothers) and Madres (mothers) de Plaza de Mayo in Argentina. Several interviewees actively engaged in bi-communal projects in the post-2003 period repeatedly drew on this argument (Interview nos 10, 15, 23). Although this contention has strong explanatory value, it should be noted that it fails to explain why the first exhumations took place without the assistance of the 'other' side, well before the opening of the checkpoints and certainly without the intervention of civil society. A closely related question is whether Cyprus qualifies as an applicable case of transitional justice.

Specifically, if one perceives the missing as a bi-lateral problem, then the non-resolution of the issue does not constitute a barrier to the process of domestic democratization or political reconciliation in either of the two communities; it is a problem of international relations, not transitional justice. One might argue that unlike post-Francoist Spain, where those associated with the Nationalists and the Republicans had to live together in the same polity; in Cyprus, most of the violence was inter-communal between Greek- and Turkish-Cypriots, who now live separately as a result of the hard partition.

Despite these realities, there are convincing indications of a willingness to construct a comprehensive political community composed of both Greek-Cypriots and Turkish-Cypriots. This is the *raison d'être* of transitional justice: to (re)establish a political community whose social bonds have been fractured by violence. And this is evident in the engagement – at least verbally – of the political leaderships of both communities in negotiations for the reunification of the island,[10] not to mention the vibrant activities of pro-rapprochement grassroots groups that have increased since the mid-2000s. In fact, this chapter, although exploring the problem of the missing in both communities, focuses primarily on the Greek-Cypriot side precisely because it has deployed an official position that a single community existed – and was violently overturned by the Turkish intervention in 1974. Meanwhile, until recently, the Turkish-Cypriot leadership denied the existence of a single community and the problem of the missing, deemed dead, thereby offering minimal commitment to the process.

Hence, this chapter focuses on the main puzzle: namely, why the RoC did not act more promptly to uncover the fate of its citizens – predominantly, the Greek-Cypriots – buried within its jurisdiction, despite the mounting popular demand. Arguably, the search was inhibited by the lack of technological/scientific knowledge. Generally, societies lacking the capacity to exhume and identify missing persons and, more generally, to unearth the truth in a scientific way prefer to keep the book of the past closed. The absence of DNA identification techniques in the 1970s or 1980s explains why early resolution was not easy. As early as 1987, Greek-Cypriots were investigating the possibility of using foreign expertise in forensic science with an unofficial mission to Canada and the United States (US) (Interview no. 86). As the following chapters indicate, this argument has significant explanatory value, but *alone* is insufficient to explain the puzzle, as other techniques of identifying human remains have been available since the early 1980s, as shown in the forensic exhumations carried out in Latin American countries like Argentina.

Another popular explanation for the delay points to the involvement of Turkey. As will be illustrated below, according to the Greek-Cypriot narrative, the issue of the missing was created by the Turkish invasion, with Turkey as the prime perpetrator. Therefore, any developments lay in the hands of Turkey and were definitely out of RoC control. In an interview, a Member of Parliament insisted: 'Here we have to deal with Turkey.... [Y]ou cannot cooperate easily with the Turks' (Interview no. 9). Although Turkey and the Turkish-Cypriot side were, indeed, responsible for the vast majority of the Greek-Cypriot missing, a number of cases could have been easily and promptly resolved.[11] In instrumental terms, it would have been a realistic policy for the RoC to promote early unilateral exhumations and return the Turkish-Cypriot missing to their relatives. Such a policy would have placed all legal and moral burdens, not to mention international pressure, on Turkey,[12] while paving the way for an early solution of the problem, based on trust in the other side. Also, it would have advanced the interests of the Republic.

Framing, transition and policy outcomes

For the RoC, the period following the Turkish invasion had all the features that societies in transition to peace and democracy usually face: urgent human rights problems as a result of political violence (refugees, missing, dead), the need to reinstate state institutions and the economy, as well as sensitive decisions to be made regarding how to deal with the violent past. These dilemmas were particularly acute in the RoC, because of the need to deal with the legacy of intra-communal violence in the Greek-Cypriot community.

More specifically, the period preceding the Turkish invasion was characterized by mounting levels of intra-communal violence within the Greek-Cypriot community, which reached its peak when a group of Nationalists in a short-lived *coup d'état*, guided by the Greek military regime, overthrew President Makarios and executed several Greek-Cypriots, predominantly leftists and those loyal to Makarios (Papadakis 1993).[13] Hence, the study of this transitory period has the potential to reveal the founding institutional tenets of the RoC: the tacit elite consensus that determined what would be remembered and what would be silenced in public discourse. This section deploys the analytical tool of framing to analyse the causal mechanisms that transformed the original elite consensus into a well-entrenched hegemonic discourse on the issue of missing persons, decreasing the possibility of comprehensive truth recovery.

To highlight the framing of the issue of the missing by political elites in the RoC, I examine parliamentary speeches, resolutions, questions and laws relevant to the subject of missing persons since the early 1970s. Analysis of parliamentary speeches has several advantages. As the previous chapter has indicated, parliamentary speeches can provide insight into the elite framing of specific issues, because they are unmediated presentations of argumentation in a specific sociopolitical context (Loizides 2009). They reflect the positions of political parties as directly expressed by their representatives, without any interventions or alternative interpretations, as could be the case with media coverage. Parliamentary debates depict the positions adopted by political parties and leaders at very specific historical instances, without the ability to alter them retrospectively.

I juxtapose the official opinions of the most proactive Members of Parliament on the problem of missing with what I learned from personal interviews conducted during two periods of fieldwork in Cyprus, summer 2008 and January to February 2009; this greatly facilitated my effort to cover any gaps in process tracing (Tansey 2007). Finally, my analysis draws extensively on the electoral programmes of presidential candidates over the last 20 years to get the full picture of the framing on missing persons.

A considerable shortcoming is that the most essential debates about issues relating to missing persons are conducted behind closed doors in the designated (ad hoc) Parliamentary Committee on Missing Persons,[14] and access to the minutes of this committee is generally barred. As illustrated below, this is part of the strategy used to frame the missing. However, I overcame this deficiency, at least partially, by arranging personal interviews with current and previous members of the committee;[15] I also gained limited access to the classified minutes of these closed sessions.

Diagnostic framing, as previously mentioned, identifies the source of a problem and attributes blame to the perceived source of the problematic situation (Benford and Snow 2000). Prognostic framing suggests ways to solve these problematic situations (ibid.). In the Greek-Cypriot community, the Turkish invasion was a catalyst for a common diagnosis of the problem of missing persons by political elites. In this framing, Turkey is held as solely accountable for the creation and perpetuation of the problem. Turkey is perceived to be responsible for the other major wounds opened during the invasion, such as the occupation of 37 per cent of the island, forcing approximately 211,000 people to become refugees and creating the problem of the 'enclaved' (Kovras and Loizides 2011). The empirical evidence from the House of Representatives, the interviews, the pre-election material and classified sessions of the designated Committee on Missing Persons all identify Turkey as the responsible actor. Since 1974, 12 resolutions have been issued by the House of Representatives, all identifying Turkey as solely responsible; all were adopted unanimously.[16] Moreover, in the personal interviews, all members of the Parliamentary Committee on Missing Persons identified the Turkish invasion as the beginning of the problem of missing persons and Turkey as the only responsible party. Finally, the electoral programmes of several candidates for Presidency of the RoC, irrespective of ideological or party affiliation, voice the issue of missing persons under the rubric of the 'Cyprus Problem', subtly sketching it as part and parcel of the Turkish invasion.[17]

In 1975, marking the first anniversary of the coup, a key debate took place in the House of Representatives. This debate led to the determination of the basic features of the pact for the transition to democracy (Parliamentary Debates 1975b: 576–591). A remarkable feature of the session was that all party leaders and Members of Parliament endorsed a common reading of the recent past, which linked the issue of missing persons to other side effects of the Turkish invasion, including refugees and the occupation of the island. That framing became a well-entrenched founding tenet of the transition to democracy in the RoC. Even 20 years after the invasion, the core diagnostic element that ascribes the causal and moral responsibility to Turkey remains intact:

> The House of Representatives of Cyprus, with the completion of the grievous anniversary of 20 years after the Turkish invasion and the creation of the tragic problem of the Missing, heavily condemns the continuous intransigent stance of the Turkish side.
> (Parliamentary Debates 1994b: 2554)

Missing frames

A good starting point for examining the complex social phenomenon of the Cypriot missing is the official legal definition of the RoC missing. Until very recently, a missing person was defined as 'the Greek-Cypriot who is still missing since July 20th 1974, due to the Turkish invasion ... and the state has no positive information that s/he died'.[18] Several interesting features of the diagnostic framing derive from this definition. For one thing, the beginning of the problem of missing persons coincides with the 1974 Turkish invasion, indicating a conscious decision to causally link the two issues. It is not a coincidence that the master narrative of the Greek-Cypriot community describes the Cyprus problem as one of 'invasion and occupation'.

However, the Turkish-Cypriots who went missing as a result of the atrocities carried out by Greek-Cypriot paramilitaries in the 1960s (Patrick 1976), although citizens of the Republic, are excluded from the definition. An examination of parliamentary debates since 1963 indicates no framing of the Turkish-Cypriot missing, arguably because by then, the representatives of the Turkish-Cypriot community had withdrawn from the parliament; this period was identified by the Greek-Cypriot narrative (as seen in parliamentary speeches) as the 'Turkish mutiny' (*Τουρκανταρσία*). The narrative sought to defend the RoC from the Turkish-Cypriot mutiny, and, thus, any human rights violations were subtly legitimized, excluding Turkish-Cypriots from the state's definition. Again, this coincides with the master narrative that eschews any reference to the Cyprus problem before the Turkish invasion. It was only in 2003, at a time of broader change of the RoC policy, that the definition of the missing changed slightly to encompass 'any citizen of the Republic', instead of explicitly mentioning Greek-Cypriots.[19]

This leads us to a third interesting point. Although the Greek-Cypriot community had several missing persons as a result of the inter-communal turbulence in the 1960s, only recently were they granted the status of 'missing', something again explained by the necessity to preserve the master narrative (Kovras and Loizides 2011).

Essentially, two important elements are omitted from the elite diagnostic framing: there is little reference either to the Turkish-Cypriot missing or to the legacy of intra-communal violence within the Greek-Cypriot community. The Turkish invasion was preceded by a spiral of intra-communal violence within the Greek-Cypriot community between the supporters of a pro-independence policy, designed by President Makarios, and the supporters of General Grivas, who followed a pro-*enosis* (union with Greece) policy.[20] This division dominated political life in the Greek-Cypriot community from 1968 until the Turkish invasion (Papadakis 1993). The intense hostility culminated in a short *coup d'état* by the supporters of a pro-*enosis* policy, assisted by the Greek junta, on July 1974, which overthrew and exiled Makarios. Several reported atrocities against the supporters of President Makarios and leftists were carried out by the pro-*enosis* faction (AKEL 1975). The decision of the political leaders to avoid any reference to this legacy of intra-communal violence constitutes a fundamental element of the consensus on which the Republic was established in 1974. Therefore, *selective memory*, or selective oblivion, became the founding tenet of the pact that facilitated the transition to peace and democracy in the RoC after 1974.

Three framing strategies to address the problem

Three overlapping framing strategies were pursued to address and redress the problem of the missing: emphasis on national unity and reconciliation by strengthening the institutions of the Republic, as the only way to overcome the division of the past and restore credibility to the RoC; emphasis on the 'culture of victimhood', as symbolized by wounds opened up by the Turkish invasion, that would enable the construction of a new common basis of unity for the whole Greek-Cypriot community; and lobbying international forums to condemn and put pressure on Turkey, so as to facilitate resolution of the problem.

Parliamentary debates on the first anniversary of the 1975 coup reveal much about this new consensus to promote unity and reconciliation. At this time, all major party leaders agreed to put aside their differences and work toward a new unity. Glafkos Glerides, leader of Democratic Rally (henceforth, DISY) and later President of the Republic, stressed:

> Today, with full consciousness of the grave dangers that the Greek-Cypriot people are facing, I insist that it is obligatory to the mental unity of Greeks in Cyprus, that we overcome party interests in order to fulfill a common struggle for the survival of Cyprus.
>
> (Parliamentary Debates 1975a: 576)

Using similar terms, the leader of the most popular party at the time – communist Progressive Party for the Working People (henceforth, AKEL) – Ezekias Papaioannou said: 'During this black anniversary ... we swear to the memory of all known and unknown heroes of Cypriot freedom to keep the flag of patriotic unity high' (Parliamentary Debates 1975c: 581). It is clearly commonly understood that the state institutions failed to prevent the twin disasters of the coup and the Turkish invasion. In fact, in the aftermath of the invasion, the only tangible asset held by Greek-Cypriot negotiators was control of the only internationally recognized entity on the island, the RoC.

The early consensus reached among all parties in the parliament on the need to preserve the RoC by strengthening the unity and the institutions of the Republic is illustrated in several resolutions.[21] Papaioannou stressed: 'One of the most fundamental reasons for the tragedy ... is the fact that since the inception of Cyprus as an independent state, we have not succeeded in establishing real state institutions'.[22] All speakers insisted on the twin pillars of this 'invented unity': the need for unity and reconciliation, coupled with respect for the institutions of the Republic.

The necessity to overcome past divisions and create a widely shared version of the past explains the strategy of accentuating the Greek-Cypriot culture of victimhood triggered by the Turkish aggression. There was an attempt to frame the missing not merely as victims of the ongoing struggle for reunification of the island, but for some politicians as the symbolic continuity of Greek suffering stemming from customary (unjustified) Turkish expansionism.[23]

This culture of victimhood, triggered by the Turkish aggression, was reinforced by the repetition of the number 1,619 (mentioned above), denoting the number of Greek-Cypriot missing persons. Although this number was not accurate, it became an illustrative symbol of Greek-Cypriot victimhood (Sant Cassia 2005: 51). During the period 1981–1999, although various lists containing different names frequently appeared, the number/symbol 1,619 remained intact,[24] becoming an important element of the framing process.

Perhaps not surprisingly, the Parliamentary Committee on Missing Persons is officially titled the Committee on Refugees-Enclaved-Missing and Adversely Affected Persons, underscoring a political strategy of linking all aspects and symbols of victimhood triggered by the Turkish invasion. What is surprising is that this committee works behind closed doors, and the minutes remain confidential. One might have expected such a body to invest in a free flow of public information, which would increase the possibilities of finding the missing and keep the public informed.[25] However, this decision constitutes an essential element of the framing strategy by subtly restricting public debate.

A third framing strategy is lobbying in international forums. Several resolutions, the minutes of classified sessions of the designated Parliamentary Committee on Missing Persons and comments made in the personal interviews show that enlightening (διαφώτιση) the international community is a central and consistent tactic of the RoC.[26] For the RoC, then, this is not a *domestic* (bicommunal) political issue, but a human rights (justice) issue. The appropriate way to pursue the battle is through international bodies, such as the UN, the European Court of Human Rights (ECtHR) and the EEC/EU. This is in line with the official view that the other side of the conflict is not the Turkish-Cypriot community (perceived to lack independent agency and the victim of Turkish expansionism), but Turkey. The 'legalistic discourse' employed by the Republic at the negotiating table (Anastasiou 2008), along with the issue of missing persons, can be explained instrumentally, because the Greek-Cypriot community controls the only internationally recognized authority on the island, and existentially, because the less powerful in a conflict frequently deploy a 'justice' discourse. A knowledgeable observer shared with me an interesting experience; in one of the first meetings of the two community leaders in the post-1974 period, Turkish-Cypriot leader Denktaş asked Makarios why he continued to play up the issue of the missing, although it was obvious that the vast majority were dead. Makarios replied, 'What other options do I have?' With his question, he implied that this legal framing of the missing (instead of dead) was an instrument deployed by the weakest part of the conflict (Interview no. 86). The tactic of international lobbying has attracted much international sympathy for the cause of Greek-Cypriots and their struggle against Turkey, even though it has had only minimal effect on redressing the demands of the relatives. Yet as Chapter 6 shows, some of the landmark decisions of the ECtHR were pivotal in catalyzing the resumption of the activities of the CMP in 2004.

Hegemonic belief

The specific framing on the issue of missing persons gradually acquired hegemonic status. Because the framing was stable and widely endorsed by the whole spectrum of political elites, it became dominant relatively easily. Following the literature, the criterion for a successful framing is the 'credibility of the proffered claim' (Benford and Snow 2000: 620), based on four elements: (1) 'frame consistency' or the correspondence between frames, beliefs and actions; (2) empirical credibility or the correspondence between the proffered claim and the realities of life (Kaufman 2008); (3) the reliability of the frame-maker (Benford and Snow 2000: 620); and (4) the importance of the 'idea' around which the framing is woven (Snow et al. 1986).

The framing of the issue of missing persons by political elites in Cyprus satisfies all of these requirements. For one thing, the frame-maker's credibility is significant; in Cyprus, the level of trust in governmental institutions is remarkably high (CIVICUS 2005: 97; Mavratsas 2003), making any challenge to the official discourse offered by the state very unlikely. Furthermore, the long-term consistency in the framing is coupled with abundant empirical evidence that Turkey was indeed solely responsible for the humanitarian disaster, ranging from the national narrative of the past to a series of decisions taken by the ECtHR condemning Turkey as the principal perpetrator. Indeed, even when it was revealed that several missing persons were buried in areas controlled by the Republic, thus challenging the core assumption of the framing, and even with the resumption of the activities of the CMP, the framing was so well-entrenched that neither the political leaders nor civil society dared to question it.

In the interviews, I found further indications of hegemonic framing. Two important pioneers in the recent demands for truth were journalists who published information about missing persons, Andreas Parashos and Sevgül Uludağ. Both told me that when they initiated the process, they received death threats; this clearly points to the hegemonic status of this specific framing (Interview nos 18, 22). In fact, Uludağ's brother-in-law, also a journalist, was killed by a Turkish-Cypriot ultra-Nationalist group some years before for his engagement in the issue of the missing.

Nor was there a clear 'counter-framing' – that is, an effort to 'rebut, undermine, or neutralize a person's or group's myths, versions of reality, or interpretive framework' (Benford and Snow 2000: 626). The only indication of a challenge to the proffered elite framing prior to 2000 was the highly symbolic act of the wives of two Greek-Cypriot missing persons who started digging up graves in a Greek-Cypriot cemetery in 1998 (where the first exhumations of Greek-Cypriot missing persons later took place), thereby overtly defying official policy.[27] Despite the importance of this initiative, the elite framing remained almost intact.

Several examples indicate that political elites were, in fact, trapped by their own discourse. As an interviewee revealed, even when the government decided to change its policy on the issue of missing persons and carry out unilateral exhumations in the Republic's zone in mid-1990s, the framing was so well-established that policymakers decided to 'leak' the information about the 'missing being buried in the Republic' to journalists, because of the objections raised by politicians and the official association of relatives of the missing who remained loyal to framing (Interview no. 18).

More importantly, this hegemonic framing reduced the flexibility of policymakers by defining 'national interest' in very narrow terms. Classified documents from closed sessions of the Parliamentary Committee on Missing Persons reveal that the hegemonic discourse was so well entrenched that even when a window of opportunity was opened, the political elites were not sufficiently flexible to use it. For example, in a classified session, six months after the resumption of the activities of the CMP in 2005, disappointing evidence from the first exhumations impelled several members of the Parliamentary Committee to raise the issue of withdrawing from the CMP, taking as given the unwillingness of the Turkish-Cypriot side to cooperate. The representative of the Ministry of Foreign Affairs stated: 'Our main objective (in COREPER) remains the same: the CMP is not the proper forum to investigate the fate of our missing', while the president of the session had reservations as to whether 'it [was] in our [Greek-Cypriot] interest to continue the function of the CMP or not'. This reveals the hegemonic distortions that narrow the conception of national interest, causing the players to be inflexible in finding solutions (Loizides 2009).

Yet five years later, the CMP had become an extremely successful bi-communal project; thus, the attempts to undermine it could be attributed to the distortions of national interest imposed by hegemonic beliefs. Elite consensus narrowed the options of policymakers, preventing adaptation to new conditions, even when elites recognized the need for a policy shift (Loizides 2009).

The following section analyses the three causal mechanisms used to prevent truth recovery, emphasizing political learning from previous experiences, the negotiated type of transition and the institutionalization of groups firmly opposed to comprehensive truth recovery. It explains why political parties with a vested electoral interest in unearthing these issues of truth recovery for political violence – predominantly the communist AKEL – did not break this silence. Finally, it shows why the Greek-Cypriot relatives' association was not as effective as its Latin American counterpart in unearthing the missing.

Political learning

The Turkish invasion was a painful political lesson used by elites to silence historical tensions within the Greek-Cypriot community. Remembering the wounds opened by the Turkish invasion became intrinsic to the transition. Unlike other political cleavages that polarize the Greek-Cypriot community, such as left versus right, the issue of the missing persons has been a unifying factor.

The primary fault line since the late 1940s in the Greek-Cypriot community has been the cleavage between left and right; it revolves around the dilemma of whether the anti-colonial struggle should be followed by union (*enosis*) with

Greece or the establishment of an independent state (Ioannou 2005; Kakoullis 1990; Katsiaounis 2008). The high level of intra-communal tensions frequently took a violent form. In the 1950s, the anti-colonial movement EOKA (*Εθνική Οργάνωση Κυπρίων Αγωνιστών*) launched a struggle which lasted four years (1955–1959) and led to the establishment of the independent RoC (1960). However, the struggle of EOKA is much more ambiguous than this would indicate. Yiannis Papadakis mentions:

> AKEL members were branded as traitors, threatened, and, in several cases killed by supporters of EOKA. EOKA's political wing was led by Archbishop Makarios and its military section by General Grivas, a Greek-Cypriot with a fierce anti-communist record from Greek Civil War.
>
> (1993: 151)

Even during the anti-colonial struggle, intra-communal conflict was explosive (Crawshaw 1978: 307; Drousiotis 2005; Panayiotou 1999; Peristianis 2006: 257; Poumpouris 1999).[28] The conflict between AKEL activists and right-wing Nationalists was a central element of political life in the Greek-Cypriot community; it ranged from intimidation to violent attacks (Papadakis 1993: 153). Tensions were so high that two football leagues were established to avoid mingling clubs of the left and right; these football clubs were created by the expulsion or conscious decision of players with a leftist ideology to leave their clubs and establish new ones with leftist affiliations (Panayiotou 1999).

A period of renewed violence/terrorism occurred in the early 1970s, when a group of extreme Nationalists, EOKA B, was formed; their sole objective was immediate *enosis* with Greece (Patrick 1976). The main cleavage in the Greek-Cypriot community was between those grouped under the leadership of Grivas, who promoted immediate *enosis*, and those under President Makarios, who endorsed the independence of the RoC as a means to a higher end (*enosis*) when the time was ripe. In the early 1970s, the levels of intra-communal violence escalated, leading to the above-mentioned short-term coup on 15 July 1974 (Attalides 1979; Papadakis 1998).

When he returned from exile with the restoration of democracy, President Makarios decided to grant a general pardon, offering an 'olive branch' to his opponents in his landmark speech of return (*Time* 1974). Whether Makarios' decision to grant immunity should be attributed to his calculation of the power of the coupists or to his desire to create a unified block, apportioning all blame to Turkey by detaching the issue of intra-communal violence, remains a contentious issue in the literature. Either explanation seems to reinforce the view of Samuel Huntington: that it is the balance of political power and the nature of the transition that determine a society's decisions on how to tackle the legacy of the past during transitions (1991: 216).

At any rate, in the RoC, the transition to stability and democracy was achieved through the subtle consensus of political elites to follow the olive branch policy pursued by Makarios and bury old hatreds and intra-communal division. Therefore, some degree of 'political learning' seems to have dictated the decision to selectively remember/silence certain aspects of the past (Hall 1993: 278). According to Bermeo, political learning

> is the process through which people modify their political beliefs and tactics as a result of severe crises frustrations and dramatic changes in environment. [...] Crises often force people to re-evaluate the ideas that they have used as guides to action in the past. The changed ideas may relate to tactics, parties, allies, enemies, or institutions.
>
> (1992: 274)

In the case of Cyprus, the source of learning was the disastrous effect of intra-communal violence that led to the Turkish invasion, but at the same time it should be noted that the democratization process was facilitated by the existence of a previous bureaucratic mechanism that efficiently managed pressing problems triggered by the war, such as the flow of refugees.

A study of parliamentary debates in the House of Representatives suggests that learning was immediate and transcended political ideologies and party affiliations. The speeches of all political leaders during this period are full of references to learning from previous mistakes. One speaker stressed:

> The tombs of the casualties from the (Turkish) invasion cannot be separated between Left and Right; and does it really hold any meaning to which party our missing persons, the enclaves and the other victims of the tragedy belong?[29]

Even communist AKEL, presumably not responsible for human rights abuses during that period, accepted and became committed to the olive branch policy of silence.[30] Since 1974, every anniversary session of the parliament on the coup constitutes a tutorial on the political learning from it and the Turkish invasion.[31]

In short, political learning became the basis for an elite consensus on what should be remembered and what should be silenced in public discourse. Elite pacts 'are relatively rare events in which warring national elite factions deliberately reorganize their relations by negotiating compromises to the most basic disagreements' (Burton and Higley 1987: 295). As pacts are a second-best solution for every party to a settlement, there is tacit agreement that particularly contentious topics – such as political violence – will be excluded from public debate, so long as they have the potential to derail the peace/democratization process by challenging spoiler groups (Burton et al. 1992: 11; Stepan 1997).

Democratization literature has noted the side effects of pacts on transitions to democracy. It argues that elite settlements, although providing a conducive environment for promoting democracy and peace, as well as the ideal environment for resolving urgent problems (economy, reconstruction, institution-building), are achieved at the expense of the quality of the emerging democracy. According to the 'frozen democracy' argument, negotiated transitions tend to concentrate power in the hands of a few political elites and inhibit open democratic procedures; they also restrain the development of a vibrant civil society and slow the pace of development of political and civil rights (Burton *et al.* 1992; Diamond 1999; Encarnación 2003; Karl 1987, 1990; Licklider 1995: 685; Linz and Stepan 1996: 56). In the words of Bermeo: 'Pacts make democracies more durable, but also make the deepening of democracy more difficult' (2003: 166).

In the case of Cyprus, there is a thread linking the framing of the issue of missing persons and the elite settlement that led to transition. The consolidation of democracy in the RoC after 1974 was remarkably successful, but it seems to have been achieved at the expense of truth, by fettering potential truth-seekers. Although the *pacted* nature of the transition cannot fully explain the idiosyncratic features of the slow development of civil society in Cyprus (CIVICUS 2005; Mavratsas 2003), to some extent, the nature of the transition had a long-lasting effect on the quality of democracy that emerged. In fact, the negotiated transition prevented any comprehensive truth recovery, not only by silencing potential grassroots truth-seekers – predominantly the domestic groups of relatives and other civil society associations – but by shaping the texture of the institutions of the Republic and its political culture in such a way as to delimit the scope of truth recovery. Any person, group or party contravening this pact was branded a traitor, and this constitutes a central feature of the political culture in the Greek-Cypriot community (Constantinou and Papadakis 2001; Mavratsas 2003). Here, as elsewhere, then, the texture of transition shaped the institutions and political culture of the nascent regime.

Institutions and political culture

Transitions constitute critical historical junctures with lasting impact on the quality of a fledgling democracy, because during these periods the shape of political elites, the texture of institutions and the nature of the political culture are determined (Manning 2007b). In Cyprus, the *pacted* nature of the transition shaped the consensual nature of political institutions, the political system and political parties, making it difficult for inconvenient questions and dissenting voices to enter the core political process.

In the period preceding the Turkish invasion, the RoC and its institutions were valued by the vast majority of Greek-Cypriots as second-best alternatives in the face of the *enosis* dream. That explains why the RoC was frequently labelled the 'reluctant republic'. However, as previously mentioned, in the aftermath of the Turkish invasion and the wounds it opened in Greek-Cypriot society, it became imperative to re-establish the RoC as the most important instrument in the struggle for reunification of the island.

The *pacted* nature of the transition provides analytical insights into the consensual texture of contemporary political institutions of the RoC. The Presidency of the Republic remains one of the most respected institutions, irrespective of who holds the seat (CIVICUS 2005).[32] The president is elected for a fixed five-year term without any checks from parliament. When we consider the 'superpowers' of the president, we have to ask why no president pursued a solution of unilateral exhumations within the Greek-Cypriot community before 1999, thus mitigating the pain of the relatives and partly resolving the issue of Greek-Cypriot missing persons. Why did the political parties that suffered from intra-communal violence, such as AKEL, not address the issue, even though AKEL had been a coalition partner in several governments?

Answers lie in the political and electoral system, which is founded on unity and alliance. A candidate must receive more than 50 per cent of the votes, and if no one reaches this threshold, a second round of voting takes place (Loizides 2009). It is virtually impossible for any party to promote its own candidate; thus, alliances, especially in the second round, are a central feature of the electoral system in Cyprus. Therefore, the strategy of all parties emphasizes two tactics: polarizing the long-standing cleavages to earn votes, while designing a flexible agenda to build bridges for collaboration with other parties in the second round (Loizides 2007b). The number one issue on the political agenda remains the 'Cyprus Problem' and as long as 'the problem remains unresolved, other issues must always be rated as secondary. Likewise, there is pressure to avoid any debate on matters ... that could harm the national cause' (Christoforou 2009: 96).

Any potential unilateral decision, such as truth recovery, that would challenge the foundations of the post-1974 consensus, is perceived as a suicide mission for any party, because it might be excluded from making alliances. It is revealing that the biggest party in the Republic, communist AKEL, only dared to put its own candidate forward in the 2008 elections because of these calculations and the aforementioned historical cleavages. In short, AKEL, and any party representing the defeated in post-conflict settings, prefers to disappoint its constituents, rather than break the elite pact of (selective) silence. Even when democracy was well consolidated and security threats that originally dictated the elite pact were absent, breaking the founding pact of the democratic regime would have decreased the prospect of forming a government by distancing potential allies. This is also observed in consecutive socialist governments in 1980s and 1990s in Greece and Spain that abstained from raising the issue of dealing with the past.

Moreover, as expected, the negotiated transition in Cyprus facilitated the creation of a 'highly censorious environment', one 'marked by taboos, intolerance and vilification of views deviating from the predominant governmental discourse and the official views of history' (Faustman 2009: 34). Of course, this political culture was not only the product of transition, but was also based on previous experience with the Ottoman Empire (1571–1878) and British rule (1878–1960) (Christoforou 2009). Since the independence of the island, this culture has been linked to national unity, fettering the development of a vibrant and vocal civil society (Mavratsas 2003; Taki and Officer 2009), which is usually the main source of truth-seeking.

This is not to say that the quality of democracy in the RoC is negligible. On the contrary, in all major international surveys of democracy, including Freedom

House and Polity IV project, the RoC ranks highly in almost every aspect measured (CIVICUS 2005).[33] Instead, I argue that the political system failed to provide venues for people to freely express their discontent if their views challenged the predominant one. As Papadakis underlines, the features of 'ethnic autism' and 'self-righteousness' constitute the twin tenets of political culture in the Greek-Cypriot community (Papadakis 1993, 2006), inhibiting any comprehensive re-evaluation, which is a prerequisite for truth recovery.

An example can illustrate how this culture forestalled the resolution of missing persons. The Turkish-Cypriots always claimed that *all* missing Greek-Cypriots died during the coup, and this was charged to Turkey (Sant Cassia 2005: 43). A central objection, which prohibited for several years the unilateral exhumation in cemeteries within the control of the Greek-Cypriot community, was the fear that revealing that missing persons were buried in the south would have exculpated Turkey. This explains the reticence of civil society to mobilize to address issues related to the recovery of historical memory.

Institutionalized victims' associations

Contrary to the experiences of other countries with 'disappeared' or missing persons where relatives' organizations became the main source of truth-seeking into human rights violations of the past, in the Greek-Cypriot community, relatives have, at times, blocked truth recovery. Paradoxically, at certain historical junctures, the Pan-Cyprian Organization of Parents and Relatives of Undeclared Prisoners and Missing Persons acted as an institutionalized group preventing recovery.

The relatives of the missing constitute a highly regarded group in the Greek-Cypriot community, because they epitomize the ongoing suffering and victimhood of the Greek-Cypriot people. Soon after the Turkish invasion, the leaders of the organization of the relatives of the missing realized the symbolic capital that the group had amassed and decided to safeguard their positions as elected leaders of the organization by accommodating the interests of the relatives (Drousiotis 2000). The government had always reserved privileged treatment for the relatives of the missing, as well as other victim groups. There are roads, parks, squares and even a museum dedicated to missing persons (Sant Cassia 2005: 157). Privileges range from positive discrimination in employment to financial support for getting a house, no property taxation and a pension for relatives.[34] This preferential treatment is not limited to the relatives of the missing, since all refugee groups, enclaved people and combatant organizations receive privileges and are highly respected groups in the Greek-Cypriot community. However, the case of the missing symbolizes the unhealed aspect of the suffering of the Greek-Cypriot community.

According to Paul Sant Cassia, such groups 'act more as a political pressure group to remind society about the national problem of the missing and primarily to direct pressure against Turkey, rather than to represent and resolve the problems of the individual relatives' (2005: 86). In post-conflict settings, victims' groups frequently become campaigners, mobilizing to attract material resources and public attention (Bouris 2007; Brewer 2004). As some of the interviewees told me, one of the most remarkable political decisions of the organization of relatives was the mobilization of April 2003, when Turkish-Cypriot leader Rauf Denktaş unexpectedly declared an 'open border' policy, opening the checkpoints and permitting the entrance to and from the north (Interview no. 23). When the checkpoint opened, hundreds of mothers and relatives of the missing, covered in black, protested at the checkpoints, putting significant psychological pressure on visitors willing to cross to the northern part of the island after more than 30 years.

For decades, the organization loyally followed the official state policy, which, as previously noted, identified Turkey as solely responsible for missing persons. However, because of the symbolic capital held in the hands of a few representatives of relatives, it became difficult for the leaders to follow the official policy shift towards unilateral exhumations (late 1990s); accordingly, they began to act in ways that contravened state policy. In several instances, the organization prevented exhumations that could have clarified the fate of a number of the missing. The leader of the organization vehemently rejected the policy of unilateral exhumations in the mid-1990s, when official policy change dictated the following: the elucidation of the list of the missing, which would have shown that the number of missing was not 1,619 but 1,493; the notification of relatives of 126 individuals that their relatives should not be considered missing but dead; and, finally, exhumations in the Greek-Cypriot cemeteries. As the minister charged with the task of notifying the relatives revealed in an interview, the leader of the relatives insisted that the policy shift was unacceptable and publicly encouraged the relatives not to 'open their doors' to the minister, in an effort to sabotage this process (Interview no. 32; Paroutis 1999; Politis 1999).

Although by 1996, at the governmental level, a decision was made to change the policy and inform the relatives of the 126 presumed dead, this was obstructed by the relatives themselves. The organization threatened the government that they would mobilize the mothers, because they feared that the government wanted to 'cover-up' the issue (Drousiotis 2000: 64). The government stepped back, and the policy was not implemented until 1999 – a significant delay. There were also cases of missing persons who, although officially recorded as 'fallen during the invasion' since the early 1990s, were considered missing by their families until 2000, chiefly because of the resistance of the Government Service for Missing Persons[35] which was closely controlled by the relatives' association.

Oded Haklai identifies two modes of state penetration by societal groups: first, 'having members of the group appointed to various positions of decision-making' and, second, 'having officials whose loyalty to the laws of the state is matched or surpassed by sympathy to the social movement's objectives' (Haklai 2007: 718). Both hypotheses hold true in the case of the relatives of the missing in the RoC. On the one hand, a government department for missing persons was established soon after the Turkish invasion to provide relief to the relatives (Sant Cassia 2005: 84). In 2005, a legal provision indicated that the designated ministry for resolving practical and material problems relevant to the relatives had to employ one member from the organization to take part in decisions that touched on the rights of relatives. Even more importantly, until recently, the designated body to handle the issue of the missing – the Government Service for Missing Persons – was run by the brother of the president of the relatives' association and represented the political agenda of the leaders of the association. On the other hand, political elites had always been sympathetic to the cause of the relatives. Every interviewee who belonged to the designated Parliamentary Committee on Missing Persons described relations with the relatives' organization as excellent. According to the committee's president: 'the role of the parliament, regarding our front [the missing] is to help retain the unity ... whenever you need it, the Parliament along with the Organization ... can become a powerful pressure group' (Pan-Cyprian Organization of Relatives of Missing Persons 2000: 25). As a member of the committee revealed: 'The demands and the positions taken by the relatives [of the missing] always constitute the compass of the workings of our committee' (Interview no. 2).

No political party or individual politician dared challenge the group, because it would compromise their ability to build coalitions. The case of the missing seems to support Hacklai's contention that when an organized societal force 'manages to penetrate the state, it can prevent state agencies from acting in a coordinated manner, cause institutional fragmentation ... and use the state to achieve group objectives' (2007: 714). In Cyprus' idiosyncratic civil society, a group perceived to be an instrument in the political struggle of 'persecuting' the 'other' side in the conflict has a semi-independent role with respect to the state (Taki and Officer 2009). An interviewee said: 'Whenever we go to international conferences on missing persons, the Greek-Cypriots and the Turkish-Cypriots are the only delegates that do not direct their demand for truth to their states, but against the "other" (community)' (Interview no. 20). This contradicts the experience of countries with similar experiences of disappearances, such as Argentina, Chile and Guatemala, where the demand for truth emerged from victims' groups and was directed against the state.

To sum up, the civil society group tasked with seeking the truth about the missing persons assumed a role of institutionalized 'spoiler'[36] and never dared challenge state discourse, because of vested interests in continuing its relationship with the state. This, coupled with an inherently weak civil society, explains why the demand for truth was never directed against the state. This reality, in combination with a censorious political culture, prevented individual relatives of the missing from taking legal action against the government for negligence in the perpetuation of unnecessary suffering over three decades.

Conclusion

Elite consensus in post-conflict settings is significantly facilitated – often dictated – by transitions that result from a pact between the major political forces. Because negotiated transitions are seen as second-best alternatives for all parties involved, contentious issues like truth recovery are often excluded, as their public debate raises the issue of responsibility (who did what to whom). Such debates could derail the whole process into a 'blame game', thereby endangering the agreement. Therefore, selective silences that meet the interests of the parties involved tend to prevail. For example, in Northern Ireland, militant Republican groups would never have agreed to a formal truth recovery process over the issue of the disappeared (and presumed killed) in the Good Friday Agreement, since that would have raised the thorny issue of responsibility.[37]

This consensus informs the institutions of the nascent democratic regime; it affects the political life/culture, because it is a key ingredient in electoral engineering and the central political institutions. The electoral system affects internal party structures and the electoral orientation of the political parties; this, in turn, affects their adaptability to the new game in town – peace. This has been the case in other pacted transitions, such as Mozambique, where the guerrilla faction Resistência Nacional Moçambicana (RENAMO) has achieved an impressive transformation into a successful political party, primarily by pursuing its electoral objectives (Manning 2007a). Hence, linking human rights issues to political settlements frequently facilitates the peace/democratization process by silencing these issues. Gradually, this silence is ingrained in the political institutions and political culture; ultimately, this framing acquires a hegemonic status that is difficult to challenge. But in the long term, this silence may be a necessary precondition for democratic consolidation.

Finally, the role of the victims' groups has *not* been thoroughly studied in transitional justice. The case of the relatives of the missing in the Republic of Cyprus is instructive. The government of the Republic provided privileges to the relatives of the missing, ranging from preferential treatment (i.e. hiring in public services) to significant material support (i.e. pensions, tax breaks) – policies designed, in other words, to accommodate victims' needs. Still, Cyprus has a dark side. The instrumental use of victims' groups by the government could accentuate the feeling of victimhood, promote mutual distrust and inhibit reconciliation.[38] More importantly, in certain circumstances, victims' groups can be transformed into institutionalized groups with an agenda that prevents truth recovery, even when the government is willing to proceed with comprehensive truth recovery and a resolution of human rights issues.

Paradoxically, the right to acknowledge the truth about the suffering of victims, which has been the central argument deployed by the international community and transnational advocacy networks to justify the implementation of transitional justice mechanisms, has often had an adverse outcome. These transitional measures often adopt a simplistic/bifurcated diagnosis of the problem (victim=good versus perpetrator=bad), which empowers the leadership of the most vocal – believed to be the most representative – victims' groups. Frequently, however, these groups may have developed a political agenda that prioritizes objectives other than the humanitarian needs of victims, such as bolstering nationalism and victimhood. Finally, guided by this humanitarian myopia (Belloni 2007), such reckless interventions, instead of democratizing the process of truth recovery, may institutionalize a specific version of the past that reflects the ownership of truth by particular societal groups.

Notes

1 According to the official lists submitted by the two communities to the CMP, the number of Greek-Cypriot missing at the time of submission was 1,493 and the number of Turkish-Cypriots missing was 502.
2 The Turkish Republic of Northern Cyprus (hereafter referred to as TRNC), established by the Turkish-Cypriot authorities in the north of the island in 1983, remains an entity unrecognized by any international legal body, with the exception of Turkey.
3 This is a paradox, as the Turkish-Cypriot leader declared them all dead; yet at the time of setting up, the CMP insisted that they be investigated as missing, probably to deflect the blame from the Turkish side.
4 The names of the Greek-Cypriot missing persons from the 1963 to 1964 period were not included in the original list of the Greek-Cypriot missing submitted to the CMP; therefore, the map does not included the 42 missing from this period (see Figure 3.1).
5 Αγνοούμενοι/missing persons whose fate is still unclear. For more information on the symbolic details of the discourse of the two communities on the issue of missing persons, see the seminal analysis by Paul Sant Cassia (2005, 2006b).
6 Approximately 115 exhumed persons were identified. The majority died and were hurriedly buried in common/mass graves in the turbulent days after the coup and the Turkish invasion; a number were previously considered missing.
7 There are indications that the National Guard – the Army of the RoC – had a detailed list with the names of all those buried in *Lakatamia*.
8 The sole exception is the exhumation of a US citizen in 1998, missing since 1974.
9 For further information on the CMP, see: www.cmp-cyprus.org/ (accessed 18 January 2014).
10 The latest reunification plan, the Annan Plan (2004), proposed the creation of a truth and reconciliation commission to clarify certain violent periods of the past.
11 Chapter 6 shows that the role of Turkey helps explain the resumption of the CMP in 2004.
12 The relatives of Turkish-Cypriot missing persons from the village of *Tochni* have sued the RoC for negligence and the non-investigation of the cases of 84 Turkish-Cypriots killed by Greek-Cypriot paramilitaries on 14 August 1974.
13 See the list of the fallen during the coup in the Ministry of Foreign Affairs of the RoC at: www.mfa.gov.cy/mfa/mfa2006.nsf/All/8FA6CC01D244E364C22571B9002BDA0 A?OpenDocument (accessed 15 January 2014).
14 Committee on Refugees-Enclaved-Missing and Adversely Affected Persons.
15 The interviews were semi-structured and included nine members of the current (2008–2009) Committee on Refugees-Enclaved-Missing and Adversely Affected Persons – the designated parliamentary body for issues related to missing persons. The interviews included several former members of this committee to examine fluctuations in the discourse.
16 See, for example, Law No. 77/1979, *Ο Περί Αγνοουμένων Νόμος*, 19 October 1979; Law No. 34/1980, *Ο Περί Ωφελημάτων Αφυπηρετήσεως Αγνοουμένων Κρατικών Υπαλλήλων*, 20 June 1980; Law No. 41/1980, *Ο Περί Κοινωνικών Ασφαλίσεων Νόμος*, 16 July 1980; Law No. 53(I)/1992, *Ο Περί Επαγγελματικής Αποκατάστασης των Αναπήρων και των Εξαρτωμένων των Πεσόντων, Αγνοουμένων, Αναπήρων και Εγκλωβισμένων*, 10 July 1992; Law No. 24(I)/1998, *Νόμος που Προβλέπει τον Υπολογισμό και την Καταβολή Συνταξιοδοτικών Ωφελημάτων στους Κρατικούς Υπαλλήλους και στους Υπαλλήλους των Οργανισμών Δημοσίου Δικαίου που είναι Αγνοούμενοι*, 16 April 1998; Law No. 178(I)/2003, *Νομος Που Περιέχει Διατάξεις σε Σχέση με την Περιουσία Αγνοουμένου και Ρυθμίζει ορισμένα Θεματα σε Σχεση με την Περιουσία του*, 28 November 2003.

17 For example, see the pre-electoral leaflets of Spiros Kyprianou (1983), Georgios Vasiliou (1988), Glafkos Clerides (1993 and 2002), Tassos Papadopoulos (2003) and Dimitris Christofias (2008).
18 See Law No. 77/1979; No. 34/1980; No. 53(I)/92; and Resolution No. 75/1982.
19 Law No. 178(I)/2003.
20 This split is known in the literature as Makariakoi (supporters of Makarios) versus Grivikoi (supporters of Grivas) and became the main fault line in the Greek-Cypriot community from the 1960s onwards, lasting until the Turkish invasion. The objective of *enosis* with Greece was widely shared by all major political leaders. However, Makarios supported the view that *enosis* should be put aside until a better time in the future, while Grivas and his supporters insisted on an immediate declaration of *enosis*.
21 Resolution no. 37/1975 and no. 46/1978.
22 Parliamentary Debates 1978: 1807; another speaker from a different ideological background said: 'The coup was successful because our political institutions and state bodies were weakened' (Parliamentary Debates 1979: 1886).
23 For example, an MP of centrist DIKO (Democratic Party) compared the Turkish invasion and the suffering that it caused to the Greek Cypriot community (missing persons, refugees, enclaved) 'with the other great national disaster in Asia Minor' (1919–1922) – a reference to the greatest collective trauma in contemporary Greek history (Parliamentary Debates 1982d: 1154).
24 According to the files submitted to the CMP, the official number of Greek-Cypriot missing persons is 1,493, with 502 missing Turkish-Cypriots. These numbers discredit the numbers offered by the official narratives of the two communities (1,619 Greek-Cypriots and 803 Turkish-Cypriots, respectively). In parliamentary debates of the early 1980s, the number 1,619 was never mentioned, and the number of the missing fluctuates at about 2,000.
25 The members of the parliamentary committee explained this decision; first, emphasizing the need to protect the sensitive personal data of the missing and, second, noting that information circumscribing the problem could not be made publicly available, because it was a matter of national interest.
26 Resolution no. 75/1982; no. 113/1992; no. 19/2007; Interview no. 17.
27 Paul Sant Cassia offers a lively presentation of this act in his book (2005).
28 According to sources, during the years that EOKA was active (1955–1959), out of the 265 executions ordered by EOKA, 131 targeted Greek-Cypriots (Grekos 1991: 272). Other investigators indicate that assassination attempts were made against 230 Greek-Cypriots (Markides 1977: 19). Recent investigations reveal that approximately 200 Greek-Cypriots were killed by EOKA (Drousiotis 2005).
29 A particularly elucidating example of this process of political learning is the intervention of the leader of DISY, Glafkos Clerides, who said:

> The primary historical lesson to be learned is ... that division and intolerance are sources of national disasters [...]. Therefore, today we shall all work hard towards decreasing the tensions of the past and build a real and universal unity.
> (Parliamentary Debates 1981b: 269)

30 In this respect, it is particularly interesting to note Ezekias Papaioannou's AKEL's leader – commitment to the olive branch policy set by Makarios just a couple of days after his return from exile, when he stressed: 'The speech of the president drew the line and the tactics that we should follow' (Parliamentary Debates 1974d: 155).
31 For example, see Parliamentary Debates: 1982i: 2785–2798, 1983: 1419–1431, 1985: 2199–2213, 1987: 2987–2997, 1989: 2955–2958, 1991: 279–289 and 1992a: 3581–3592.
32 The many assassination attempts against Makarios made political elites reticent to publically express their dissenting views (Ker-Lindsay 2009a: 116); this should be

attributed to the consensus to avoid any repetition of the legacy of intra-communal violence that led to the disastrous invasion, according to prognostic framing.
33 The annual reports of Freedom House can be accessed online at: www.freedomhouse.org/reports#.UtrGKfbFJdg (accessed 18 January 2014); the POLITY IV project can be accessed online here: www.systemicpeace.org/polity/cyp2.htm (accessed 18 January 2014).
34 Cyprus House of Representatives Laws: No. 53(I)/1992; No. 34/1980; No. 24(I)/1998; No. 178(I)/2003.
35 The designated body of the state to handle issues of the missing.
36 Although the term is normatively charged and frequently refers to violent groups, drawing on the work of Edward Newman and Oliver Richmond (2006), a broader definition of spoiling activity is adopted in this context to include non-violent activities used deliberately to stall peace processes.
37 In Northern Ireland, 13 persons went missing during the 'Troubles' (mainly, during the 1970s); the process was handicapped by the unwillingness of dissdent Republican groups to provide information on the location of the graves of these missing (McDonald 2007).
38 As Marie Smyth notes, because victims act as 'moral beacons', they may accentuate a culture of victimhood that deserves sympathy and 'foments counter-violence' or 'spoiling' activity under the guise of a noble cause (Breen-Smyth 2007; Bouris 2007).

4 Cases compared
Hegemonic silence and the 'linkage trap'

The first chapters deployed two outlier cases – that is, two cases where no transitional justice measures were implemented – namely, Cyprus and Spain. The major finding is that an early elite consensus on how to tackle the past, most frequently informed by partial political learning from past experiences, leads to strong institutionalization, subsequently becoming a hegemonic belief and excluding dissenting voices.

The analytical tool of 'elite framing' is essential to identify the fundamental ideological tenets upon which an elite consensus is constructed. As Figure 4.1 indicates below, elite consensus is significantly facilitated – often dictated – by transitions that result from a pact between the major political forces. In cases of 'pacted transitions', there is a need to set a least common ideological denominator upon which to build the consensus for the new political regime.

A decision to 'silence' contentious incidents of the past, such as the Spanish Civil War, or 'selectively remembering' the past in a way that accentuates a culture of victimhood, as in Cyprus, are frequently identified as the most appropriate bases for consensus in transitions to democracy. This consensus informs the institutions of the nascent democratic regime; most importantly, it affects the political culture, because this consensus is a key ingredient in the electoral system and the central political institutions. The electoral system affects internal party structures and the electoral orientation of the political parties; this, in turn, affects their adaptability to the 'new game' in town – peace. This has been the

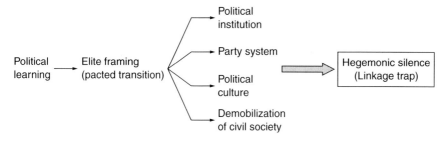

Figure 4.1 Schematic presentation of the construction and maintenance of (hegemonic) silence.

case in other 'pacted transitions', such as in Mozambique, where the guerrilla faction RENAMO has achieved an impressive transformation into a successful political party, primarily by pursuing its electoral objectives (Manning 2007b).

In this causal mechanism, the central role is reserved for political parties and political elites. In transitional periods, political parties are expected to undertake multi-task initiatives, such as (1) contribute to democratic consolidation; (2) establish internal party structures; and (3) achieve demanding electoral objectives. In the new and uncharted field of democratic politics, they must be careful not to challenge the consensus upon which the whole structure (i.e. political system) is based. Because negotiated transitions are seen as second-best alternatives for all parties involved, contentious issues like truth recovery are often excluded, as their public debate raises the issue of responsibility (i.e. who did what to whom). Such debates could derail the whole process into becoming a 'blame game', thereby endangering the agreement. Therefore, selective silences that meet the interests of the parties involved tend to prevail. For example, in Northern Ireland, militant republicans would never have agreed to a formal truth recovery process over the issue of the 'disappeared' (and presumed killed) in the Good Friday Agreement, since that would have raised the thorny issue of responsibility.[1]

Electoral considerations often explain why political parties possessing a profile conducive to truth recovery – such as AKEL, PCE and PSOE, all of which were the unacknowledged 'victims' of violence – abstain from promoting such a policy. More importantly, the earlier an elite consensus is formed and the deeper its roots, the more institutionalized and stable it becomes (Hartzell 1999). However, paradoxically, with greater institutionalization, the more difficult it becomes to challenge it; simply stated, it becomes the founding tenet of democratic political life. For example, Spanish democratic parliamentary life has been constructed to a large extent around the so-called *pacto de silencio*, which took on a life of its own. Even though the circumstances have radically changed, and Spain is now a consolidated democracy, the '*pacto*' remains taboo, and all parties refrain from touching on it. In Cyprus, the case of the 'missing' – highlighting the culture of victimhood within Greek-Cypriot political culture – embodies the unity of the (Greek) Cypriot people in the face of unjustified and continuous Turkish aggression and has become a legitimizing tenet for the Republic.

At the same time, the cases of Cyprus and Spain reaffirm the 'frozen democracy' argument, which holds that 'pacted transitions' tend to be efficient in consolidating democracy, but that the quality of the emerging regime is handicapped (Encarnación 2007). The most significant side effect of 'pacted transitions' is the demobilization of civil society. This is important for the study of truth recovery, because the main source of truth-seeking in post-conflict/post-authoritarian regimes is usually the civil society groups associated with the victims. However, when an early elite consensus is transformed into a hegemonic belief, dissenting voices are silenced. Marie Breen-Smyth remarks: 'Truth-tellers are a threat to politicians, because they have the power to disrupt hegemonic versions of truth'

Cases compared: hegemonic silence 69

(2007: 175). This hegemonic discourse can only be challenged by the mobilization of civil society, whose capacities remain significantly limited in pacted transitions.

To be sure, an early elite consensus and its 'institutionalized discourse' is a double-edged sword in negotiated transitions. On the one hand, the deep institutionalization of the consensus excludes dissenting voices and prevents original truth recovery. On the other hand, it may be a necessary evil to achieve a certain minimum level of democratic consolidation and peace. This can be labelled a 'linkage trap'. Linking human rights issues to political settlements frequently facilitates the peace/democratization process by silencing these issues. Gradually, this silence is ingrained in the political institutions and political culture; ultimately, this framing acquires a hegemonic status that is difficult to challenge. But in the long term, this silence may be a necessary precondition for democratic consolidation. Alternatively put, there is an inherent paradox in consensual institutions: *they are oriented towards reproducing the consensus (hegemonic belief), which silences the victims and civil society at large, but at the same time they often cultivate democratic institutions, which provide the tools necessary for potential domestic truth-seekers* (such as civil society groups) *to challenge this pact, albeit in the long term.*

Another tension noted by this study is that between the urgent call for national reconciliation, in which consensual institutions build trust between former enemies, and the necessity to create a competitive political system. This analysis notes the casual mechanisms through which political elites in both Cyprus and Spain attempt to bridge the often conflicting demands of transitional societies.

An equally interesting finding of this comparative analysis is the role of 'ideas' in negotiated settlements. The role of institutions in transitions has been addressed in both democratization and conflict resolution literature, but the role of ideas and how these become institutionalized is largely ignored. As Marc Ross puts it: 'Most research has little to say about how interests are developed and defined in different societies' (2007: 1). In fact, interests are not pre-given, and their institutionalization should be meticulously studied. Remembering and forgetting the past are constitutive elements of collective identities rooted in past experiences. The key question is why certain elements of the past are accentuated while others are excluded from public consideration. Here, the role of ideas is central. For example, the process of 'partial political learning' from past experiences has been central in Cyprus and Spain. The painful experiences of the past have been transformed into instructive lessons for the political elites who have translated these lessons into policies. More importantly, the 'invented unity' gave birth to the 'founding legitimizing myths' of these nascent democratic regimes.

All nations seek a narrative to make sense of the past and create social cohesion (Brewer 2006). These narratives act as 'legitimizing moments' and shape the character of the nation's regime (Gibson 2006; Norval 1998: 251; Wilson 2003). As the experiences of Cyprus and Spain indicate, 'foundational myths' do not have to be based on factual truths. So long as collective memory is socially constructed, however, it is important to understand the dynamics of its formation and institutionalization. As this analysis indicates, in negotiated transitions, political elites frequently draw lessons from painful experiences of the past, thereby altering their preferences/priorities and creating policies of consensus.

Equally important at the 'ideation' level is the role of political leaders. However, this also remains underexplored. For example, the leadership of Nelson Mandela and his ideological inclinations clearly influenced post-apartheid South Africa's framing as 'the rainbow nation'. So, too, the ideas and arguments of scholars and epistemic communities 'have heavily influenced the development of the literature' (Vinjamuri and Snyder 2004: 346). It is not coincidental that the diffusion of retributive and restorative norms has come at a period of increased influence of transnational human rights groups and international legal bodies or that this diffusion is dominated by legal scholars who set as their primary/non-negotiable objective the comprehensive screening of the past (Hirsch 2007).

This study recruits the analytical tool of 'framing' to explore the causal mechanism that transforms ideas into institutions and policies. However, it is also important to understand why a society decides to 'silence' certain aspects of the past and how these silences are incorporated into institutions, since this will help the effort to design institutions that will allow truth-seekers to insert their demands into the public discourse more easily. A better understanding of the processes of the formation of these foundational myths is essential when societies decide to democratize the process of memory – that is, when they allow divergent or conflicting discourses to enter the public discourse. This is happening today in Cyprus and Spain, as will be discussed in the ensuing chapters.

The rule of law and amnesties in transitions

A central assumption in the literature on transitional justice that has recently gained currency is that a comprehensive screening of past human rights abuses through retributive (i.e. trials, ad hoc tribunals, policies of lustration) or restorative policies (i.e. truth commissions, apologies, reparations) constitute preconditions for the establishment of the rule of law and, subsequently, the consolidation of peace and democracy. Some argue that 'tackling the past' facilitates the efforts to reconstruct a morally just order; strengthen the rule of law – an extremely important task in nascent democracies (Landsman 1997); deter potential abuses in the future (Kim and Sikkink 2010; Rosenblum 2002); and avoid collective stigmatization by individualizing (Robinson 2003). Following this line of argumentation, truth-telling has a legitimizing function for the new regime; educating the citizenry about past human rights abuses strengthens the respect for the rule of law (Hayner 1996). The reverse argument sustains that 'forgetfulness is the enemy of justice' (Shriver 2003: 28) and, as such, any transition failing to 'address the past' is not only morally reprehensible, but is less likely to achieve democratic consolidation and sustainable peace. In essence, there is a causal relationship between truth recovery, justice and the consolidation of peace/democracy. As one scholar notes: 'A promise of impunity may well lead to a cease-fire; but a lasting peace can only be built over a foundation of truth, justice and meaningful reconciliation' (Méndez 2001: 32). Yet a comparative analysis of the experiences of two societies where transitions are characterized by the absence of any transitional justice measure provides minimal support for these claims.

The linear relationship between truth, justice and peace/democratic consolidation has not been fully explored, nor is it backed up by empirical evidence. As Borer comments, this literature has 'equated aspiration with empiricism' (2006: 27). Although it is taken for granted that a coherent policy combining elements of retributive and restorative justice facilitates peace-building and democratic consolidation, the present analysis offers a different explanation – namely, that it is a certain minimum level of peace and democratic consolidation that permits any retributive or restorative measures to be implemented. This argument will be further explored in the ensuing chapters. However, it is evident from this analysis of two societies where amnesty – or 'impunity' – has been the method of dealing with the past that lasting peace and democratic consolidation do not depend on truth or justice. Instead, these objectives are closely linked to democratic stability and the development of democratic institutions.

Several authoritative international monitoring bodies rank the Republic of Cyprus and Spain among the world's leading countries with respect to human rights and democratic institutions. Since 2003, Freedom House, perhaps the most reliable independent body, has been awarding both countries the highest rating in the categories of 'Political Rights' and 'Civil Liberties', and both polities are characterized as 'Free'.[2] Equally, the 'Polity project' – another important project collecting worldwide data – ranks Cyprus and Spain quite highly and characterizes both as 'consolidated democracies'.[3]

Apart from the high rankings of the two societies in various monitoring projects, the pacification of social life is a significant illustration of their successful transitions. The level of violence in Spain and Cyprus has been minimal: intragroup violence has not erupted since 1974 in the RoC;[4] in Spain, only ETA's terrorist violence remained (until recently) to sully the transition. Nor did the absence of truth recovery mechanisms prove fertile ground for the formation of an anti-system party or faction that would undermine the legitimacy of the regime – with the exception of ETA.

Hence, it is not always true that a comprehensive screening of the past is a necessary precondition for democratic consolidation. The study reveals that a full-blown consolidated democracy with respect for human rights can be established even in the absence of any form of justice (*de jure* amnesties in Spain; de facto immunity in Cyprus). This is not to suggest that amnesties work well in every post-conflict setting. However, amnesties should not be excluded out-of-hand in peace-building and transitional justice initiatives, since under certain circumstances an amnesty can be a useful tool for democratic consolidation (Mallinder 2007). More specifically, amnesties could be useful in situations where (1) the transition is achieved by a negotiated settlement; (2) there is a relative balance of power between the former enemies; (3) the involvement of citizens and political elites is extensive; or (4) there is a 'memory' of unsuccessful judicial screening in the past.

It is a tragic irony that amnesties are most necessary and most frequently deployed in situations where human rights violations are widespread and the call for justice more urgent. According to a database of post-conflict justice since World War II, compiled by Lie *et al.*, the single most important factor in determining the transitional justice measure is the 'balance of power' between former enemies (2007). From 98 cases of trials identified by the study, 68 took place following a victory by one side, verifying the argument developed by Samuel Huntington that dealing with the past is principally a political decision reflecting the balance of power between the (former) enemies (1991: 211).

Amnesties can create political space for a 'safe exit' of the incumbents of the *ancien regime* and create space for the reintegration of political elites in political life. This is especially important, as it may be preferable to reintegrate extreme political elites into the new 'electoral game', rather than to exclude them; the latter move could impel them to undermine the 'new game in town' by extra-constitutional means. For example, consideration of the stability of the fragile Republic of Cyprus could explain Glafkos Clerides's decision to establish a new centre–right party (2007) that integrated repentant coupists. And in Mozambique, the transformation of RENAMO from an armed group into a successful political party (as mentioned above) is partly explained by the institutional bridge opened up through amnesties (Manning 2001). Similarly, the civil war that erupted between the supporters of Vichy and the resistance groups in France after the liberation (1944) was diminished as a result of a reconciliation strategy put forward by General De Gaulle, again guided by pragmatic considerations, such as the staffing of bureaucracy (Gildea 1996).

Finally, in cases where previous attempts to democratize the country have been deemed unsuccessful, and where stability takes precedence over justice, amnesties may be useful tools with which to build trust. The 'disastrous' experience of the Second Republic in Spain offered a negative example of how transitions work; therefore, stability was the overarching objective of the Spanish transition. Equally, the turbulent years (1963–1974) that stigmatized the young Republic of Cyprus made the stability of the regime a priority after the Turkish invasion. The two societies considered here learned how to resolve societal conflicts in a peaceful way in the absence of any policy of truth recovery or retributive justice; this is the essence of democratic consolidation.

To be sure, this is not a normative argument. I am not arguing that amnesties are better suited to address the realities of post-conflict settings. Rather, I contend that amnesties constitute a de facto solution in many conflicts, and, subsequently, they deserve more coherent analysis if they are to become a useful policy tool (see Mallinder 2008; McEvoy and Mallinder 2012). This study shows that amnesties should not be disqualified; with certain preconditions, they can be an instrument for democratic consolidation. As noted above, the quality of democratic institutions and the respect for human rights in Cyprus and Spain are comparable with other societies that have no experience of civil war.

A central argument resulting from the present research is that in post-conflict settings, it is difficult to distinguish the 'perpetrators' from their constituencies. Therefore, in the absence of credible judicial institutions, a retributive policy might end up penalizing people who are vocal yet non-violent opponents of a particular regime. Under certain circumstances, then, amnesties can help to avoid 'collective scapegoating'.

'Revealing is healing'?

This section evaluates another central premise of the literature of transitional justice – namely, that a comprehensive screening of the past, including official acknowledgements, apologies and truth-telling mechanisms, is a precondition for societal healing and reconciliation (Assefa 2001; Humphrey 2003). It has become a 'conventional wisdom' in the literature that *truth* and *justice* are central elements of any reconciliation initiative: on the one hand, they restore moral equality between the victim and the perpetrator, which subsequently appeases the will for revenge (Hayner 2002; Theissen 2004; Dyzenhaus 2000); on the other hand, unaddressed past injustices tend to fester, triggering spirals of revenge and violence (Harris 2002; Minow 2002; Scott 2000). The rationale for adopting a policy of screening the past is that collective memory and collective identities of the belligerent parties should be renegotiated in post-conflict settings to address past misdeeds and create a more inclusive vision for the future. Martha Minow notes: 'Failures of collective memory stoke fires of resentment and revenge' (2002: 28).

This argument has been transformed into a policy recommendation promoting truth commissions, which has been adopted by several international bodies, including the UN. For example, the authoritative Institute for Democracy and Electoral Assistance (IDEA) in its 'Reconciliation after Violent Conflict' report directly links reconciliation to truth-telling mechanisms and the pursuit of justice (2003). However, at the same time, there is no compelling clinical or sociological evidence that 'revealing is healing' (Hamber 2006; Hamber and Wilson 2002; Mendeloff 2009). In fact, a growing strand of the literature questions the necessity of dealing with the past as a precondition for reconciliation. Such critics argue that a thorough accounting for the past may prolong the return to 'normality' by maintaining enmity in public life and not allowing the wounds of the past to heal (Newman 2002). David Mendeloff asks: 'Is "truth" the best glue to hold these (post-conflict) societies together'? He clarifies: 'Mythmaking based on historical distortion and omission is the most common basis for national identity. In divided societies emerging from violent conflict the truth can be a source of danger' (2004: 371).

The study of Cyprus and Spain provide only partial support for the thesis that 'revealing is healing'. One could insist that the 'failure' of the Greek-Cypriot community to address the violence (both intra- and inter-communal) that accompanied EOKA's struggle (1955–1959), as well as the violence that marked the first days of the independent Republic of Cyprus, contributed to the tragedy of 1974. One might well conclude that this failure had a long-lasting impact – the formation of mutually exclusive collective identities that interpret new events in the light of the past (Heraclides 2001). Nevertheless, since 1974 and the de facto partition of the island, it is difficult to evaluate the effects of (non)truth recovery on inter-communal (non)reconciliation, since the outcome can be explained by the decades-old division of the island.

When the analysis shifts to the intra-communal aspect, a completely different picture appears – one that does not lend credence to the argument of the literature that truth constitutes a central element of reconciliation. As previously illustrated, the primary strategy of the Greek-Cypriot political elites following the Turkish invasion was the doctrine '*Δεν Ξεχνώ*' ('I don't forget'; see Politis 2009), referring to issues that accentuated the community's culture of victimhood and to the absence of any critical reflection into, or reference to, the intra-communal violence. Still, it is hard to argue that the Greek-Cypriot community is haunted by divisions or sentiments of revenge. In fact, intra-communal reconciliation has been achieved in the absence of any comprehensive dealing with the past.

For its part, Spain pursued a paradigmatic transition that involved 'silencing', but still managed to achieve societal reconciliation. Of course, a counter-argument might be that the search for truth by the grandchildren of the victims 70 years after the conclusion of the civil war proves the necessity of truth recovery in post-conflict settings. As noted previously, this analysis does not offer a normative argument. Instead, it suggests that truth recovery is a noble cause to be pursued, but only when the ground is fertile. Reconciliation in Spain has been achieved in the absence of any truth recovery mechanism.

Remembering and forgetting are instrumental processes and there are degrees of each. Essentially, 'societies use both strategies: recovery and eradication.... Societies, at particular times, slip into one or another of those modes' (Cohen 2001: 243). But it is important to examine why certain aspects of the past are accentuated, while others are downplayed or 'silenced'. This decision is frequently influenced by the 'lessons' of the past. In fact, it may be the *learning process* that explains how a society determines its balance between 'remembering' and 'forgetting'. This point will be further explored below.

Hagiography of victims

It has been argued that airing the truth about the past constitutes a moral obligation to victims, since: (1) some may be able to forget, but the victims cannot; (2) if a government does not concentrate on victims, it fails in one of its most basic political duties (i.e. to protect its citizens) (Biggar 2003; Kaminski *et al.* 2006); and (3) grievances that are not addressed/redressed are carried over to future generations. Hence, a privileged position in transitional justice literature is reserved for victims' groups; indeed, the field is victim-oriented (e.g. Barton

2000; Huyse 2003). Since the pursuit of truth recovery by relatives of *desaparecidos* in Latin America, victims' groups have been highly vocal, frequently forming social movements in the pursuit of justice, while academic research has closely followed this trend.

The study of Cyprus and Spain verifies only certain arguments in the literature. It is true that even in situations where there is a blanket decision made to let bygones be bygones – most frequently, by silencing contentious aspects of the past, such as human rights violations – it is impossible for victims and their relatives to forget. In fact, these painful memories may transcend generations, as in Spain, where unearthing the truth of the civil war is being carried out by the victims' grandchildren. In Cyprus, as well, 30 to 40 years after the original violent events, the mobilization of society to 'recover' the missing is very much alive. However, the role of the victims' groups has *not* been thoroughly studied in theoretical terms. For one thing, the lack of compelling empirical evidence does not permit us to draw safe conclusions on the 'constructive role' of victims' groups in recovering the truth. Although it is certainly the moral duty of the state to address victims' needs, the literature of transitional justice seems unable to understand that post-conflict settings or transitions to democracy deviate from 'normality' and constitute a 'state of exception' – to paraphrase Carl Schmitt. States frequently prioritize the establishment of the nascent regime's legitimacy; once this is accomplished, it will be able to effectively address victims' needs. The still-fragile democratic venture in Spain of the late 1970s did not have sufficient legitimacy to address the suffering of the victims of Francoism.

Societies in transition have resorted to different processes, from comprehensively addressing victims' needs (i.e. truth commissions) to maintaining complete silence over their suffering. This decision usually reflects (1) the balance of power of the groups previously in conflict; (2) the type of transition; (3) the distance between the transition and the original commission of atrocities; and (4) the political culture of the society (which may be victim-oriented).

Even when a government decides to address and redress the victims' needs, there is insufficient empirical evidence to support the view that this will facilitate a process of truth recovery. The case of the relatives of the missing in the Republic of Cyprus is instructive. The government of the Republic provided privileges to the relatives of missing, ranging from preferential treatment (i.e. hiring in public services) to significant material support (i.e. pensions, tax breaks) – policies designed, in other words, to accommodate victims' needs. Still, Cyprus has a 'dark side'. The 'instrumental' use of victims' groups by the government could accentuate the feeling of 'victimhood', promote mutual distrust and inhibit reconciliation. More importantly, in certain circumstances, victims' groups can be transformed into institutionalized groups with an agenda that prevents truth recovery, even when the government is willing to proceed with comprehensive truth recovery and a resolution of human rights issues.

The 'bad civil society' argument has been insufficiently addressed in the transitional justice literature (Chambers and Kopstein 2001), where a 'hagiographical' presentation of victims excludes certain inconvenient questions from consideration. Who is the victim in post-conflict settings? Should demands from the 'bad civil society' be incorporated in truth recovery initiatives? If the government does not address victims' needs, does it fail to meet one of its most basic political duties? However, this Manichean view of victims versus perpetrators is an endemic feature of the new 'humanitarianism' characterizing peacebuilding literature and practice (Belloni 2007; Richmond 2005a).

Paradoxically, the right to acknowledge the truth about the suffering of victims, which has been the central argument deployed by the international community or transnational advocacy networks to justify the implementation of transitional justice mechanisms, has often led to precisely adverse outcomes. These transitional measures frequently adopt a simplistic/bifurcated diagnosis of the problem (victim=good versus perpetrator=bad), which often empower the leadership of the most vocal – believed to be the most representative – victims' groups. Frequently, though, these groups develop a (political) agenda, which prioritizes objectives other than the humanitarian needs of victims, such as bolstering nationalism and victimhood. Moreover, guided by this 'humanitarian myopia', such reckless interventions, instead of democratizing the process of truth recovery, often institutionalize in the public discourse a specific version of the past that reflects the 'ownership of truth' by particular societal groups. Needless to mention, this argument does not diminish the often invaluable role of victims' groups in promoting human rights and democratic consolidation in post-conflict settings (Robbins 2013). Instead, the focus shifts to humanitarian organizations and transnational advocacy networks, which, in their effort to attract the attention of international organizations in a very competitive field that would secure financial resources to efficiently pursue their (humanitarian) goals (Barnett and Snyder 2008), frequently empower the most vocal victims' groups, often at the expense of broadening the process of truth recovery.

Finally, the literature has abstained from defining who is considered a victim, thereby implying that victims' demands overlap with the demands of the wider society in the aftermath of a conflict or authoritarian regime. In essence, the literature frequently confuses the demands of certain victims/civil society groups with what society demands. For example, in Uruguay, the amnesty law (1986) appeared in a referendum ratified by the people – although certain vocal groups demanded truth and/or justice instead of amnesty. The lack of sufficient empirical evidence does not permit us to draw safe conclusions, but an informed guess would say that in Spain there was widespread support for the amnesty law of 1977; in fact, the opposition considered it a priority. In any event, victims are sensitive and highlighting their demands may cause problems elsewhere. As noted, there is insufficient empirical evidence, but this analysis of Cyprus and Spain suggests that victims' associations often inhibit a comprehensive truth recovery if that contradicts their version of truth.

Notes

1 *Irish Times*, 7 December 2009.
2 Freedom House has two broad categories of assessment: 'Political rights' and 'Civil liberties'; the numerical ratings range from one (highest degree of freedom) to seven (lowest level of freedom). Cyprus and Spain have been assigned one in both categories and have been described as 'free' countries. For more information, see: www.freedomhouse.org/template.cfm?page=1 (accessed 15 January 2014).
3 The 'Polity score' assesses the democratic institutions and the quality of the democratic regime. For more information, see: www.systemicpeace.org/polity/polity4.htm (accessed 15 January 2014).
4 Although before 2003 the de facto division of the island explains the lack of intercommunal violence, it is impressive that in the post-2003 period – with the opening checkpoints and free transit – there have been no violent incidents.

Part II
Post-transitional justice

5 The crumbling of the pact of silence in Spain

Decades before contemporary debates about the value of unearthing the remains of Lorca, the exhumation of another prominent victim of the civil war – this time, from the victors' side – monopolized public attention. In 1959, amidst the Francoist dictatorship, when the Valley of the Fallen (*Valle de los Caídos*) was constructed, the remains of José Antonio Primo de Rivera, founder of the Phalange – a fascist organization established in the interwar period – were exhumed and reburied in a salient place in the newly established Valley. Sixteen years later, it was the turn of *Caudillo* (Franco) to be buried next to Primo de Rivera. Since then, on the anniversary of the death of these two leaders (20 November), members of the Phalange gather in the Valley of the Fallen to pay homage to both leaders by singing their anthem (*Cara al Sol*) – a ritual of nostalgia for the regime.

Recently, a heated debate has surrounded these events. On the one hand, some Spaniards believe that such ceremonies should be prohibited, holding that the Valley remains an abhorrent relic of Francoism. The monument was built in the aftermath of the Spanish Civil War (1936–1959) by the forced labour of approximately 20,000 defeated Republicans. Besides, although the declared intention that the construction of this awe-inspiring monument was to honour all those that died during the war, it has been argued that the Valley remains as a surviving reminder of Franco's regime. Thousands of forced (Republican) workers died during construction, while the tombs host primarily those victims that died 'for God and Spain' (*por Dios y España*), excluding Republicans. Therefore, it cannot be seen as an act of reconciliation. On the other hand, an important segment of Spanish society insists that latest developments in the recovery of historical memory constitute persecution, while the Law of Historical Memory, legislated by the Socialist Government in 2007, constitutes an effort to revise national history. Either way, several developments indicate that the pact of silence has long been broken.

A new social movement, the Association for the Recovery of Historical Memory (ARMH), was formed in 2000 with two primary objectives: first and fundamental, to unearth the remains of those lying in unmarked mass graves and provide them with a decent burial; second, to exert pressure for the promotion of policies of public acknowledgement for the suffering of (Republican) victims of

82 Post-transitional justice

the Spanish Civil War and, more generally, the recovery of historical memory. Both these objectives were achieved with notable success. More specifically, by the end of 2007, more than 3,000 victims had been exhumed and identified (Congram and Steadman 2009: 162), while by the first quarter of 2010 more than 1,850 mass graves had been reopened (see Figure 5.1). Also, in October 2007, the Socialist Government passed the Law of Historical Memory, which satisfies most of the demands of the association. These include: (a) denouncing Franco's regime; (b) banning public symbols that commemorate Franco or his allies; (c) mandating local governments to finance exhumations of mass graves; (d) declaring as 'illegitimate' the summary military trials held during the Spanish Civil War and Francoist dictatorship; (e) opening up military archives; and (f) other measures of moral, symbolic and economic repair to all victims of the war (Law 52/2007).

Both truth recovery of the civil war and the struggle for the recovery of historical memory have become central elements of Spanish politics. First, in 2002, the parliament passed a resolution that, for the first time in Spanish history, condemned Franco's insurgency in 1936 as illegitimate. By the mid-2000s, more and more people became interested in the silenced past. In an opinion poll in

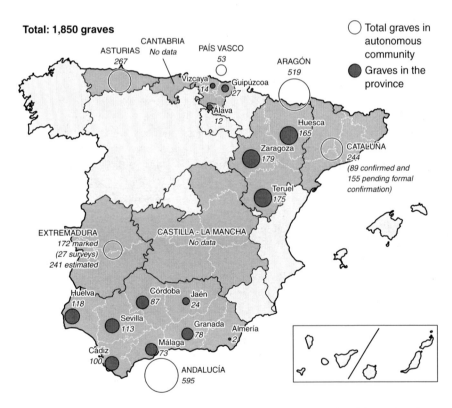

Figure 5.1 The map of exhumations in Spain in 2010 (source: Spanish Ministry of Justice).

2005, 53.3 per cent of respondents replied that 'the victims of the civil war have been forgotten and now it is time to repair this injustice' (CIS 2005). Also, there has been a 'wave of remembering' in such diverse fields as novels, movies, documentaries and conferences, tackling the issue of the civil war, while some of these focus exclusively on the subject of *desaparecidos* of the civil war (Black 2008: 230).[1] It is estimated that despite a weak civil society in Spain, today more than 300 civil society associations are mobilized for the recovery of historical memory. These range from associations of ex-prisoners; the lost children of the war (*niños de la Guerra*); refugees of the civil war; forced labour battalions; to veterans of the International Brigades (Gálvez-Biesca 2006).[2] Revealing the 'thirst' of society to recover historical memory is the headline story in December 2005 that the winning lottery number was 14431 – that is, the date of the establishment of the Second Republic (14/4/31) (Cuesta 2008: 298). For some, this was a positive omen, since 2006 was declared by parliament as a 'Year of Historical Memory'. As Francisco Ferrándiz has aptly said, 'the memory industry' is flourishing in Spain (2008: 189).

The puzzles

These recent developments give rise to certain puzzling questions: why did Spanish society decide, almost 70 years after the end of the civil war, to open the door to truth recovery? More specifically, how did it become possible to overcome the hegemonic pact of silence that prevented truth recovery for several decades? In a similar vein, how did the issue of the *desaparecidos*, neglected for several decades, become a central issue on the political agenda? Other similarly puzzling questions follow: why was the first significant rift in the hegemonic pact of silence opened during the Conservative (and non-accommodative to victims' demands) Government of Aznar, with the 2002 resolution that condemned Franco's coup? Finally, what accounts for the remarkable *volte face* of the Socialist Party's (PSOE) approach to the civil war in the post-2004 election period, contravening (previous) decades' long policies that (passively) preserved the pact of silence? The objective of this chapter is to provide a coherent answer to these questions. Finally, it is important to examine how, contrary to unsuccessful attempts in the late 1970s, demand for exhumations originating from grassroots organizations have been successfully incorporated into the political agenda.

In what follows, two alternate explanations are presented briefly, as well as reasons why they fall short in unravelling these puzzles. Then an argument is put forward that the successful socialization of Spanish political elites in international human rights norms, in combination with a new favourable equilibrium in the political opportunity structure, facilitated efforts of truth-seeking groups to enter their demands onto the mainstream political agenda. This chapter fully explores the catalytic role of international institutions in supporting grassroots truth-seeking initiatives. The explanation deploys analytical tools of 'contentious politics' and focuses on the parameters that shaped a positive equilibrium in the 'political opportunity structure', including new political allies for truth-seeking groups; the coming into power of a friendly government in the period after 2004; as well as the assistance of influential (judicial) allies. It is also argued that opportunities were not always external, but that in several instances these associations created new opportunities by pursuing innovative actions. The second part of the chapter investigates the development of the elite discourse on the issue and reveals a gradual revision of the hegemonic pact of silence maintained since transition. Analysis will show that the majority of left-wing and regional–nationalist parties promoted a revised version of the pact of silence, which 'delinks' the issue of human rights abuses from overall political transition. Equally, the study of elite framing highlights the levels of socialization of political elites into international human rights norms.

Alternative explanations

Amongst domestic scholars investigating the process of recovering historical memory in Spain, two (overlapping) explanations remain particularly popular. The first account adopts a post-materialist explanation for the recent remarkable change. According to post-materialist theory, societies that experience an increase in levels of wealth, development and job security tend to gradually shift their interests, priorities and values from purely materialist to post-materialist texture, such as concerns about environmental degradation and human rights (Inglehart and Welzel 2005). As such, it could be argued that a shift to post-materialist concerns in Spanish society, including acknowledgement of victims of the civil war, is due to growth in the economy and achievement of high levels of wealth over the last three decades.

It should be made clear though, that the post-materialist argument refers primarily to job security, rather than wealth or development rates. It is primarily job security that makes people active in civil life and capable of pursuing post-materialist objectives. However, high levels of unemployment have been a permanent feature of the Spanish economy, and this might provide an explanation for the weakness of civil society in Spain. As Omar Encarnación (2009) has argued, this hypothesis seems to be quite feeble, taking into consideration that although democratic consolidation and high levels of (materialist) development have been achieved, Spanish civil society is still very ineffectual. Although there is an element of truth that people today have more time and technological knowledge to address the past, such as the internet, it is incoherent to argue that the same society that showed only minimal interest in several important post-material problems, as the 'anaemia' of civil society reveals (ibid.), at the same time mobilized to promote the issue of the recovery of historical memory.

Another quite popular explanation for the contemporary recovery of historical memory points to the 'generational hypothesis'. This argument draws on social psychology literature, which insists that there is a cycle of memory that enables remembrance of traumatic events after a period of 20 to 30 years (Pennebaker and Banasick 1997). Following this argument, the period between 12 and 25 years old is very influential in the development of a person's cognition. Hence, when the generation who experienced a traumatic event during its adolescence takes centre stage in political, economic and social life, usually after 20 to 30 years, these events will surface in the collective memory. Thus, it has been argued, that the generation of those involved in the recovery of historical memory in Spain do so precisely because during transition (1975) they were infants and had no personal living memories of Franco and therefore were not committed to the 'pact of silence'. In fact, Iguarta and Paez have found that there is a correlation between the production of films concerning the Spanish Civil War and the above-mentioned model (1997).

Although the passage of time is of central importance in catalyzing the revision of the hegemonic pact of silence, this is not necessarily related to specific generations. However, as will become clear in the analysis, the passage of time, although not a causal determinant, facilitated the recovery of truth (narrowly defined), by changing the normative context that created new opportunities for domestic truth-seeking groups. Explaining 'why now' needs to focus not merely on the aspect of time, but also on the (new) opportunities available to these actors to promote comprehensive screening of the past. Therefore, analysis will now proceed to presentation of contentious political literature, which will serve as the primary tool of analysis.

Political opportunities

The literature of contentious politics focuses on political processes of social change and, as such, it is best-suited to help us explain the recent deconstruction of the hegemonic 'pact of silence'. This section sheds light on the interesting process through which demands of associations promoting truth recovery – more precisely, the (pioneering) ARMH, managed to successfully legitimize their demands in political debates.

According to the relevant literature, there are three main preconditions that determine the degree of success of collective action. First, the group should define the situation as *one in which moral principles have been violated* and, therefore, subsequently, perpetuation of this unjust situation is unacceptable (Klandermans 1997: 40; Gamson 1992). This constitutes the 'injustice component' of collective action. However, defining the situation as unjust does not suffice for the emergence of collective action. '[A] consciousness that it is possible to alter the conditions or policies through collective action' (ibid.: 7) is necessary to stimulate the belief that *changing the current situation is possible*. This second component refers to the 'agency' of the group. Finally, the *'identity'* component frames the situation in confrontational terms with a clearly defined *'we'* versus *'they'*, thus bolstering the distinct collective identity of the group (Klandermans 1997: 40).

However, the emergence of a social movement is not sufficient per se to instigate change, since other more powerful political actors frequently object to its demands. Contentious politics focuses on explaining the process through which marginalized interests within a society form collectives and struggle to promote a specific political agenda in order to accommodate their demands (McAdam *et al.* 2001: 5; Tarrow 2001: 7). The central problem that claim-makers experience is the lack of regular access to powerful institutions (Tarrow 1998). This lack of access, in combination with the challenging nature of their demands ('change' is always challenging), explains the centrality of political opportunities in facilitating or constraining the prospect of success. Contentious politics literature focuses on these changing conditions that encourage or discourage efficient promotion of collective claims in the political agenda.

The central idea of the contentious politics approach is that 'political opportunity structure' influences the strategies of claim-makers and, subsequently, their degree of success in promoting their demands in political terrain (Kriesi 2004: 69). 'Political opportunity structure refers to the features of regimes and institutions that facilitate or inhibit a political actor's collective action and to changes in those features' (Tarrow and Tilly 2007: 440). In essence, a change in political opportunities might either pave the way for successful political action or, conversely, restrain collective action. It should be mentioned that although the term 'structure' may sketch a static picture of opportunity, most opportunities/constraints are *situational* and affected by actions of contentious groups. This fluidity of political process increases the chance of successful collective action (Tarrow 1998: 77). The literature identifies four broad factors that determine the political opportunity structure.

First, the *degree of openness of institutions in a political system* is of central importance, because it determines the degree of access to power by social movements. The most evident parameter of institutional access to power is the territorial organization of a given state. Federal, or decentralized, states contain diffused centres of decision-making, which subsequently increase space for formal access. On the contrary, unitary states provide fewer points of formal access to power. An equally important factor determining the degree of access to power remains the electoral system. It is a common wisdom that, usually, proportional representation increases the number of parties in national parliaments, which ultimately increases the number of social groups represented (Kriesi 2004: 70).

The second important factor is the *presence of influential elite allies* that can 'act as a friend in the court, as guarantors against brutal repression, or as acceptable negotiators on behalf of constituencies' (Tarrow 1998: 79). Generally, the most important allies in these processes are political parties that embrace claims of the grassroots movement. Still, other influential allies may include international advocacy networks, international institutions, media groups or even favourable judicial bodies, such as the case of sympathetic state officials (i.e. judicial bodies) to the cause of Jewish settlers in the West Bank (see Haklai 2007).

A third, overlapping factor in the political opportunity structure is the *stability of elite alignments*. If the political system has reached a firm equilibrium where political affiliations are well-established, the prospect of making new allies and accessing power is minimal. Most frequently, electoral instability or polarization in the political terrain disrupts political equilibrium and paves the way for new alliances.

Finally, the fourth factor is the *state's propensity to repression*. If a state's 'prevailing strategies' are *exclusive*, this increases the cost of collective action for a social movement and therefore acts preventively on the successful accommodation of grassroots' demands (Kriesi *et al.* 1995: 35). On the other hand, a state that has an *integrative* repertoire of action will facilitate the incorporation of collective claims into the political agenda. However, extreme repression can sometimes increase the level of sympathy for the group and, subsequently, might open a window of opportunity for new alliances. Finally, a remaining important aspect is the existence of a 'counter-movement'; the main objective of which is to prevent successful accommodation of the demands of a prototypical movement. The emergence of a counter-movement may, on the one hand, polarize political debate and create more space for new political allies, but at the same time this polarization might alienate the group from mainstream politics and moderate sectors of society that could potentially be sympathetic to its claims.

Social movements are not simply powerless actors whose fate is determined by exogenous political opportunities. In fact, grassroots organizations also have the capacity to create opportunities at the most rudimentary level by creating controversy and attracting media attention (Gamson and Meyer 1996: 276). Equally, the transmission of information relevant to their activities and demands paves the way for new alliances. Hence, the content of the activities of grassroots associations is of crucial importance, since these may enhance the opportunities or, inversely, if provocative, provide fertile ground for the establishment of counter-movements that oppose their demands and, as such, shrink the prospect of success (Tarrow 1998: 72).

In what follows, first, the puzzling and remarkable change of the Conservative Government from intransigence to partial accommodation will be unveiled using the tools of contentious politics. Then analysis will illustrate the favourable shift in the political opportunities' equilibrium, which facilitated the institutionalization of the demand for exhumations of 'desaparecidos'.

The volte face of Aznar

Indications reveal that from the mid-1990s until early 2000s, the issue of the civil war has re-emerged in Spanish society. It is revealing that in several questions in the special survey on Francoism and transition carried out by the Centre of Sociological Studies – *Centro de Investigaciones Sociológicas* (henceforth, CIS) – in 1995, almost half of the respondents believed that the 'divisions created by the civil war have not been forgotten yet' (CIS 1995a: 2201). In the meantime, the prospect of extraditing Pinochet to Spain had stirred allegations in several Latin American countries that Spanish society had adopted a 'hypocritical stance' in judging the non-prosecution of human rights violations in other societies, although at the same time Spain had abstained from addressing its own past (Encarnación 2007). In fact, for a segment of Spanish society, the Pinochet case acted as a catalyst for critical reflection over the reasons behind the decades' long reluctance to talk about the past.

As public debates about the past began to surface, the first exhumation and identification of a civil war victim took place. In the first weeks after the re-election of Aznar with an absolute majority, Emilio Silva, a journalist, carried out the exhumation of his grandfather, along with another 12 buried victims, who were executed during the civil war in the region of *El Bierzo* in Leon (McCoy 2002). The exhumation attracted significant domestic and international media attention. After the identification of his relative, he wrote an article in a local newspaper describing how the 'disappearance' of his grandfather affected his family (2000). Immediately, he was inundated by emails and letters from different parts of the country from people who were also motivated to trace the remains of their relatives and provide them with a decent burial. In his book, Silva explains that this increased demand convinced him of the urgent need to establish an association that would tackle these issues in a comprehensive manner. Subsequently, he decided to establish the Association for the Recovery of Historical Memory – *Asociación para la Recuperación de la Memoria Histórica* – (hencefore, ARMH) (Silva and Macias 2009). Since 2002, ARMH has been the main channel of communication among relatives of the disappeared, although hundreds of other civil society associations with objectives related to the recovery of historical memory have since emerged (Ferrándiz 2006; Richards 2002).

ARMH, along with other civil society groups calling for exhumations, repeatedly demanded that the government accommodate certain demands – most importantly, to provide the financial support necessary to carry out exhumations. ARMH insisted that the state had a moral and legal obligation to rectify the unjust situation created by the unequal treatment of victims of the civil war by the Spanish state, since victims of Nationalists were located, identified and returned to their relatives immediately after the termination of the civil war (see Chapter 2). The non-accommodative stance of the People's Party (PP) infuriated the leadership of the association, most significantly because of the perceived double standards in the management of the issue by the government (Interview no. 44). More specifically, the Conservative Government ordered the exhumation and repatriation of the remains of (approximately) 5,000 dead members of the '*Division Azul*' (Blue Division) that fought alongside the Nazis on the Eastern Front during World War II (Ferrándiz 2009: 83). It is estimated that, between 1997 and 2003, approximately 1,162 persons were repatriated (ibid.). The unequal treatment reserved for victims of the two sides further frustrated the members of ARMH.

This perception of unequal treatment, along with the non-accommodative stance of the government to the demands of the relatives of *desaparecidos*, convinced the leadership of ARMH of the need to internationalize their cause. This strategy has become common practice in the repertoire of human rights associations who face repressive regimes. The role of transnational/international institutions and the processes through which they facilitate the efforts of domestic NGOs to realise their objectives has been investigated by Kathryn Sikkink, Thomas Risse and Margaret Keck. According to Keck and Sikkink, transnational advocacy networks expand the opportunities of domestic human rights groups, since they provide useful information; highlight the symbolic aspects of their cause; and, more generally, cultivate a sympathetic international audience, while at the same time increase the cost of non-compliance for national governments (1998: 17). It can be argued that they legitimise the claims of these groups (Risse and Sikkink 1999).

In August 2002, the leadership of ARMH decided to internationalize the issue. At that time, ARMH decided to apply to the UN Working Group on Enforced and Involuntary Disappearances (henceforth, WGEID), based on UN resolution 43/133 (1993), which underlines the obligation of states to investigate the fate of the disappeared (Silva and Macias 2009). In effect, it was expected that the UN would act as leverage on the Spanish state to fulfil its international obligation to bring an end to the discriminatory situation by (a) exhuming the bodies of those disappeared; (b) publicly acknowledging the memory of those that could not be recovered; and (c) setting up a fact-finding judicial mechanism (Blakeley 2005: 48; Kovras 2008). Eventually, the UN recognized the right of the relatives 'to know the truth' – a norm that has gained international currency over the last two decades.[3] The UN working group did not examine the cases of *desaparecidos* of the civil war, since its jurisdiction does not extend to the period preceding its inception (1945). Subsequently, the scope of examinations focused exclusively on the period of the Francoist repression (1945–1975).

The UN not only verified that the Spanish state had a duty to fulfil these obligations, but also decided to include Spain in the list of countries with missing persons – something that constituted a major embarrassment for a country-member of the most prominent international clubs. It was also a personal disaster for the international profile of Aznar, since the justification for following the 'coalition of the willing' in deposing Saddam Hussein was founded on the premise that dictators should not evade punishment. The sincerity of this argument would have been significantly challenged if Aznar continued abstaining from any (symbolic) condemnation of the domestic dictator, Franco. Thus, almost concurrently with the decision of the UN working group, in November 2002, PP, as an indication of its willingness to comply with the UN's decision, decided to back a parliamentary resolution that (unanimously) condemned, for the first time in Spanish history, the coup of Franco as illegitimate. The fact that internationalization of the issue was the most significant reason in explaining this remarkable *volte face* is also reinforced by the fact that just a couple of months prior to the adoption of the resolution, the government refused to accommodate a similar demand put forward by a number of parliamentary groups in opposition (Diario De Sesiones del Pleno (Congreso) 2002a: 4–6). It seems, though, that the change in the attitude of PP was merely instrumental, since a year later in 2003 it refused to dedicate a part of the 2003 budget to sponsor these exhumations (Blakeley 2005: 55).

Still, the resolution that condemned Franco in 2002 should be seen as the single most important development and paved the way for further advancement on the issue of truth recovery. Since the transition, the PP has remained reluctant to denounce historical affiliations with Francoism. However, in 2002, Aznar made this decision, in order to wash away the label of 'Francoism' and become a competitive party in the liberal democratic arena. Also, this decision was dictated by Aznar's eagerness to join the 'coalition of the willing' in Iraq and, as such, going to war to depose a dictator without previously condemning a domestic dictator would have seriously delegitimized the cause. Whatever the reasons for this change, it seems that, ultimately, it had reverse effects for PP. Instead of closing the debate about the past once and for all, the 2002 resolution motivated parties of the left who were previously hesitant to break the pact of transition and who were fearful of the reaction by the establishment (military and the church) when talking about the past and legitimate victims of the war. Hence, the PP's decision should be considered extremely important in paving the way for truth recovery, precisely because it legitimized, in mainstream political discourse, debates about the past.

To explain the subsequent successful accommodation of the demands of the ARMH, and other associations active in the recovery of historical memory, into mainstream political debate, it is important to analyse strategies of the growing memory movement, as well as the change in the political opportunity structure.

'*Desaparecidos*' and the split in the memory movement

It would have been misleading to present a picture where exclusively exogenous factors (such as party politics) explain the successful accommodation of the agenda of the memory movement in Spain. These associations followed a very careful strategy in order to finally present an 'attractive' issue to political parties. The decision to set the issue of exhumations of *desaparecidos* as the primary topic in this wider effort to recovery historical memory is of major strategic importance.

As several interviews from my fieldwork indicated, there is some sort of strategy involved in this decision. First, there was a necessity to frame claims not merely in terms of historical justice, but in terms of human rights. As explained before, the issue of the *desaparecidos* became a very efficient legal tool that enabled the internationalization of ARMH's demands. Moreover, framing the issue in terms of 'disappeared', still missing (instead of 'dead' or 'victims'), highlights the ongoing nature of the problem, which needs (urgent) political accommodation. It is interesting to examine the terminology deployed by the different sections engaging in the debate about the recovery of disappearances in Spain. As the leader of ARMH revealed in an interview (Interview no. 44), the use of this term is calculated. So long as there has been no official acknowledgement of those executed or a policy to identify their whereabouts, the term has been instrumentally employed to indicate that this is a pending problem. Besides, the term serves as a bond among the members of these associations, as well as an identifier to the society. On the other hand, sceptics insist that they are not 'disappeared', but merely a process of restoration of the individual memory of the deceased. An overlapping argument would point to the fact that previous decisions of international courts on cases of enforced disappearances in other countries secured a solid legal precedent upon which the associations could build on.

The symbolic power of image, which makes certain issues much more attractive to the public than others, should also be taken into account. There is a growing demand for emotionally powerful images of exhumations, which are projected to a global audience (Ferrándiz and Baer 2008). Finally, Spanish society was already sensitive to the phenomenon of enforced disappearances, since it was familiar with the drama of relatives of *desaparecidos* in Latin American societies, with which there are close cultural ties. Therefore, in strategic terms, the decision to frame truth recovery primarily as a demand for the recovery of the *desaparecidos* was very successful and enhanced opportunities for success by presenting their cause in 'attractive' terms both to the Spanish (and global) audience, but also to its potential political allies. This strategy explains the success of a grassroots movement with such a provocative agenda, despite the remarkably weak civil society in Spain.

At this point, it is important to highlight another significant aspect of societal mobilization over the issue of the recovery of *desaparecidos*. Since the establishment of ARMH – the first association of its kind – in 2002, a major split has taken place in the memory movement. More precisely, a new group called *Foro Por La Memoria* (Forum for Memory), affiliated to the Spanish Communist Party, was established with similar objectives to the ARMH's. Since then, a heated argument has divided the memory movement. The leaders of 'Foro' significantly disagreed with the approach pursued by ARMH, since they believed that the struggle against 'oblivion' should be framed in terms of recovery of democratic/collective memory. This thesis deviates from ARMH, which was organized under the objective of satisfying the individual rights of relatives to 'know the truth'. Thus, the central point of divergence between these two groups, which remain the most important in the field, is that for 'Foro' these acts of exhumations should be a political instrument to unearth the 'Republican memory' (of the Second Republic), while ARMH adopted a more individualist approach, which was thought to be 'apolitical' by 'Foro'. As a leading member of 'Foro' argued in an interview, the process of exhumations is a means for 'the Left here in Spain to recover its point of reference' (i.e. its democratic precedent in the Second Republic and its anti-Francoist resistance) (Interview no. 50). In essence, members of 'Foro' accused ARMH of 'privatizing memory' (Interview no. 45).

Furthermore, as in every 'success story', leading figures have developed a sense of 'ownership' over the process, which frequently becomes a source of conflict. More recently, a new split took place within the 'Foro', in which one segment is willing to collaborate with ARMH, at least on certain objectives, while the *Federación de foros por la Memoria* adopted a more intransigent stance. Finally, other (marginal) groups have developed a discourse that resists the very process of exhumations, since they believe that graves are places of memory and, subsequently, exhumations 'revise the past'. Therefore, it is important to note that the strategy of the memory movement to prioritize the issue of disappearances has been very successful, despite the fact that currently these exhumations have been interpreted in different ways by different groups. The analysis now turns to the process through which polarization of the political scene in Spain facilitated the adoption of the issue of the missing by political parties.

Polarization and political opportunities

As previous analysis has illustrated, in Spain access to power through institutional means is rather *closed*. The electoral system rewards major parties, while there is no institutionalized mechanism for informal democratic participation. This has led to the demobilization of civil society, while trust in political institutions by the Spanish public remains remarkably low. It is noteworthy that in an opinion poll in 1995, 84 per cent lent credence to the view that MPs promote their own personal interests and the interests of their party (CIS 1995b: 2154). These statistics point to the same conclusion: Spaniards hold an image of a rather 'closed' political system, with limited institutionalized access points for the promotion of new demands from 'grassroots' organizations or movements. Therefore, analysis now moves to an examination of the remaining three factors in the political opportunity structure – that is, (a) stability of elite alignments; (b) presence of elite allies; and (c) a state's capacity/propensity for repression.

As analysed above, the non-accommodative stance of the PP Government led to internationalization on the matter of Spanish *desaparecidos* and subsequent flexibility by the government. However, this is only one part of the explanation. Several questions remain to be answered, such as why the PSOE decided to change its policy from non-accommodation throughout its 14-year governance into becoming a vocal advocate of truth-seeking groups in the 2000s? What was the role of regional–nationalist and left-wing parties?

To provide a coherent answer to these questions, it is essential to turn to the unprecedented polarization that characterized the second Aznar administration (2000–2004), as well as the subsequent redrawing of the map of party politics, which drastically shifted traditional axes of alignment. Throughout the second term of the Aznar administration, left-wing parties increasingly attacked the government for taking unilateral steps to promote a specific (revisionist) reading of history – primarily, by sponsoring specific cultural events. This contravened previous consensus to abstain from using the past as an instrument of politics (Gálvez-Biesca 2006: 34).

The most significant illustration of this break with previous political consensus in certain key policy areas was the unilateral decision of Aznar to abandon the traditionally Europe-oriented foreign policy of Spain and join the 'coalition of the willing' in the war against Iraq (Woodworth 2004: 12). This was a major turning point, decided without any consultation of opposition parties. Equally, this decision infuriated a particularly sensitive domestic audience concerning the use of violence for conflict resolution, derived from the collective trauma of the Spanish Civil War. The extraordinary mobilization of Spanish people against the war in Iraq in 2003 acted as a catalyst for the resumption of historical memory in mainstream politics. During these protests, for the first time since the consolidation of democracy, flags of the Second Republic were flown widely on the streets of major Spanish cities (Cuesta 2008: 298). This was an illustration of two overlapping, significant political developments that facilitated the insertion of the agenda of associations for the recovery of historical memory into mainstream politics: the reconstruction of identities of regional–nationalist parties and the unprecedented polarization of the political system.

A new body of high quality historiographic accounts of the civil war and the subsequent Francoist repression emerged throughout the 1980s and especially in the 1990s. The main feature of this new wave of historiography is the focus on local history, using innovative tools such as oral history and analysis of municipal archives. As a prominent historian highlights:

> the principal impetus came from resurgent nationalist movements in Catalonia, the Basque Country, and Galicia. Writing history from the 'periphery' was a form of identity politics whose target was not only the National-Catholic myth of 'eternal Spain', but also the teleological narrative of national unification that liberal historians had crafted in support of Spanish nationhood in the nineteenth century.
>
> (Boyd 2008: 137)

The persistent demand by the *Generalitat de Cataluña* (the Government of Cataluña) to the state to return archives of the civil war from Salamanca to Barcelona lends credence to this argument. Hence, the subject of recovering historical memory overlapped with the effort to develop local identity in peripheral nationalisms in Spain during the 1990s and especially in the early 2000s. In the ensuing analysis of elite discourse, it becomes obvious that regional–nationalist parties were the most proactive advocates for the recovery of historical memory and promoted numerous political initiatives relevant to the recovery of historical memory and, more concretely, the recovery for *desaparecidos* (Juliá 2006). Therefore, associations promoting truth recovery had support from parliamentary groups of regional–nationalist parties, who became the new influential political allies.

The other major development that significantly altered the political opportunity structure in favour of the memory movement was the polarization of the political system, which changed the electoral strategy of left-wing parties. There are two competing explanations about the reasons behind this polarization. One school of thought supports the view that polarization is the result of the PP's electoral strategy. According to this view, the majority of Spanish voters place themselves in the centre-left part of the political spectrum. As such, the PSOE has a comparative asset in electoral terms. In order to alter this situation, the PP had to design a confrontation strategy with the Socialist Party, in order to strengthen electoral support of right-wing voters and, simultaneously, polarize the political debate by emphasizing 'negative' issues, in order to frustrate the electorate and increase abstentionism – something that will increase the possibility of the PPs gaining a majority (Blakeley 2008; Fundación Alternativas 2007). Fundamentally, the PP's strategy was simple: the lower the turn out, the better the chance of success.

The other school of thought suggests that, in fact, it was the PSOE that, for the first time, in the election of 1993, employed the strategy of polarization in order to win the elections. Framing the election as a battle of democratic forces versus fascist fossils enabled the PSOE to maintain power (Barreiro and Sánchez-Cuenca 1998). Irrespective of which of these two theories carries more explanatory value, the reality is that Spanish politics entered a 'competitive turn', in contrast to the 'consensual' period that characterized party politics in the late 1990s. It is important, though, to examine this remarkable change of the PSOE on the issue of victims of the civil war, which will subsequently help us investigate the process through which the PSOE became an ally of these memory movements.

Following the relevant literature on party politics, parties 'change' either because significant changes are taking place within the party (i.e. a new balance among different factions) or because of broader environmental changes in the political system (Poguntke 2004; Ramiro and Morales 2004). Equally, successive electoral failures lead to changes in leadership. According to Encarnación, a major factor in the renovation of the PSOE was the emergence of a generation of new leaders within the party, primarily Rodriguez Zapatero, who had a completely different image of politics from that of the older generation of *Felipistas* (Gonzalez) and did not feel committed by the pact of transition. Equally, since the transition, all major grassroots associations were orbiting around *Izquierda Unida* (henceforth, IU). Subsequently, for PSOE, a potential way of winning the 2004 election was to keep the centrist profile, in order not to alienate the traditional electorate of the party, but also to promote left-oriented policies, so as to gather votes from the left spectrum.

In essence, a significant reason that explains the renovation of the PSOE was the need to accentuate old cleavages (left–right). In a 1994 opinion poll, 65 per cent responded that, in essence, parties are all the same, while 83 per cent had never thought of becoming a member of a party (CIS 1994: 2124). Equally, in questioning feelings about politics, replies were indicative of revulsion towards politics (distrust: 48.9 per cent; indifference: 25.5 per cent; boredom: 27.9 per cent) (CIS 1995b: 2154). Furthermore, in 1995, 56.7 per cent of respondents believed that political parties may be vocal, but in reality are all the same, while this percentage increased to 65 per cent in 1998 (CIS 1995b, 1998). Besides, the literature of party politics has highlighted the fact that increasingly, over the last few decades, the centre of decision-making has moved to international/transnational institutions (Poguntke 2004). This limits the flexibility of national parties to pursue radically different policies, which subsequently further cultivates the opinion that 'all parties are the same'. Faced with this reality, domestic political parties have resorted to 'symbolic politics' and accentuation of the personality of the leader (ibid.: 5).

All these indications reveal that although the PSOE had a favourably inclined (centre-left) electorate basis, it could not win the elections, largely due to the homogeneous public perception of political parties. Therefore, a solution to this problem could have been the renewed salience of old cleavages, by bringing new problems into the agenda that would accentuate an image differentiating the PSOE from the PP. As previously shown, this electoral strategy was also followed by the PP. In essence, although after transition elections were won by capturing the centre, this has not been the case since the late 1990s. So, in order for the PSOE to win an election, it had to win both the centre and the left (Fundación Alternativas 2009). The data provided by the World Values Survey are revealing. On the scale of self-positioning (where one stands for left and ten for right), although in 2000 more than 45 per cent of the Spanish electorate positioned itself in the centre, in 2007, this percentage had shrunk to 30.5 per cent (see Table 5.1). It is clear from the relevant graph that the electorate representing this percentage has moved, primarily, to the centre-left and centre-right (see Figure 5.1). It is revealing that the percentage of those identifying themselves as centre–left reached an unprecedented 38 per cent.

Table 5.1 Self-position of the Spanish electorate (%)

Year	Left (1–2)	Centre-left (3–4)	Centre (5–6)	Centre-right (7–8)	Right (9–10)
1981	10.50	30.60	39.10	16.50	3.40
1990	13.70	33.00	34.00	14.30	4.80
1995	9.60	31.80	40.20	15.00	3.20
2000	10.90	29.30	45.10	11.80	3.00
2007	12.10	37.90	30.50	16.60	2.90

Primary source: World Values Survey.

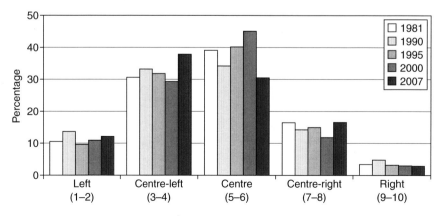

Figure 5.2 Self-positioning of the Spanish electorate (primary source: World Values Survey).

Accordingly, the PSOE's electoral agenda in 2004 was significantly revised to become a neo-left manifesto (Encarnación 2009), which also highlighted symbolic aspects of the (forgotten) left-wing tradition of the party. This was a major facilitator for the efforts of truth-seeking groups. However, the PSOE did not embrace the memory movement until the 2004 election. This was a turning point.

The 2004 election and the 'second transition'

The election of 2004 saw the peak of a wider transition from consensus politics to 'polarized politics' (*política de la crispación*) (Field 2008: 44; Gunther and Montero 2009: 136). The election was marred by the bombings of Madrid commuter trains, just a couple of days before the election, where 191 people were killed. This became known as the 'September 11th of Europe' (Garton Ash 2004). The (then) governing party (PP) originally identified the Basque terrorist organization ETA as responsible for the attacks. Over the next few days, though, processing of new information revealed that Jihadists were responsible for the attacks and 'justified' it as a reaction to Spanish involvement in the Iraq War. Also, a conspiracy was subtly hinted at by the governing party that the attacks were the product of a secret collaboration between ETA and the PSOE, so as to oust the PP from government (Tremlett 2006). Although in the period preceding the election, opinion polls were predicting a comfortable win for the PP, the management of the crisis infuriated the Spanish electorate and gave the PSOE a (minority) government.[4]

The coming into government of the PSOE was of great importance for the accommodation of demands by the memory movement, since during the two consecutive socialist governments (2004 and 2008) several laws would address these demands. However, what is even more important is to examine the way through which the PSOE managed to form a government in the 2004 election. Reckless management of the terrorist attacks by the (then) government mobilized Spanish society and convinced many people who originally had decided to abstain from voting to cast their ballot. In this process of 'constructive voting', the priority of some citizens of the so-called left was to get rid of the PP Government (Field 2009). Hence, the PSOE capitalized on votes from originally apathetic voters; the mobilization of new voters; and finally from voters of other left-wing parties (Colomer 2004). However, the PSOE did not receive an absolute majority and therefore it was in search of new allies.

This unprecedented polarization paved the way for the establishment of a broad coalition government that included left-wing parties and several regional–nationalist parties. Previous polarization, such as mobilization for the war in Iraq, ignited electoral support for these parties. For example, *Esquerra Republicana de Cataluña* (henceforth, ERC) increased its members in parliament from one to eight and, for the first time since the transition, formed a separate parliamentary group (Field 2009). As previously mentioned, these parties were already proactive advocates/allies in the recovery of historical memory. Hence, it was the insistence of parties such as IU and ERC to trade the promotion of this specific cause for support to the government that eventually promoted the topic onto the political agenda. In its electoral programme of 2004, the PSOE made no references to the issue of historical memory or *desaparecidos* (Aguilar 2008: 427; Blakeley 2008: 318; PSOE 2004). This verifies the argument that the original boost for insertion of the issue as a core political agenda was given by the left and regional–nationalist parties and was later adopted by the PSOE. This also confirms the theoretical hypothesis that new social movements are particularly dependent upon the support of left-wing parties. Their demands produce considerable possibilities for success when these parties/allies become members in a coalition government (Kriesi 1995).

The support of left-wing parties for the formation of a government majority was conditional upon the fulfilment of an obligation to promote a comprehensive law for the accommodation of the matter of the *desaparecidos* and, more generally, the recovery of historical memory (Juliá 2006). Throughout the second government of the PP (2000–2004), IU and ERC had submitted several laws, questions and initiatives on this topic (Diario De Sesiones del Pleno (Congreso) 2002a: 4–6; Diario De Sesiones del Pleno (Congreso) 2002d: 9–11; Diario De Sesiones del Pleno (Congreso) 2002c: 6–8; Diario De Sesiones del Pleno (Congreso) 2002g: 10–11).

Apart from satisfying the demands of his government allies, Zapatero also had to design a long-term policy that would keep the majority of those (left) voters that did not belong to the PSOE, but in 2004 had voted for the Socialist Party. The remarkable success of left-wing parties in 2004 expanded the target group of potential voters of the PSOE to the left. Thus, after the 2004 election, it was expected that a long-term policy to increase voters from the left would have a double benefit: keeping occasional voters of the left loyal to the PSOE and building a new centre–left electoral basis, while at the same time getting votes from the left increased the possibility of forming a majority government in the 2008 election.

The decision of Zapatero to pursue radical policies in several areas should be attributed both to issues endogenous to the party (new generation of leaders, etc.), but also to a landmark change in the political landscape of the 2004 election. Table 5.2 presents a very clear picture of this new profile of the PSOE electorate. In the question measuring intention to vote for the PSOE in the period after the 2004 election of the Socialist Party, those positioning themselves on the left and centre-left were much more positively inclined to vote PSOE than centrist voters – this constitutes a significant change from the party politics of the 1990s. Equally, it is worth noting that in the month the Law of Historical Memory was passed (October 2007), left voters seemed to 'reward' the PSOE with a remarkable increase in intention to vote (see Table 5.2).

Last, but not least, it should be taken into account that the grandfather of the prime minister was a captain of the Republican Army and was executed just days after the opening of the civil war (Crawford 2007). Zapatero, in one of his first speeches as prime minister, referred to a letter his grandfather wrote before

Table 5.2 Intention of voting PSOE (%)

Month/Year	Left (1–2)	Centre-left (3–4)	Centre (5–6)	Centre-right (7–8)	Right (9–10)	Non-aligned
January 2005	58.62	77.97	54.11	5.58	7.69	30.00
April 2005	48.19	74.68	47.22	3.14	0.00	26.76
July 2005	53.70	74.21	48.03	2.91	0.00	23.12
October 2005	54.70	71.49	44.32	2.34	0.00	21.00
January 2006	54.86	69.30	42.89	2.62	3.57	21.48
April 2006	61.97	73.27	51.23	3.87	7.46	23.36
July 2006	44.17	73.40	37.67	3.37	5.40	21.12
October 2006	52.57	74.51	37.62	2.26	2.86	16.49
January 2007	52.56	67.36	38.54	3.44	0.00	16.48
April 2007	53.59	72.58	36.45	2.47	2.12	19.31
July 2007	51.63	70.53	43.67	3.07	5.55	20.88
October 2007	61.76	71.53	41.83	5.10	5.71	26.55
April 2008	52.51	76.00	45.01	4.42	7.41	24.81
July 2008	46.20	70.40	33.67	3.00	7.84	22.83
October 2008	53.53	66.66	44.69	2.99	2.00	25.32

Primary source: Fundación Alternativas (2009).

being executed in which he asked his family to 'clear his name when the time is right' as his personal motivation behind getting involved in politics (Newsweek 2007: 32). Hence, the style or preferences of the leadership constitutes another new opportunity facilitating the truth-seeking activities in the post-2004 period.

Zapatero pursued radical policies in several areas perceived to be 'untouchable' since transition. For this reason, the first term of the Zapatero administration (2004–2008) was called the 'second transition' (Field 2009). During the first weeks after formation of his government, Zapatero fulfilled the central electoral commitment – namely, the withdrawal of Spanish troops from Iraq. Additionally, he ordered the withdrawal of all religious symbols from public places; recognized the use of stem cell research from embryos; legalized same-sex marriage in 2005 – Spain became the first Catholic country in Europe to do so; passed a gender equality act; expanded autonomy in six regions; legislated the facilitation of divorce procedures; and finally, but most importantly, institutionalized the end of silence over the past by passing the Law of Historical Memory in 2007 (Field 2009: 379).

In June 2004, the new government set up an inter-ministerial commission to investigate the situation of victims of Francoism and promote measures to regulate rectification of this problem, which would be enshrined in law (Royal Decree 1891/2004). After several delays, a draft law was presented in July 2006 and was passed in 2007. The most significant provisions of this law consist of: (a) declaring as illegitimate the military tribunals that condemned thousands of people to death because of their political beliefs; (b) state assistance in exhuming mass graves; (c) banning public symbols and removing names of streets that commemorate Franco and his allies and turning the Valley of the Fallen into a monument representing all casualties of the war; and finally (d) opening up the military archives on the civil war (Crawford 2007: 26; Law 52/2007).

To recapitulate, three significant developments created a favourable equilibrium in the 'political opportunity structure', which facilitated successful incorporation of the demand for truth recovery into the core political agenda: the emergence of several (left-wing and regional–nationalist) parties as vocal advocates for grassroots organizations; the wider polarization that changed the traditional cleavages and culminated in the results of the landmark 2004 election, which permitted the participation of 'allies' in government; and the new design of the PSOE's agenda that competed for left voters.

The 'super judge'

Although the law of 2007 was perceived to be a 'full stop' for the Socialist Government, the ARMH and their political allies were frustrated and perceived this as the first step in an ongoing process. The spokesperson of ERC, frustrated by the poor implementation of the Law of Historical Memory, went as far as to characterize PSOE's efforts as 'decaffeinated' (Diario De Sesiones del Pleno (Congreso) 2006a: 8609). The ARMH decided to present its complaints exclusively to Garzón, investing in his global reputation as an audacious human rights advocate – a title obtained when he implemented the universal jurisdiction to extradite the Chilean dictator Augusto Pinochet (Ferrándiz 2009: 64). Subsequently, in contentious political terms, this was a strategic decision by these associations to establish a new influential ally.

Garzón obviously had a pro-truth-seeking profile. It is worth noting, for example, that in 2005 he argued in favour of the establishment of a fact-finding committee on the civil war and Francoist repression. His more proactive involvement, though, begins in 2008, when the ARMH, along with 12 other associations and the anarcho-syndicalist union (CGT), demanded his assistance over exhumations. Immediately, Garzón ordered the exhumation of 19 mass graves (including one where the remains of Lorca allegedly lay) and asked government agencies and several mayors to collect all relevant information regarding the disappeared (Ferrándiz 2009; Guardian 2008; Tremlett 2008). The Platform of Victims of Forced Disappearance during Francoism (a recently established platform of various truth-seeking groups) replied on 22 of December by providing 143,353 names (Ferrándiz 2009: 64). In one motion, Garzón argued that the systematic nature of extermination of these people constitutes a crime against humanity, and, therefore, the 1977 amnesty law is inapplicable to these cases (Motion 399/2006). Equally, he argued that preferential treatment of victims of the victors by the Spanish state and the non-accommodation of demands of the 'defeated' constitutes an ongoing violation of human rights. His position was further reinforced by the UN, which called Spain to abolish the 1977 amnesty law and establish a fact-finding committee (United Nations 2008b, 2009). Furthermore, in 2006, the Council of Europe condemned the grave human rights violations that took place in Spain during and after the civil war and urged the government to rectify this discriminatory situation (Council of Europe 2006).

The possibility of overturning the founding tenets of the transition – that is, the amnesty law and the pact of silence – created heated debate and renewed polarization. In 2009, two far-right groups (*Manos limpios* and the advocacy group Liberty and Identity Association) charged Garzón with exceeding his jurisdiction under Spanish state laws. In February 2010, the Criminal Law Chamber issued a ruling that Garzón might have exceeded his authority, which means that Garzón faced the prospect of expulsion by the judicial body. On February 2012, the Supreme Court cleared Garzón of the charge of the abuse of power (Tremlett 2012). However, what is important is that even after 70 years, truth recovery on the civil war is still a contentious issue.

The potential of expelling Garzón provoked wider public (and international) debate within Spain about the quality of a democracy that preserves a (amnesty) law that contravenes the most fundamental international laws.[5] In essence, these debates constitute the clearest example that contemporary Spanish society is undertaking a process of truth recovery, albeit a belated one. Finally, it is important to note that, for the first time, the issue of international human rights norms entered centre stage of political debates. Socialization into human rights constitutes the other central explanation of the timing of truth-seeking initiatives. In order to further illustrate these unprecedented changes, analysis will turn to elite discourse, which is one more variable of the explanation.

Elite framing

The investigation of elite discourse is based on analysis of parliamentary debates – primarily, on the issue of the *desaparecidos* and, more generally, the recovery of historical memory. It is further enriched by interviews with several members of the designated committee that drafted the Law of Historical Memory (2007), as well as the laws that circumscribe the topic. Analysis reaffirms the hypothesis that the specific framing, which acquired a 'hegemonic' status and became the founding tenet of the political system, had gradually been revised by left-wing and regional–nationalist parties. This ultimately led to deconstruction of the 'institutionalized pact of silence'. Perhaps the single most important new element in this discourse is the frequent recourse to international human rights norms and comparison with the experience of other countries who successfully managed to 'tackle their past'. Still, the PP is the only party with parliamentary representation that remains loyal to the transitional settlement, framing produced in the 1970s.

PP's framing: linkage to the 'spirit of transition'

Analysis now turns to diagnostic framing of the PP, which is the only party that remains 'loyal to the spirit of transition'. The single most important element in the PP's discourse is attachment to the successful transition as its point of reference. According to the PP, successful transition, the constitution and democratic consolidation culminated in national reconciliation and resolved these issues once and for all. Therefore, the PP remains loyal to the linkage between elements of transition and 'silence' over the past. As an MP of the Conservative Party remarked: 'the arrival of democracy and the Constitution of 1978, meant to leave history to the historians and never use it as a political weapon easily used by one against others' (Diario De Sesiones del Pleno (Congreso) 2006f: 9400–9401).[6] In essence, transition put a 'full stop' to all these considerations. This desire of the PP to put an end to new questions on this issue was the main rationale behind its decision to support the resolution that condemned Franco in 2002. According to their spokesperson:

> With the resolution that will be unanimously approved today, we want to remove the issue from political debate, to put an end to it, to close [...] for the benefit of all, the benefit of the victims and the benefit of future generation.
> (Diario De Sesiones del Pleno (Congreso) 2005c: 20515–20517)

This was reproduced on several other occasions by the PP,[6] such as in 2006, when it was argued that 'the unanimous agreement of the Constitutional Commission on November 20th, 2002, closed the debate ... closed it once and for all, and represented a meeting point for parliamentary groups' (Diario De Sesiones del Pleno (Congreso) 2006c: 8613–8615).

It is to be expected that the prognostic framing qualified by the PP rejects any effort to 'delink' the debate over the past from the transitional pact of 'silence'.[7] In essence, for the PP, what should be done is to keep the book of the past closed and to look forward. Perhaps the most illustrative example is the above excerpt from a debate in 2006:

> its (law's) purposes contradict each other. In theory its objective is to suppress division, but the sole existence of the law is a factor of division and confrontation. It talks about reconciliation and coexistence but that, gentlemen, has nothing to do with stirring the mud. [...] On the one hand it says that it is time to honor the victims. Did we not do so with the transition? Did we not do so during the last thirty years? Did we not do so with the Constitution? Did we not do so with what this room has repeatedly done? Did we not solemnly do so on the 20th November 2002? [...] Why reopen a chapter that was successfully closed in the transition?' The presentation of the transition as a 'full stop' to all these considerations is repeated in each and every debate in parliamentary intervention of members of the PP.
> (Diario De Sesiones del Pleno (Congreso) 2007a: 14627–14630; Diario De Sesiones del Pleno (Senado) 2006e: 4967–4971)

Centre-left and regional–nationalist parties' framing: delinkage

What is even more interesting, though, is to present the 'prognostic framing' of those parties that challenge the discourse of the PP. Eventually, then, in which direction do these parties want to direct truth recovery? Three central elements characterize their framing on how to disengage from this problematic situation: truth, justice and repair.

The central element of 'prognostic framing', shared by regional parties and parties of the left, is delinkage of the amnesty law and, more generally, the success of transition from the acknowledgement of these human rights abuses, which is perceived to be unjustified. More precisely, the single most important element of hegemonic framing that predominated Spanish politics until the late 1990s was founded on linking the success of wider political settlement (transition) with the amnesty and institutionalization of silence over the past human rights abuses. This reading has been considerably challenged since the early 2000s, which subsequently facilitated the deconstruction of its hegemony.

In essence, it has been argued that the transition and amnesty law that accompanied it were both instruments utilized to achieve two very specific objectives – namely, the consolidation of democracy and national reconciliation. So long as these objectives have been (successfully) met, the perpetuation of this situation is affecting the quality of democracy and subsequently should be altered. As the spokesperson of the PSOE argued: 'the democratic transition confused pardon with oblivion' (Diario De Sesiones del Pleno (Congreso) 2006d: 8615–8617). This is also echoed in the law that declared 2006 as the 'Year of Historical Memory', in the preamble of which is stated that:

> The experience of more than twenty-five years of democratic practice permits us today to approach, in an open and mature way, our relation with our historical memory, keeping in mind that to recover that memory is the most stable way to settle our future of coexistence.
>
> (Law 24/2006)

Equally, all interviewees that participated in drafting the law verified this 'delinkage' hypothesis from the past. For example, a member of a regional–nationalist party argued that '[t]he problem was the interpretation of transition in the 1980s [...] we confused pardon with oblivion and the amnesty with amnesia' (Personal Interview no. 48).

Third, it is important to note that there are also different perspectives adopted by different parties. The most significant of these refers to the level of analysis. The PSOE adopts an individualist/legalistic approach, which lends credence to the view that injustice is done to individuals, so the state can only acknowledge the recovery of 'individual memory'. This is depicted in the final Law of Historical Memory in 2007, the provisions of which apply to individuals. On the contrary, regional–nationalist and leftist parties insist that this injustice is not limited to individuals, but also to the collective memory of groups that suffered persecution during the civil war and the Francoist regime. More precisely, the regional–nationalist parties and IU, both of which trace their legitimacy to the Second Republic, have started challenging the legitimacy of the transition itself, which is perceived to be a continuation of Francoism. More precisely, as Franco died in his bed and hand-picked his successor (King Juan Carlos), there was no rupture. Therefore, these parties have sought to establish a linear legitimacy that links contemporary Spanish democracy with the Second Republic. This explains why IU usually refers to the *recovery of 'Democratic Memory'*, pointing to the loyalty of the party of the Second Republic, and ERC refers to the *recovery of 'Republican Memory'*, an even more explicit reference to the Republic. This element of delinkage has also come up in several interviews.

The moral acknowledgement/repair for the suffering of victims constitutes a *sine qua non* element in the effort to 'delink' the legacy of transition from the resolution of human rights violations. In these efforts, a central position is reserved for the *desaparecidos* (see, for example, Diario De Sesiones del Pleno (Congreso) 2002c: 6–8; Law 52/2007).

What is even more interesting, though, is the frequent reference to international human rights norms in order to legitimize arguments. For the first time, truth recovery and justice are presented as indispensable elements of societal healing. A transition founded on the institutionalization of silence prevented the healing of the nation and, as such, it is perceived to be unjust and inefficient. Hence, truth recovery is presented as the best vehicle through which to move forward and heal the wounds of the past. This rationale transcends the argument of truth-seeking parties. IU supports that

> ...this conflict, in which we have come to speak of the 'two Spains', will not finish until we restore the whole truth about what happened and we recognize all those relatives and the pain they suffered and still suffer, by returning to them the remains of their loved ones so that they can be given a decent burial.
> (Diario De Sesiones del Pleno (Congreso) 2002e: 20503–20505)

Equally, ERC suggests that: 'the plain and effective exercise of the right to truth offers a fundamental safeguard against the repetition of such violations' (Diario De Sesiones del Pleno (Congreso) 2006f: 9400–9401).[8] Finally, PSOE's spokesperson provides a vivid account:

> Can the official Spain of 2006 [...] look to its past and restore it with sincerity, extracting the consequences that the passing of history offers to us? [...] because truth, that is always hard and distasteful, is also liberating; because truth, as the classics say, will set you free [...] we say it (the truth) with no negative intentions, without sectarianism, without party considerations, without opening wounds, because history does not hurt people, it makes them great and it corrects them, avoiding the repetition of errors.
> (Diario De Sesiones del Pleno (Congreso) 2006d: 8615–8617)

The starkest illustration of this rationale is found in the Law of Historical Memory of 2007, which states that:

> [...] reconciliation is not founded on forgetting but only on remembering [...] for some years now there have been not two Spains but only one, the one we have known for the majority of the living generations, is reasonable in this Spain to lament, to remember, and to repair the dignity and memory of all victims.
>
> (Diario De Sesiones del Pleno (Congreso) 2007b: 14633)

Finally, it should be noted that most politicians I interviewed highlighted the importance of truth as a precondition for successful and comprehensive reconciliation (Interview nos 39 and 37).

This new element – the 'healing function of truth' – should be linked to the wider (normative) debate that surrounds international human rights. Compliance to international institutions' recommendations is qualified because elites have been socialized to these norms and they feel that compliance is the right thing to do. Analysis of elite discourse highlights the importance of human rights norms (truth and justice) in challenging and, eventually, revising the pact of silence.

Finally, the logic of precedent-setting dictates the process of truth recovery at a political level as well. Every time a new demand emerges from a left-wing party, it is justified on the existence of a previous one, which is presented as imperfect and in need of further improvement. For example, a prominent member of the IU in a personal interview commented that: 'in a country that had never seen something like that before (i.e. law) this is a point of departure not an ending point' (Interview no. 46). This is a persistent element in the argument of truth-seeking parties: the law of 2002 was the first step to condemn Franco, but did not touch on the issue of the disappeared. Therefore, an inter-ministerial commission was established in 2004 to examine the issue. The declaration of 2006 as a year of 'Historical Memory' was also founded on the 2002 law, which was implemented poorly. Finally, the 2007 Law of Historical Memory was justified by the creation of an inter-ministerial commission (2004). So, there is a gradual and slow process of breaking the silence. This logic of gradually demanding more concessions is also derived from the interviews. For example, a leader of the local branch of the ARMH in Granada insisted that 'the Law is just the beginning of a difficult task ... it should be improved' (Interview no. 42).

Conclusion

The emergence of legal instruments/norms, the existence of a conducive international (human rights) agenda and the availability of new political allies were previously absent and significantly assisted the emergence of the politics of exhumations. Equally, the advancement of forensic techniques to identify human remains, which were not available before, considerably facilitated the process of truth recovery. All these developments are closely related to the passage of time, which changed the normative context within which these debates are framed in international politics, creating new opportunities for truth-seekers. The investigation of the discourse of political elites revealed the gradual process of revision of the hegemonic pact of silence. Equally, the study of elite framing illustrated the level of 'socialization' of political elites into international human rights norms. Overall, a critical scrutiny reveals that the single most important facilitative factor that was missing before was the creation of a normative international context, which legitimized domestic (truth-seeking) actors. Truth and justice are new elements that were not previously present in the repertoire of political leaders. Hence, comparisons with other societies that had similar experiences, but who did manage to address their past, acted as role models for domestic elites.

Notes

1 Indicative examples include documentaries: *Los niños perdidos del franquismo* and *Las fosas del Silencio* of Montse Armengou and Ricard Belis; the most successful novels include the worldwide bestseller *The Soldiers of Salamis* by Javier Cercas and *La Voz Dormida* by Dulce Chacón; The Academy Award winning film of Guillermo Del Toro, *Pan's Labyrinth* (2006), is another indication of this new interest in the past. Finally, since 2001, the weekly series *Cuéntame Como Pasó* (*Tell Me How It Happened*), focusing on the adventures of a family during the Francoist dictatorship, has been a remarkable success.
2 Sergio Gálvez-Biesca has estimated the number of these groups to be 300 (Interview no. 47).
3 For an insightful analysis on the topic, see Kyriakou (2012).
4 Although the bombings significantly influenced the final outcome, it should also be mentioned that political issues that divided and polarized Spanish politics in the period from 2000 to 2004 were also important in explaining the change of government (Blakeley 2008).
5 International media took the debate further, arguing that the perseverance of these laws in EU countries decreases the credibility of the International Criminal Court in judging contemporary human rights violations in other conflict-ridden countries, since this sets a double standard.
6 Also, see similar views, as expressed in the amendments proposed by PP in the 2002 Resolution (20–11–02); Diario De Sesiones del Pleno (Congreso), no. 76 (122/000008), Atencia Robledo, 15 March 2005a, p. 2645.
7 See Diario De Sesiones del Pleno (Congreso), no. 76 (122/000008), Atencia Robledo, 15 March 2005b, p. 3645; Diario De Sesiones del Pleno (Congreso), no. 222 (121/000099), Atencia Robledo, 14 December 2006g, pp. 11259–11262.
8 For a more representative presentation of the arguments of the ERC, see also: Diario De Sesiones del Pleno (Congreso), no. 172 (122/000180), Cerda Argent, 27 April 2006b, pp. 8609–8611.

6 The success story of the Cyprus problem

During my fieldwork in Cyprus (summer 2008 and winter 2009) the Greek-Cypriot newspapers featured, on almost a weekly basis, announcements of the funerals of identified missing persons from 1974, indicating the remarkable progress of the Committee on Missing Persons (CMP). In August 2004, the political agreement that reactivated the CMP set this ineffective and long-dormant group on the road to becoming the single most successful bi-communal project in Cyprus. By December 2013, 1,012 bodies had been exhumed and 477 identified through its activities (CMP 2013).[1] The progress of the CMP is reflected in an upswing in public opinion. For example, in an opinion poll undertaken by the UN in 2007 (see Figure 6.1), 92 per cent of Greek-Cypriots and 74 per cent of Turkish-Cypriots evaluated the presence of the CMP on the island (UNFICYP 2007) as positive. In the same poll, 91 per cent of the Greek-Cypriot respondents and 68 per cent of Turkish-Cypriots said that the exhumations and subsequent identification of the remains were essential processes (ibid.).

To backtrack a bit and establish the historical context, the Committee on Missing Persons was formally established in a bi-communal agreement in 1981,

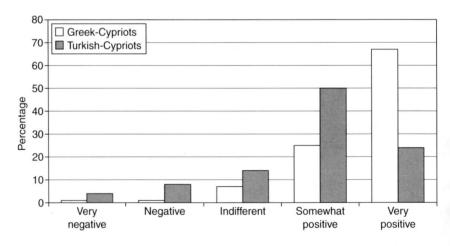

Figure 6.1 Evaluation of the CMP (source: UNFICYP 2007).

under the auspices of the UN (UN 1981).[2] The Committee was comprised of a humanitarian representative of each community, with a third member directly appointed by the Secretary General of the UN from a pool of experts on the International Committee of the Red Cross.[3] The primary objective of this tripartite mechanism was to investigate the fate of Greek-Cypriot and Turkish-Cypriot persons who went missing during the violent years (1963–1974). Despite its early promise, the CMP did little until 2004, primarily because of the lack of genuine cooperation from the Turkish-Cypriot leadership, as several UN Resolutions reveal.[4] In 1997, the relatives' hopes were rekindled when the two community leaders, Clerides and Denktaş, reached a significant bi-communal agreement on exchanging information and, where possible, assisting efforts to locate burial sites. However, once again, the agreement died on the negotiating table, largely because of Denktaş's lack of cooperation. The Turkish-Cypriot leader repeatedly recruited the Turkish-Cypriot martyrs/missing (*Şehitler*) as the symbol of the impossibility of peaceful coexistence between the two communities, thereby legitimizing his policy of partition (Sant Cassia 2005: 22) and sabotaging the CMP. Despite these obstacles, in 1999 the Republic of Cyprus carried out unilateral exhumations in two cemeteries within its jurisdiction (southern part). Through these exhumations, 24 persons considered missing were identified. Then, in 2004, a landmark agreement was reached by the leaders of the two communities to resume the activities of the CMP.

Despite the absence of a political settlement, paradoxically, a breakthrough has been achieved regarding one of the most sensitive and intractable aspects of the Cyprus problem – namely, the issue of the missing. As noted above, in the summer of 1999, the Republic of Cyprus carried out unilateral exhumations in two cemeteries within its jurisdiction, thereby revealing that several Greek-Cypriot persons considered missing were buried in these common graves. What accounts for this remarkable change that contravened the decades-long official policy of the RoC identifying Turkey as the only agent able to provide a solution to the problem of the missing? The situation becomes even more puzzling if we take into account that this decision was made before Greco-Turkish rapprochement began in 1999, at a time when several contentious issues divided the Aegean neighbours.[5] This climate of tension cannot be considered to have been conducive to unilateral gestures of goodwill.

Even stranger is the process that led to the resumption of the activities of the CMP in 2004. Although this body was established by a UN General Assembly Resolution in 1981, it remained inoperative until 2004; not a single grave was dug up in 23 years.[6] Which factors explain the transformation of the CMP from an inoperative mechanism into the most successful – and, as the polls reveal, popular – bi-communal project on the island, despite the non-solution of the Cyprus problem? It is perplexing that the agreement to resume CMP activities was reached a mere three months after the negative outcome of the referendums for the resolution of the Cyprus problem (Annan Plan), when bi-communal trust reached a low point.

The literature of transitional justice gives us little help in resolving these conundrums, as it has paid little attention to how complex human rights issues can become stepping stones to reconciliation. Resolving sensitive human rights issues that carry enormous symbolic capital can pave the way for meaningful reconciliation in frozen conflicts, as in Abkhazia, Nagorno-Karabakh, Kashmir and Lebanon. Transitional justice literature, though, has not considered how to incorporate the management of sensitive human rights issues into political negotiations in peaceful democratic transitions.

This chapter takes a close look at each of these puzzles, arguing that the *passage of time*, although not causally determinant, *changed the normative context of decision-making* at the executive level of all major actors involved, and this ultimately facilitated the formulation of a new policy that 'delinked' this humanitarian issue from the wider political negotiations. Political learning from the marginal gains of the preceding policy, in combination with the prospect of EU accession and the emerging legal and political norms in the management of enforced disappearances globally, culminated in a radical policy change. The credibility of the proffered policy was enhanced by developments in the field of forensic science, which enabled the undisputed identification of human remains. The new policy of 'truth and transparency' set a powerful precedent, committing future political leaders to the policy and making it difficult for them to deviate. The chapter also investigates the radical shift in Turkey's domestic politics and the country's EU orientation as two factors behind its *volte face*. It explores the mobilization of the Turkish-Cypriot community during the 2003–2004 period and the bottom-up demand for a proactive solution. Finally, it shows how the successful transformation of the Cypriot CMP proves that a policy delinking humanitarian exhumations from political settlement facilitates positive transformation in protracted human rights and opens up a window of opportunity for grassroots truth-seeking actors in 'frozen conflicts'.

Linkage negotiations

To this point, transitional justice literature has not substantially considered how to incorporate sensitive human rights issues into complex political negotiations. Negotiation theory posits two alternative approaches to reaching agreement on complex political issues. On the one hand, under certain circumstances, it is better to link all issues being negotiated to a wider settlement that will comprehensively address all problems (Bazerman and Neale 1993: 16). According to this integrative view, different issues can be linked in innovative ways to create room for participants to manoeuver (Loizides 2014). In essence, participants can make concessions on issues of secondary importance in exchange for return concessions on what are, to them, more vital issues (Lohman 1997: 41). For example, Loizides and Antoniades (2009) have proposed a novel linkage strategy for the Cyprus problem, providing incentives for Greek-Cypriot refugees to return in exchange for territorial readjustments, naturalization of Turkish settlers and Turkey's EU accession.

However, 'cross-issue' linkage can often lead to a deadlock in negotiations. Frequently, in adversarial relationships, 'negotiation over a specific issue tends to be enmeshed in the wider web of the bilateral relationship', and the 'solution of one problem comes to depend on the solution of one or more other problems' (Martin 2002: 57). An illustrative example is the debacle over the status of Jerusalem in the Middle East. More generally, issues of high symbolic and emotional value, such as territorial or identity, become entangled in broader political considerations and obstruct comprehensive agreement.

Under these circumstances, mediators delink issues assumed to be interlocked in an effort to break a multifaceted problem into smaller components and avoid sticking points (Lohman 1997: 48; Martin 2002: 57). Delinkage strategies have proved successful in bilateral cooperation on environmental issues, territorial disputes and international treaties. A good example of delinkage of environmental issues from peace negotiations is the Indus Waters Treaty signed in 1960 between India and Pakistan, under the auspices of the World Bank. The Indus Waters Treaty secures a form of distribution of water between the two countries (Ali 2008). This riparian cooperation untied the Kashmir dispute from the problem of water allocation and has worked quite efficiently. The treaty has become the strongest link of bilateral cooperation, and water distribution has continued, even during the three waves of conflict over Kashmir (Ali 2008: 171). Another interesting example of decoupling is the return of Sinai to Egypt during the Camp David negotiations. The Sinai question was delinked from the Golan Heights, the West Bank and the wider Palestinian question (Vasquez and Valeriano 2008); at the same time, the return of Sinai to Egypt was delinked from its future remilitarization (Loizides 2014). Such an approach has the advantage of 'reducing the number of actors needed to reach an agreement', while simultaneously 'not holding the solution hostage to the most hardline group' (Loizides 2014: 205). The case of the missing persons constitutes another interesting and successful example of the utilization of delinkage strategy to resolve human rights issues during transitions.

The limitations of the 'linkage' strategy in the RoC

In the immediate aftermath of the 1974 invasion, a long-term political and legal strategy was drawn up by the Greek-Cypriot leadership. The strategy had two primary objectives: the protection of the sovereignty of the RoC as the only legitimate actor on the island; and the politicization of legal decisions in international forums to put pressure on Turkey to withdraw its troops. It assumed that legal instruments would be the most effective tools in the battle against a politically and militarily more powerful actor. And it surmised that interstate applications underlining the violations of the European Convention on Human Rights (henceforth, the Convention) by Turkey would greatly enhance the Greek-Cypriot strategy, as Cyprus had been a member of the Council of Europe since 1961.

The tangible political gain deriving from the European Commission's (henceforth, the Commission) verdict on the first two interstate applications was the affirmation of the legitimacy of the Republic of Cyprus and its uninterrupted sovereignty as the only recognized entity on the island.[7] This, coupled with the acknowledgement of the gross violation of human rights committed by the invading Turkish Army, became a valuable legal and political tool in the strategy to internationalize the Cyprus issue and pressure Turkey to reunify the island. Although the decision of the Commission was a precedent-setting diplomatic victory, the lack of mechanisms that could force Turkey to take remedial action limited its practical implications. In fact, the 1979 Resolution of the Committee of Ministers of the Council of Europe linked the solution of the human rights problems in Cyprus to the overall political settlement, verifying the precedence of 'the logic of consequences' over normative considerations.[8]

The first three interstate applications – although not directly referring to the missing – are of pivotal importance to the issue. For one thing, the early success achieved by deploying human rights issues to support political objectives set a precedent that trapped subsequent policymakers: this legalist strategy guided the policy of the RoC Ministry of Foreign Affairs in every aspect of human rights violations, including the missing. Undoubtedly, this linkage strategy was encouraged by the political approach that underpinned the resolutions of the Commission in the consecutive interstate applications, linking the resolution of human rights problems to developments on the political settlement (Council of Europe 1978, 1987). This rationale was likely influenced by the exigencies of the Cold War – a time when international institutions prioritized order and stability over the implementation of human rights and the rule of law. Therefore, any effort to force Turkey to comply with the decisions regarding human rights breaches had the potential to alienate Turkey – a traditional Western ally – or even trigger regional instability.

Another consideration is the *efficiency of the strategy*. Although it could be argued that, in political and diplomatic terms, the Republic of Cyprus benefitted from this strategy, by the early 1990s, several politicians and well-informed observers were challenging its ability to resolve human rights problems. The policy only minimally improved the human rights of refugees, the enclaved and the relatives of the missing. Nor did the repeated resolutions of the UN Security Council and the Commission trigger any radical attempts to marginalize Turkey in the international forum, forcing Ankara to withdraw its troops from Cyprus.

At the start of the 1980s, the goal of EU accession became a priority of the Cypriot Ministry of Foreign Affairs. EU membership would safeguard the security and legitimacy of the Republic of Cyprus; this, in combination with Turkey's potential EU membership, could become a 'catalyst' for the solution of the Cyprus problem (Demetriou 2004). As a result, a number of informed observers highlighted the need to enhance the legalist strategy, by taking unilateral steps that would contribute to the solution of issues burdening the candidacy of the Republic of Cyprus, including human rights.

In this chapter, I argue that the 1999 exhumations were the culmination of a coherent policy of delinkage originating in the mid-1990s and enacted by a small group of policymakers in the Ministry of Foreign Affairs. This policy was partly informed by the influential role of European institutions in the RoC and their desire to achieve EU accession. The socialization of domestic actors (top bureaucrats and diplomats) into emerging legal and human rights norms played an equally significant role. In arguing for and tracing this process, I rely on interviews with principal participants and other well-informed sources. I also had privileged access to limited material and memos prepared by the Ministry of Foreign Affairs. However, 'process tracing' was difficult, primarily because of the sensitive nature of the issue, but also because the developments are recent and have not attracted media or academic attention.

The first indications of delinkage at the Ministry of Foreign Affairs

In the mid-1990s, a group of top bureaucrats in the RoC Ministry of Foreign Affairs planted the seeds of an alternative policy on the missing. The first person to openly state that official policy was problematic and ineffective was Xenophon Kallis, originally a CMP official. Kallis had first-hand experience of the policy's flaws and the disorganized way in which the issue was handled: the list of the missing remained a classified document; there was a lack of updated information for each missing person; and finally, the cases of the Turkish-Cypriot missing had received only minimal attention, since there was no genuine interest in their case. Kallis's first effort to advocate change came in 1993, when Leandros Zahariades was nominated Commissioner of the Department of Humanitarian Issues (Interview no. 29). As a source from the CMP revealed in an interview, Kallis convinced Zahariades of the necessity to remove the chaos that swirled around the lists of the missing – still considered confidential documents – and to clear the cases of the missing for whom significant information demonstrated that they were dead (Interview no. 54). During my fieldwork, I acquired privileged information from special reports prepared for the Ministry of Foreign Affairs in the mid-1990s making it clear that some of Kallis's recommendations were very close to the provisions that govern the Clerides-Denktaş Agreement of 1997 and, more significantly, the CMP after 2004.

Turkish-Cypriot leader Rauf Denktaş always said that all persons whom the Greek-Cypriots considered missing had died in the intra-communal violence that accompanied the coup in July 1974. In fact, this was the permanent justification of the non-cooperative stance of the Turkish-Cypriot side in the CMP. In order to get around the problem, Zahariades – who closely collaborated with Kallis – reached a subtle oral agreement with the third member of the CMP, Paul Wurth, according to which the two sides would exchange information on burial sites and, if possible, exhume and identify the remains. A parallel process would prepare the list of Greek-Cypriot fallen during the coup, re-evaluating the list of the missing and removing all those verified as dead. Hopefully, this would overcome Denktaş's intransigence. But after a fierce reaction from the official organization of the Greek-Cypriot relatives of the missing who argued that exhumations would lead to a cover-up, implementation of the agreement was halted (Drousiotis 2000: 54).

In 1996, Leandros Zahariades died, but a new proactive actor became involved in the issue of the missing – Tasos Tzionis, a career diplomat. After his return from a position in Brussels, he received a transfer within the Ministry of Foreign Affairs to become the designated official for the management of the issue of the missing persons. In an interview, he revealed that there was an element of personal motivation behind his engagement, since an army friend who was killed in 1974 was still considered missing. In addition, he was informed that several graves in military cemeteries were labelled as 'unknown'; this convinced him of the urgent need for change (Interview no. 53). Almost immediately, there was an unofficial alliance between Kallis and Tzionis (Interview no. 18).

By 1997, there was clear agreement between the two players on the main tenets of an ideal policy. Although it was still true that without the cooperation of Turkey any comprehensive solution was impossible, there was room for some unilateral steps – most importantly, the identification of those unidentified lying in common graves in Greek-Cypriot cemeteries. But any unilateral step was considered anathema, since, according to public opinion, it would have exculpated Turkey from its responsibilities. This hegemonic belief obstructed the implementation of their proffered solution.

The turning point

The window of opportunity for these players to gain political support opened with the appointment of Ioannis Kasoulides as Minister of Foreign Affairs in early 1997. Kallis and Tzionis convinced the young and ambitious minister to subscribe to a common reading of the problem. This was a turning point.

At the time, the application of the Republic of Cyprus for EU accession was being considered. During the Luxembourg Summit of the European Council in December 1997, Cyprus became an official candidate, which was one of the minister's top priorities. Diplomats with a good grasp of developments in other candidate countries were well placed to discern that their European counterparts would put increasing pressure on Cyprus to resolve pending human rights issues. A new policy was required.

Facilitating the efforts of the triumvir to revise the policy was the passage of time. Time reshuffles the deck and creates new opportunities. In this case, three decades had passed since the implementation of the official policy on the missing, yielding few results. Clearly, the policy's poor track record, combined with the EU orientation of the Republic of Cyprus and the pressing demand of relatives to bury their loved ones, dictated change.

Hence, while the original legal argumentation remained intact, a new policy of transparency seeking to solve those cases under the jurisdiction of the RoC was pioneered. In essence, the unilateral decision to proceed to exhumations was a clear indication of delinking the truth from political negotiations. The policymakers' proffered policy was framed in such a way as to highlight the need to protect the national cause of EU accession from obstacles; as such, it gained the support of previously reluctant officials and politicians (Kovras and Loizides 2012). As Featherstone argues, one of the most important functions of the process of 'Europeanization' is its enhancement of the legitimacy of domestic actors to frame their chosen policy as strengthening the path to the EU (2003). The 'soft power' of the EU can not only influence the priorities of domestic agents, but, most significantly, has the potential to act as a catalyst for domestic change by framing the agenda of these actors in reference to EU norms and the potential costs of non-compliance for the national interests.

Another result of the passage of time was that advancements in forensic anthropology made the policy of delinkage both feasible and credible. Since the mid-1980s, new forensic techniques had been implemented in Latin American countries to identify the remains of the *desaparecidos*. The impressive results of a leading team of forensic scientists of the American Association for the Advancement of Science (AAAS) exported this knowledge to other Latin American societies with similar problems, seeking to train local forensic scientists (primarily anthropologists and archaeologists) at the same time (Simmons and Haglund 2005). By 1996, forensic exhumations had become an established tool of the international institutions in addressing the violent past; two ad hoc international tribunals – ICTY and ICTR – deployed these forensic tools to provide evidence of genocide in Rwanda and ethnic cleansing in Bosnia (Srebrenica) (Stover *et al.* 2003: 663–664). The rapid global diffusion of technical expertise helped to create new norms regarding the appropriate way to tackle the issue of the disappeared.

Kallis was closely pursuing these developments. He knew the deficiencies of the present policy and was aware of the unprecedented window of opportunity recently opened up by technological advancement. All memos prepared during this period (mid-1990–2000) contained recommendations indicating his familiarity with these developments – most importantly, the provision for the collection of genetic material from relatives so that a genetic Data Bank could be established for future use (i.e. when exhumations were implemented). The interviews indicate that Kallis had already been familiarized with these norms, since he had closely followed the techniques implemented by two patriarchs of the forensic sciences – namely, Clyde Snow and Eric Stover (Joyce and Stover 1991). Indeed, by the time an ambitious DNA identification programme commenced its activities in former Yugoslavia (2000), the Republic of Cyprus had already implemented its own policy of unilateral exhumations (1999) under the guidance of the Physicians for Human Rights.[9] It seems, then, that the formulation of a new policy proposal and its credibility were enabled by significant scientific advancements and the socialization of domestic actors into these norms.

The 'missed chance' of 1997

Within a couple of months, on 31 July 1997, a landmark agreement was reached between the two leaders, Glafkos Clerides and Rauf Denktaş, to resolve the issue of the missing. In this agreement, for the first time, Clerides and Denktaş officially adopted a humanitarian approach, delinking the resolution of this specific problem from the wider political settlement. Equally importantly, the agreement included provisions for exchanging information over burial sites on both sides of the divide and facilitating the exhumation and identification of the remains.[10] For the first time, Turkey and the Turkish-Cypriot authorities signed an agreement that agreed to carry out exhumations in the north, thereby leading to a possible resolution of the problem. Sadly, the Turkish-Cypriot leadership torpedoed the agreement.

How can we explain this initial failure? It would be absurd to surmise that someone would invest resources and political capital in a venture with only minimal possibility of success. For one thing, the agreement was reached only a few months before the presidential election in the RoC, and, to a significant extent, the process was motivated by electoral considerations. This is evident in Clerides's electoral strategy; in the 1998 election, he insisted that a final resolution was approaching and that he was the most appropriate candidate to handle negotiations at this critical juncture. Following this rationale of *grand finale*, every new positive development, such as a solution of the problem of the missing persons, would be credited to Clerides. In addition, the media presented the United States as favouring the re-election of Clerides, calling him a moderate leader with the capacity to solve the Cyprus problem.

Hence, it seems that electoral considerations dictated the 1997 agreement, and, as such, it was doomed to fail. Still, this failed agreement set a useful precedent that facilitated efforts to implement the new policy of delinkage. My interviews indicated that the triumvir perceived this as a unique opportunity to entrap Denktaş in the process. Knowing that he had no alternative but to sign the document, they arranged an agreement with maximalist demands, to which he would not have agreed at any other time. In this fashion, they ensured the commitment of the Turkish-Cypriot leader and set a powerful precedent (Interview no. 52).

The implementation of delinkage policy

The policy proposed by Kallis–Tzionis–Kasoulides had presidential support and led to the unilateral exhumations in the summer of 1999, which should be seen as the unilateral implementation of the 1997 agreement and the first indication of the policy of delinkage. Of course, implementation was not easy, because the hegemonic frame was so well-entrenched. In one instance, the triumvir had to leak information to friendly media to overcome negative political and bureaucratic reactions (Interview no. 18). Still, as shown below, the unilateral exhumations had the unintentional consequence of silencing the official organization of the relatives and led to the emergence of a new actor – the anonymous and politically unmotivated relatives, who supported any development that could provide an answer to the whereabouts of their kin.

In his authoritative book *Bodies of Evidence*, Paul Sant Cassia presents a fascinating account of the struggle of two Greek-Cypriot women, Androulla Palma and Maroulla Siamisi, to find the remains of their missing husbands (Sant-Cassia

2005). Having credible information that their husbands were buried in a Greek-Cypriot cemetery, in a highly symbolic act during the summer of 1998, the women decided to go alone to the cemetery to unearth the graves of those labelled as 'unknown soldiers fallen in 1974' in the pursuit of their husbands. Although they were stopped by police, their provocative act drew public attention (Drousiotis 2000). By the summer of the next year, the state had invited Dr William Haglund of Physicians for Human Rights, which shared the Nobel Peace Prize in 1997, to organize the exhumations and identification of the remains buried in two cemeteries[11] in the part of Nicosia under RoC jurisdiction (Drousiotis 2000: 81). Of the 55 persons exhumed, 24 were considered missing. One was Zinon Zinonos, considered missing for 26 years; it turned out he was a 16-year-old who fought against the Turkish Army and was hurriedly buried in the cemetery during the turbulent month of the Turkish invasion.

These revelations led to the first official apology of the state to its citizens for negligence (Alitheia 1999; Anastasiou 2008: 149). However, the exhumations were just the tip of the iceberg of the revised policy adopted by the Ministry of Foreign Affairs. The decision of the RoC Council of Ministers on 4 May 2000 epitomizes this delinkage, which can be labelled – from its main new features – one of truth and transparency. The new measures included: (1) publication in the *Gazette* of the official list of the Greek-Cypriot and Turkish-Cypriot missing from the 1963–1974 period (Gazette of the House of Representatives 2000: no. 3418; Gazette of the House of Representatives 2003: no. 3713); (2) the re-evaluation of the list of missing, primarily to inform the families of 126 individuals for whom they had valid information that their relatives were dead, not missing, and therefore were excluded from the list; and (3) the creation of a committee to prepare a list of Greek and Greek-Cypriot persons who died in the coup and as a result of the Turkish invasion in reply to the long-standing allegation of the Turkish-Cypriot leadership that all Greek-Cypriot missing were dead as a result of intra-communal violence (Paraschos 2009).[12]

Based on the two tenets of delinkage and transparency, the new policy did not end with the 1999 unilateral exhumations. Rather, these exhumations marked a starting point. In an interview[13] and a seminar dedicated to the issue of the Greek-Cypriot missing in 2000, Kasoulides explained the main aspects of this policy as the following. First, with respect to delinkage, this policy would have been a disaster, he said, if 'the issue of the missing [were] to become one of the aspects of the Cyprus Question and enter a labyrinth that will not lead us where we want to […]'. About truth, he added: 'It is necessary to convince (the international community) for our sincerity over the handling of the issue as a purely humanitarian one […]'. Finally, in a discussion of transparency, he commented:

> At this point, I have to say that there was a period when our side, indeed,… our intentions were not sincere in pursuing truth and that there was a political nuance in the political handling, […]. It is not sufficient to come here every time and say to the relatives of the missing look at the Turkish

intransigence, there is nothing we can do'. First of all we have to examine all these actions that we can do, in order to force the other side to follow.

(Seminar 2000)

In a 2006 seminar, he said: 'The fact that we put some order in our own cemeteries was an indication of our political will to prove that we do the best we could to proceed to the investigation and we are ready to do so' (Seminar 2006).

Briefly stated, a new policy that significantly deviated from the previous one was underway. Path-breaking changes related to domestic politics in Turkey and the Turkish-Cypriot community, as well as the prospect of EU accession, jump-started the CMP.

Overcoming the debacle in the CMP

Despite the unilateral policy change, the CMP remained inoperative until 2004. In the meantime, however, the executive branch of the government worked on implementing the policy of truth and transparency. The families of the 126 persons considered dead were given updated information on their relatives by the state and received detailed legal advice on their new legal status (i.e. pensions and other benefits); the lists of the Greek and Greek-Cypriot fallen in the coup and the Turkish invasion were published; lists with the names and details of both the Greek-Cypriot and Turkish-Cypriot missing persons were published in the *Gazette* by 2003; and starting in 2000, an intense effort was underway to collect blood and genetic samples from the relatives of Turkish-Cypriot missing – both in Cyprus and abroad – to establish a genetic material bank that would facilitate DNA identification. For the first time, the same provisions applied to the Turkish-Cypriot citizens of the Republic. In addition, the Republic of Cyprus began a unilateral investigatory exhumation in the Alaminos region, where there was information that a number of Turkish-Cypriots missing were buried.

In 2004, the rejection of the Annan Plan by the Greek-Cypriot community[14] increased the level of distrust between the two communities. Paradoxically, a couple of months after voting against the reunification plan, and despite a climate of frustration and mutual suspicion, both communities agreed to resume the activities of the CMP.

The agreement was preceded by a Turkish-Cypriot initiative to approach the Secretary General of the UN. More specifically, Turkish-Cypriot authorities declared their readiness to participate constructively in the resolution of the problem of the missing persons. Following this initiative, on 23 July 2004, Kofi Annan sent a letter to both leaders urging them to identify the remains of the missing. Both replied positively (Christou 2004). But why did President Papadopoulos, who showed an uncompromising attitude throughout the negotiations and referendum campaign on the Annan Plan, concede on this issue?

This concession is even stranger if we consider Papadopoulos' persistent reluctance to attribute any responsibility to the Greek-Cypriot community over the violence of 1960s. In fact, in a 2004 interview, he denied any atrocities were committed by Greek-Cypriots in the 1960s, stating that: 'in fact, the Turkish Cypriots were the ones who committed massacres and in 1963 we asked to increase the police patrols, but they refused. From 1963 to 1974, how many Turkish Cypriots were killed? The answer is none' (cited in Charalambous 2004). An interesting explanation of his apparent change of heart came up in several interviews. Informed observers argued that the primary reason for Papadopoulos's conciliatory stance on the issue of the missing and his constructive attitude should be attributed to the influence of Tasos Tzionis, the mastermind of the new policy, who was one of his closest aides. As the literature of bureaucratic politics suggests: 'whose views are reported to the president and who is informed in advance that a decision is to be made' is of crucial importance (Halperin and Kanter 1991: 409). Tzionis had direct access to President Papadopoulos and was trusted by him. The mutual trust is evident in the appointment of Tzionis as the head of the Greek-Cypriot team in the negotiations for the Annan Plan. More importantly, in relation to the issue of the missing, Papadopoulos abolished the Commissioner for Human Rights – previously the designated body to manage the issue – as an indication of his full support of Tzionis's efforts to resolve the problem (Interview no. 53). This elevated institutional position enabled Tzionis to set the agenda and prioritize the issue of the missing in meetings with international/European organizations and the Greek Government. As an interviewee revealed: 'with the election of Tassos (Papadopoulos), Tzionis was the one that secured continuation (of the CMP workings)' (Interview no. 18). Hence, by 2003, this was the official and undisputed policy of the RoC.

A puzzle remains, though. Why did Turkey change its decades-long policy of non-cooperation and agree to resume the CMP? Four developments underpin the policy shift: (1) the radical changes in domestic Turkish politics and the new EU orientation of the government of Justice and Development Party (henceforth, AKP); (2) the successive European Court of Human Rights (ECtHR) judgements, translated into political pressure by consecutive Resolutions of the European Commission for Human Rights; (3) the change of leadership in the Turkish-Cypriot community; and (4) the effects of the Greek-Cypriot policy on Turkish and Turkish-Cypriot considerations.

The volte face of Turkey under AKP

The first and perhaps most fundamental reason for Turkey's cooperation on the issue of the missing stems from the radical shift in the country's domestic politics, which significantly altered its approach to the Cyprus problem. From 1974 until roughly the early 2000s, the official position of consecutive Turkish governments was that the Cyprus problem had been de facto resolved in 1974. This left little room for compromise on peace initiatives and presented an image of Turkey as 'dragging its feet'. At the same time, the Turkish-Cypriot leader Denktaş took advantage of this position to design national policy according to domestic political considerations (Heraclides 2006: 229; 2010). The 1990s were a turbulent decade for Turkey; on several occasions, the country teetered on the brink of war with Greece, and Cyprus remained a serious bone of contention. These troubles, along with long-term political considerations, convinced a significant portion of the political elite that the policy needed revision, especially when the EU orientation became the country's central political objective.

The greatest problems that Turkey had to overcome to become a member state of the EU were related to improvements in the fields of democratic governance, human rights and the judiciary, as expressed in the Copenhagen Criteria (Müftüler Baç 2005: 21–25). From 1999 until 2004 – a period of crucial importance for the Cyprus problem as well – path-breaking reforms were implemented by the AKP Government, most of which complied with the European Commission, making extensive references to previous judgements of the ECtHR.[15] Since 1999, the institutional influence of the National Security Council has been significantly weakened, while extensive reforms in the judicial system have taken place. The executive organ for screening the progress of the reforms, the General Secretariat for the European Union, was also established and was attached to the office of the prime minister (Grigoriadis 2009: 80–85; Müftüler Baç 2005: 21–25). Hence, after 2002, moderation and attempts to comply with the requirements of the EU entered Turkey's foreign policy, albeit interrelated with domestic political processes. For this reason, it is important to understand ECtHR's new perception of the Cyprus problem and the impact of Turkish domestic political confrontations on Turkish-Cypriot politics.

The ECtHR and Turkey's moderation

Another critical factor explaining the Turkish change of attitude relates to the revised approach of international/transnational institutions to the issue of the missing in Cyprus, reflecting a wider normative change towards what could be called the 'logic of appropriateness' (Vinjamuri and Snyder 2004). Oddly enough, the same provisions that made the CMP an unworkable venture in 1981 proved to be the central ingredients in the success of 2004. A new element that facilitated the 2004 breakthrough was consecutive legally binding decisions of the ECtHR that condemned Turkey for human rights violations. Through these decisions, for the first time the issue of the missing was delinked from the developments in negotiations for the resolution of the Cyprus question. As the relevant literature notes, one breakthrough was the domestication of international human rights norms, primarily through binding decisions of the international judicial and political bodies and the socialization of domestic actors into these norms (Finnemore and Sikkink 1998; Risse and Sikkink 1999).[16]

Since 1989, the bodies of the Council of Europe have had the authority to interpret the European Convention on Human Rights and monitor the implementation of the decisions made by the European Court of Human Rights, primarily through the Committee of Ministers (Greer 2006; Kokkinakis 2002: 18).[17] In 1998, the ECtHR became the most rigorous supranational judicial body to provide legal recourse to individuals when their human rights were violated by one of the signatory parties of the Convention (Helfer 2008). Clearly, issues of human rights and democratic governance are now central priorities of European society.

If Turkey is to belong to this European society, it must domesticate these norms or at least indicate an effort to comply with the suggestions of its European counterparts. Briefly stated, the ECtHR decisions set the compass for Turkey in its EU path. Although landmark decisions were made by the ECtHR throughout the 1990s[18] – for example, on the properties of the Greek-Cypriots under occupation in northern Cyprus – it was only when EU accession became a central priority of Turkish foreign policy that these decisions were taken seriously. More precisely, after the 1999 EU Council Summit in Helsinki, when Turkey was attributed the status of a candidate state, Turkey intensified its efforts to comply with the decisions of the ECtHR and the follow-up resolutions of the Committee related to progress in implementation.

In this significantly revised normative context and with the altered priorities of the Turkish foreign policy, the ECtHR made a landmark decision on 10 May 2001,[19] which was directly related to the issue of the missing persons in Cyprus. In its decision, the court found Turkey responsible for the violation of Article 2 (right to life) of the European Convention, judging that Turkish authorities failed to conduct 'effective investigation into the whereabouts and the fate of Greek-Cypriot missing persons who disappeared in life-threatening circumstance' (para. 136) (cited in Hoffmeister 2002). In the same judgement, the ECtHR found Turkey responsible for violating Article 5 (right to liberty and security), because Turkish authorities failed to conduct an effective investigation into the fate of the Greek-Cypriot missing persons, even though 'there was an arguable claim that they were in Turkish custody at the time of their disappearance' (para. 150). There was also a breach of Article 3 of the Convention (prohibition of inhuman or degrading treatment), in regards to the treatment of the relatives of the missing persons (para. 158). Furthermore, all these violations had a continuing nature, meaning that every day that passed without Turkey's compliance, the country remained accountable. Finally, the judgement reaffirmed the property rights of the refugees and ruled that Turkey, rather than the Turkish-Cypriot authorities, was responsible for the violations of human rights in the northern part of Cyprus (ibid.).

Even more interesting, the judgement was followed by several resolutions of the Committee of Ministers that reflected the consistent political pressure exerted by the Council of Europe. It should be clear that the decisions taken by the international bodies of the Council of Europe neither have an institutional affiliation with the supranational EU, nor officially determine Turkey's route to the EU. Even so, these resolutions were a litmus test for evaluating the progress – or the absence thereof – of human rights, which constitutes a significant precondition for EU accession. They also indicate a change in the priorities of the European Union, which for the first time backed up legally binding decisions with political force. In essence, Turkey's accession to the prestigious international club depended on its compliance with international human rights norms.

In all resolutions, the Council of Europe demanded that Turkey set up a fact-finding committee that would meet the standards of Articles 2 and 5 of the

Convention (Council of Europe 2003a). In essence, the CMP was perceived to be insufficient by itself to comply with the judgements of the ECtHR. For example, in the Resolution of 7 June 2005, the Committee of Ministers insisted:

> Although the CMP procedures are undoubtedly useful for the humanitarian purpose for which they were established, they are not of themselves sufficient to meet the standard of an effective investigation required by article 2 of the convention, especially in view of the narrow scope of that body's investigations.
>
> (Council of Europe 2005a)

This was a response to Turkey's ongoing argument that the CMP was the best mechanism to address and resolve the issue of the missing persons (Council of Europe 2003b, 2004, 2005a).

The combination of these legal and political developments convinced Turkey that cooperation on the CMP constituted the less painful scenario, demonstrating its commitment to human rights norms and strengthening its EU orientation. Even more importantly, ECtHR decisions and the Resolutions of the Committee of Ministers empowered domestic reformist players in Turkey to frame and legitimize their demands to their domestic audience (Müftüler Baç 2005: 17). Persistent unwillingness to comply with ECtHR's decisions would seriously curtail Turkey's EU prospects.

Ousting Denktaş

Turkish policy change was also dictated by bottom-up pressure exercized by the unprecedented mobilization of the Turkish-Cypriot community in the early 2000s. Mehmet Ali Talat's coming to power in 2003 lay behind this change. More specifically, the prospect of a resolution of the Cyprus problem that would automatically be translated into EU membership mobilized the majority of the Turkish-Cypriot community in support of this leftist candidate who could oust the rejectionist Denktaş. This was the prelude to the vocal 'Yes campaign' that culminated in an impressive 64.9 per cent of the populace supporting the Annan Plan in 2004 in the northern part of the island. This mobilization, in combination with the opening of the checkpoints, facilitated bi-communal interactions and led to the surfacing of long-suppressed issues, such as the missing (Interview no. 6). This was especially important for the Turkish-Cypriot community, since, for the first time, bottom-up pressure demanded a change in policy and facilitated consent to the resumption of the CMP.

In any event, Talat's moderate profile, in combination with the support of Turkey, led to pro-active engagement in the CMP in 2004. It is interesting that the 1997 agreement – signed by Denktaş – legitimized Talat's decision to activate the CMP, without being stamped as a traitor by hardliners. Rather, he was implementing a popular demand.

The agreement of 2004 is also the outcome of the consistent implementation of the policy of truth and transparency, which influenced the calculations of the Turkish-Cypriot leadership and tilted the balance in favour of the CMP. Since 2003, and definitely before the agreement to resume the CMP, the Republic of Cyprus had opted for truth and transparency – a significant aspect of which was the equal treatment of Greek- and Turkish-Cypriot relatives of the missing.

Although the Turkish-Cypriot official discourse on the missing treated them as dead/martyrs (*Şehitler*), for the relatives, the issue was never closed. Therefore, developments after the late 1990s were treated as a unique opportunity for Turkish-Cypriot families to trace their relatives, linking the missing issue to the individual/family (Sant Cassia 2006a). The policy measures taken by the Republic were evaluated positively by Turkish-Cypriots, convincing them that they finally had the opportunity to unearth, identify and bury their relatives. As a result, the relatives triggered bottom-up (political) pressure on their leaders, an effort facilitated by the mobilization of civil society over the Annan Plan.

Delinking exhumations from truth recovery

The resumption of the activities of the CMP was also facilitated by technical advancements in forensic exhumation. More precisely, the DNA identification of human remains made possible the delinkage of exhumations from wider truth recovery. Before this time, any exhumation was inextricably linked to the testimony of a human witness; this entailed some sort of legal or moral responsibility, which acted to prevent exhumations. In addition, when they lack a sound scientific method for uncovering the truth societies often prefer to keep the book of the past closed. However, advancements in DNA testing enabled the so-called 'humanitarian exhumations' (Blau and Skinner 2005: 450) – that is, exhumations with the objective of identifying and returning the remains to relatives – without legal proceedings.

In the case of the missing persons in Cyprus, this factor was of paramount importance, since some of the perpetrators were still alive and would be extremely reluctant to participate in a process leading to their prosecution. To overcome this problem, the CMP was established on the premise of 'de facto immunity' for those providing information. A decision of the RoC Attorney General guarantees that any person who provides any sort of information to the CMP will not be legally or politically liable, nor will such information be used against those responsible for the disappearances (Solomonidou 2010).[20] Equally, there will be no attribution of responsibility for the disappearance, and the cause of death will not be revealed.

These developments made it easier for Turkey and the local perpetrators to accept the resumption of the activities of the CMP. Furthermore, as will become clear in the next section, the exhumations facilitated the credibility of the proffered framing and, as such, were warmly welcomed by the political elites. As mentioned, technological advancements enabled exhumations without wider truth recovery and the ensuing attribution of responsibility, thus facilitating the political delinkage of exhumations from the political settlement.

The emergence of a new vocal actor: relatives across the divide

Perhaps the most unexpected outcome of the revised policy of delinkage was the emergence of a small but visible and vocal bi-communal movement with a pro-rapprochement profile that transcended the divide. Deploying the tools of contentious politics (Tarrow 1998) and taking advantage of a change in the political opportunity structure, a grassroots movement with a truth-seeking profile emerged in Cyprus. The first and most obvious change was the official adoption of the delinkage policy. By the late 1990s, the issue of the missing was such a well-entrenched feature of the Cyprus problem that only the authorities on both sides of the divide and Ankara had a say in the resolution of the problem. Any effort by civil society to demand the truth and cooperate with the relatives of the 'other' would have been rejected as treacherous (Kovras and Loizides 2011). When the RoC delinked this policy in the late 1990s, the problem was gradually depoliticized and reframed in human rights terms (Yakinthou 2008). The official reframing of the problem legitimized – even encouraged – grassroots actors who had remained silent for a remarkably long period to mobilize and demand the truth. In contentious politics terms, the regime abandoned its long-term policy of discouraging grassroots' activities; by adopting this delinkage strategy, it facilitated collective claim-making (Tarrow 1998: 53).

The political changes within both Cypriot communities since 2003 have been cataclysmic and, to a significant extent, were facilitated by the 'crossings' of the Green Line (Hadjipavlou 2007b). One of the most notable developments has been the emergence of the civil society movement noted above (Trimikliniotis 2007).[21] This nascent bi-communal movement attempts to appropriate the drama of the missing and create a new narrative that focuses on the common pain of relatives on both sides of the divide, leaving aside the official discourses on the issue of the missing. For the first time, victimhood is used *not* to bolster ethnic identities (Hadjipavlou 2007a), but to *surmount the divide* and make redundant the 'discourse of self-righteousness' (Papadakis 1993: 150).

The point of departure and the *raison d'être* of the bi-communal initiative was the reaction to the ethnic monopoly of suffering that deprived victims' groups of being independent agents able to manage their suffering according to their free will. In symbolic terms, the decision to mobilize on the issue of the missing to deal with the past is very important. As McEvoy and Conway put it: 'the question of who "owns" the dead is not simply a question of the exclusive exercise of authority over the remains but is inextricably linked to the notion of "who" owns the past' (2004: 545). Members of the bi-communal initiative were disappointed in the handling of the issue by the official organizations of the 'Relatives of Missing' of both communities, as they followed an exclusionary approach, ignoring the agency of the relatives of the 'other' community. Furthermore, a gender aspect was a central element of the 'crossings' that started in 2003 and is particularly relevant in the activities of this grassroots initiative, since the role of motherhood in suffering is a focal point of the association (Hadjipavlou 2007b).

The single most important objective was to challenge the predominant discourse and promote an alternative discourse about their suffering. As the president of the initiative said in an interview:

> A growing number of people has started to realize that all these years the relatives have been exploited for political reasons [...] we have realized that – even before 2003 but definitely – since 2004 when the relatives meet each other from the two sides they start talking about the issue [the missing] they easily understand each other because they have a common element, which is the common suffering and this common pain shows that it is a chain linking people [...] these persons realize that they have the same problem and that all these years everyone tried to resolve it separately and suddenly we come to the conclusion that 'we have the same problem!'
>
> (Interview no. 28)

The initiative has adopted a strategy of low-profile activities to promote its objectives. Sevgul Uludag, a constitutive member of the initiative, describes this process as 'peeling the onion', where the objectives should be moderate – such as abstaining from ascribing individual responsibility – to avoid frightening people from speaking out, as this could endanger the whole truth-recovery process. It is remarkable that the Turkish-Cypriot member of the CMP, Plümer Küçük, identified the cooperation of the people as the single most important ingredient in the functioning of the CMP when she said: 'This project is working because grassroots people are giving us information and if we start dealing with punishment, these people are not going to give us any more information' (Interview no. 20).

Broader political changes within both Cypriot communities since the early 2000s have been cataclysmic in facilitating change. For a significant portion of the population, the frustration at the failure of 2004 Annan Reunification Plan was turned into an opportunity to address past human rights abuses at a grassroots level (Interview no. 7). A Turkish-Cypriot lawyer handling some of the most important cases of relatives of the missing and a member of Turkish-Cypriot Human Rights – a local NGO – identified the mobilization for the Annan Plan as a stepping stone in the bid to put the issue of human rights centre stage:

> We started after the referendum. Basically we were all pro-Annan and we were pro-Yes, and we were pro-changing leadership ... and it doesn't matter if there is no solution, we must implement human rights to the best of our ability within our area ... it's not an excuse the non-solution. So this was our mission as an NGO.
>
> (Interview no. 8)

Civil society learned tactical and policy lessons from the failure of the Annan Plan – notably, that the political discourse on both sides of the divide was so well entrenched that it had to be challenged from a grassroots level.

Another overlapping change in the opportunity structure was the coming into power of moderate leftist leaders on both sides of the divide: Mehmet Ali Talat and Demitris Christofias. As the literature of contentious politics suggests, the availability of influential political allies can lead to successful mobilization (Tarrow 1998). Traditionally, the island's left-wing parties were vocal advocates of bi-communal grassroots initiatives, especially when these were related to their persecution in the violent past (Ireton and Kovras 2012; Papadakis 1993). Leftist parties on both sides of the divide were sympathetic to addressing the past.

Finally, the abrupt decision of Turkish-Cypriot leader Rauf Denktaş to open the checkpoints in 2003 was instrumental. The open checkpoints policy created an unprecedented opportunity for relatives of missing persons to build an effective organization structure, meet and exchange ideas regularly and organize collaborative events (Interview no. 9). Deprivation of access, restricted communication and limited exchange of ideas with the 'essential' ally on the other side of the divide had prohibited these activities for more than 30 years.

Conclusion

Despite the decades-long inaction, the recent resumption of the CMP should be seen as a relative 'success story', which stands in stark contrast to the overall stalemate in the political negotiations for the Cyprus problem. The above analysis has presented the story of this change, focusing on the factors that contributed to the policy of unilateral exhumations by the Republic of Cyprus in 1999 and the set of factors that convinced Turkey, Turkish-Cypriots and the Republic of Cyprus to participate in the CMP.

One of the main tenets of the hegemonic belief constructed in the Republic of Cyprus subtly connects the (resolution of the) issue of the missing with an overall settlement, based on the belief that human rights issues are useful in the blame game against Turkey. Hence, 'delinking' humanitarian issues like the missing – where the Republic of Cyprus had a moral advantage – was previously considered to weaken or even damage the overarching Greek-Cypriot strategy for the reunification of the island. Although not a causal determinant, the *passage of time* constituted a significant reshuffling of the cards. Learning lessons from past policy failures, technological advancements that support a revised policy, modification of the framing and the domestication of new (legal and human rights) norms all contributed to the resumption of the CMP.

The passage of time is also closely connected to the Turkish perception of the problem in the post-2000 period. Political learnings from the minimal gains and continual international condemnation of the official policy on the Cyprus issue – namely, that the 1974 'peace operation' (invasion) provided a solution to the problem – has led to growing (domestic) demands for a revised policy. Emerging human rights norms have been recruited by domestic actors in the battle against the Kemalist/military establishment. Therefore, decisions by the ECtHR condemning Turkey's management of the issue of the missing have acquired new significance in the AKP Government. In addition, domestic shifts in the balance of power within the Turkish-Cypriot community and bottom-up pressure from the grassroots (relatives of Turkish-Cypriot missing) initiatives have led to Turkey's more active participation in the CMP venture.

To conclude, the passage of time and the radical developments on the issue of the missing since 2004 has legitimized new versions of the past that were previously unacceptable. For example, in 2009, a Greek-Cypriot history professor in an interview publicly shared his childhood memories from the 1963–1964 massacres carried out by Greek-Cypriot extremists against Turkish-Cypriots (Haravgi 2009). Although the reaction by certain politicians was furious, arguing that such initiatives undermine the overall Greek-Cypriot political efforts to resolve the problem, the majority of the media and the mainstream politicians did not subscribe to this view. In fact, some (previously) predominant discourses were delegitimized. It has become a conventional wisdom that these crimes were de facto recognized by the Republic of Cyprus, especially so long as the list of the Turkish-Cypriots missing has been published in the *Gazette* of the House of Representatives. Hence, despite the remaining political stalemate, the developments on the missing have instilled in the public and political discourse critical re-evaluation over responsibilities for the past – an element previously 'missing'.

Notes

1 Of the 477 identified persons, 358 are Greek-Cypriots and 110 are Turkish-Cypriots.
2 Several resolutions of the General Assembly related to the 'missing persons' problem – calling for the creation of an investigatory body – preceded the establishment of the CMP, including UN Resolutions 3450 of 9 December 1975; 32/128 of 16 December 1977 and 33/172 of 20 December 1978.
3 See the 'Terms of Reference' of the CMP, as established in 1981, online at: www.cmp-cyprus.org/about-the-cmp/terms-of-reference-and-mandate/ (accessed 20 January 2014).
4 See, for example, UN General Assembly Resolution A/RES/37/181 of 17 December 1982.
5 Perhaps the two most contentious issues of the time were the dispute over the control of the Aegean islet Imia/Kardak in 1996 and the declaration of the RoC of its intention to purchase and install S-300 missiles in Cyprus, which provoked another hot debacle in the Aegean in 1997.
6 The only exception is the exhumation of an American citizen in 1998, 'missing' since 1974, which was not carried out by the CMP.
7 The first interstate application (6780/74) was lodged in 1974. The RoC argued that, as a result of the invasion and occupation, Turkey was breaching articles 1–8, 13, 14 and 17 of the Convention. Although the term missing is absent, it accused Turkey of 'detaining in Cyprus and Turkey hundreds of persons arbitrarily and with no lawful authority ... subjecting the said persons to forced labour under conditions amounting to slavery or servitude'. The second interstate application (6950/75) came as a reaction to the 1975 unilateral proclamation of the Turkish Federal State of Cyprus by the Turkish-Cypriot leadership in the northern part of Cyprus.
8 The third interstate application (8007/77), lodged in 1977, shifted attention to the continuation of human rights violation, even after the cessation of hostilities. The publication of the resolution of the Committee of Ministers in 1992 reaffirmed the previous political and legal gains by the Republic of Cyprus (Council of Europe 1992).

126 *Post-transitional justice*

9 Physicians for Human Rights is a non-profit international organization of health professionals that was established in 1986 and is strongly involved in forensic exhumations in post-conflict societies. In 1997, it was awarded the Nobel Peace Prize, while Dr Haglund, who is also an established figure in the field, was the leader in the organization of the exhumations in Cyprus in 1999.
10 For more information on the agreement, see online at PIO: www.pio.gov.cy/MOI/pio/pio.nsf/all/4632228BBD701DA4C2256D6D00314114?opendocument (accessed 20 January 2014).
11 These include the military cemetery of Lakatamia and the cemetery of Konstantinou ke Elenis.
12 Paradoxically, as Sant Cassia points out (2005), although the number of the missing was always known, there was not an official number of the fallen. Subsequently, the publication of the list of the fallen (λιστα πεσόντων) constitutes an important development. The lists can be found online at: www.mfa.gov.cy (accessed 20 January 2014).
13 Interview with Neo Loizides, 19 July 2010.
14 Two separate referendums were held on 24 April 2004, where almost 76 per cent of the Greek Cypriots and 35.1 per cent of the Turkish-Cypriots rejected the proposed plan.
15 It is worth noting that in all reports, a specific section is dedicated to the developments of the Cyprus problem. See, for example: Commission of the European Communities, *Regular Report on Turkey's Progress Towards Accession*, 13 November 2001, p. 30; *Regular Report on Turkey's Progress Towards Accession*, 9 October 2002, p. 43; *Regular Report on Turkey's Progress Towards Accession*, 10 October 2004, p. 51.
16 For more detailed analysis on the recent legal developments on the issue of the 'enforced disappearances', see Scovazzi and Citroni (2007) and Citroni and Scovazzi (2009).
17 Even this mechanism, though, until the ratification of Protocol 11 – in 1998 – strengthened the 'linkage' of human rights to political developments, since the Commission for Human Rights initially invited the parties involved to reach a friendly settlement. It was only after 1998 and the adoption of Protocol 11 that (legal) judgements were taken by the ECHR, detaching the whole mechanism from political considerations (Greer 2006).
18 In the landmark decision of the ECHR in the case of Titina Loizidou (Loizidou v. Turkey, 40/1993/435/514), Turkey was found responsible for the denial of the applicant to access her property in the northern part of Cyprus.
19 Fourth Interstate Application of the Republic of Cyprus vs. Turkey, 10 May 2001. Application no. 25781/94. This was preceded by three previous interstate applications in 1976, 1983 and 1999, consecutively (Nos 6780/74, 6950/75, 8007/77, 25781/94).
20 This has not been legislated yet; so, relatives may lodge lawsuits in the future based on this gap of legality.
21 The name of the group is: Bi-Communal Initiative of Relatives of Missing Persons, Victims of Massacres and other Victims of War.

7 The Greek puzzle

In the summer of 2012, I decided to do fieldwork in Florina in northern Greece. My fieldwork coincided with two of the most important national elections held in Greece since the consolidation of democracy in 1974. During this period, public debates were dominated by Greece's ailing economy and militant street protests. Undertaking field research on the Greece Civil War at this time turned out to be a clever move. From the debates, I realized that the civil war is vividly remembered today, especially in rural areas, and that many Greeks continue to draw analogies with the past to make sense of the economic recession and political polarization.

I selected Florina because one of the biggest unopened mass graves in Europe is just outside this town. Northern Greece, in general, and the region of Florina, in particular, paid a heavy toll in human lives during the Greek Civil War.[1] One of the most decisive battles was fought in Florina in February 1949. The Democratic Army of Greece (henceforth, DSE) – formed under the auspices of the Greek Communist Party – made the strategic decision to capture Florina in an effort to build a 'fortress' from which to organize its military operations in northern Greece and to secure a safe retreat to the Yugoslavian border, just kilometers from Florina, if a retreat proved necessary. From late 1948 onwards, the DSE had been on the defensive, because of successive attacks by the opposing Government (national) Army against DSE strongholds in the neighbouring mountains of Grammos and Vitsi. DSE estimated that capturing Florina was the last chance to secure breathing space, while the Government Army perceived this to be a critical battle that could signal the end of the war. Both sides mobilized thousands of soldiers in Florina in February 1949. The DSE suffered a total defeat.

It is not going too far to say that the battle of Florina shaped the collective memory of the civil war. Although more than 60 years have passed, the battle is still vividly remembered by the locals. It had symbolic value for both parties. For the winners, it led to a 'communist-free' Greece and validated the territorial integrity of Macedonia (Gounaris 2002). The latter point requires some explanation: although the Greek Civil War was not an ethnic conflict – in sharp contrast to Spain – Slav-Macedonians were important players in the region. Since the 1930s, the Greek state had persecuted Slav-Macedonian citizens, forbidding them to use their language or follow their customs. As a result, many Slav-Macedonians argued for the self-determination of Macedonia (Danforth 1993). As the Greek Communist Party was the only party to endorse the prospect of an autonomous Macedonian region, it is hardly surprising that a sizeable number of Slav-Macedonians joined forces with the DSE fighters (Koliopoulos 1999; Rossos 1997). However, the autonomy of Macedonia was anathema for the Greeks; therefore, the victory of the Government Army in Florina was seen as safeguarding the territorial integrity of northern Greece. Until the early 1980s, 12 February was an official local holiday with a parade and other commemorative activities. But for the defeated, Florina represented the beginning of a traumatic period marked by the massive exile of thousands of DSE combatants to neighbouring communist countries and the persistent persecution of leftists who stayed in Greece.

It is interesting that, in symbolic terms, Florina reflects the memory of both camps. The military cemetery is on the top of a hill, just a kilometre outside Florina; fallen soldiers of the Government Army are placed in individual graves, interspersed with other well-preserved tombs (Figure 7.1). Until the early 1980s, an annual national memorial service was held here; local political and religious elites delivered lively speeches praising the sacrifice of the fallen Greek soldiers (Antoniou 2007). Just 400 metres below the military cemetery, in a plain field, lay the remains of 700 to 800 DSE fighters, buried in the aftermath of the battle (see Figure 7.2). The only visible object is a marble monument with a sign mentioning the dead; even locals who are aware of the existence of the graves do not know their precise location (Interview no. 65). Although this is one of the

Figure 7.1 Military cemetery in Florina (11 June 2012).

Figure 7.2 Field where the victims of the battle of Florina are buried (11 June 2012).

biggest unopened mass graves in Europe, the prospect of opening it and providing a decent burial for the victims has never been introduced into the political agenda.

The Greek Civil War left open wounds, some of which remain unaddressed. Approximately 100,000 from both sides of the conflict are dead (Kalyvas 2008: 255) and 140,000 are in exile (Close 2003: 337). Thousands of children were taken away from their families or sent to other countries.[2] And as the Greek Civil War was part of the larger Cold War, the central political cleavage in the postwar period was between 'national-minded' Greeks (*ethnikofrones*) and communists; the latter (leftists) faced severe repression and persecution decades after the end of the conflict (Mazower 1995). The Greek Communist Party was outlawed until 1974, and, among those who had left, thousands were deprived of their Greek citizenship and precluded from returning to the country (ibid.).[3]

Yet the impact of the Greek Civil War was relatively less severe than that of the Spanish Civil War. As Stathis Kalyvas points out, it is analytically incoherent to compare the Greek to the Spanish Civil War, since the logic of violence (conventional versus irregular warfare), the central cleavage (Republicans/Nationalists versus left/right) and the international order (prelude of World War II versus prelude of Cold War) was considerably different in the two cases (Kalyvas 2008). However, if we shift our focus to the long-term management of the human rights abuses of traumatic experiences in the distant past – the objective of this chapter – it makes sense to compare them.

In reality, the Greek case challenges regional experience, conventional wisdom and the relevant hypotheses of the literature. For one thing, Greece is the only country in the region that has not addressed the problem of the missing. Recently, Turkey established a parliamentary commission to trace the fate of missing Turkish citizens (primarily of Kurdish origin), during a period wherein there was a broader judicial screening of the violent past (Interview no. 79). In Bosnia, the International Commission for Missing Persons (henceforth, ICMP), with its strong international (logistic, political and financial) support, has already unearthed and identified more than one-third of the persons that went missing during the Bosnian War in the 1990s.[4] But Greece, despite being a country member of the EU, has not addressed pending human rights abuses linked to the civil war, including identification of those buried in the mass grave in Florina, acknowledgement of the rights of political refugees or destruction of the personal files of the secret police.

The Greek experience also contradicts the literature. In democratization literature, the Greek transition to democracy in 1974 is seen as a 'textbook case'; the collapse of the military junta was followed by a 'clean break' with the authoritarian past, including trials of military personnel and policies of lustration (Sotiropoulos 2010). Many argue that the implementation of transitional justice policies educates citizenry in the virtues of human rights and bolsters respect for the rule of law (Elster 2004; Méndez 2001; Minow 2002); thus, we might expect Greece to be proactive and effective in addressing human rights issues pending from the civil war. This did not happen. Meanwhile, after 40 years of Francoism, Spain followed a successful yet 'negotiated' transition (based on an amnesty law), managed to unearth victims of civil war and implemented a policy of post-transitional justice that overturned prolonged silences.

This leads to a number of puzzling questions. For one thing, why did the Greek political parties representing the defeated prefer to disappoint their constituents, rather than push for policies that would acknowledge their suffering? This question becomes even more intriguing if we take into account that parties of both the left and centre–left held power in the country after 1981. In addition, although the unprecedented mobilization of civil society groups is probably the most visible element of the processes of the recovery of historical memory in Spain, in Greece, this seems limited to an academic debate, within which civil society and the relatives of the missing are largely absent from the conversation. Hence, Greece challenges the experience of other countries in South and southeastern Europe, where graves are being dug up in an effort to address painful past chapters.

In short, Greece is an interesting 'control' case study. Despite similar background conditions, Greece remains resistant to the emerging 'post-transitional justice' norm. In what follows, I give a number of alternative explanations, all of which ultimately fail to account for the puzzling situation. I go on to argue that Greece's resistance stems from three overlapping factors: the Greek path to

The Greek puzzle 131

reconciliation, the linkage of truth recovery to a sensitive national issue and the limited socialization of Greek political parties to human rights norms.

Alternative explanations

In my fieldwork interviews, a prevalent explanation of the minimal demand for exhumations and, more broadly, for the problem of the missing of the Greek Civil War than in Spain was that there were considerably fewer missing persons in the former than the latter. Of course, the 'logic of violence' in the two cases is considerably different (Kalyvas 2006). Mass executions and other forms of organized violence were part and parcel of the conventional warfare of the Spanish Civil War (Balcells 2010: 294). As indicated in previous chapters, *paseos* and other types of executions, which created the problem of the *desaparecidos*, were systematized tools of terror used to control local populations. These tools of terror were exercized even a decade after the conclusion of the war, leaving enduring trauma. Because the Nationalist/Francoist camp overthrew the legitimate (Republican) government, the use of intense violence to 'purify' Spain was part of a broader strategy to legitimize the new Francoist regime. Meanwhile, in Greece, the 'legitimate' government won the war. Therefore, official executions ceased soon after the end of the war in 1950, although other forms of severe persecution persisted (Close 2003). We might plausibly expect, then, that the greater number of the disappeared, along with the systematic use of terror, would bolster the demand for truth recovery in Spain. At the same time, however, the irregular nature of warfare in Greece and the absence of a permanent front made civilians the primary target of violence, so that the two camps could control specific regions (Kalyvas 2010: 238). Subsequently, the legacy of violence (and clandestine executions) is still vivid in Greece, especially in rural areas.

In any case, it is necessary to refer to empirical evidence if we are to make any kind of comparison. In Spain, researchers have published rigorous local studies estimating with relative precision the number of disappeared, but in Greece it is impossible to make an informed estimation, thus revealing the marginal academic and policy demand for information. To overcome this problem, I attempted to compile figures of 'disappeared' from the monthly magazine published by the official DSE.[5] However, this proved impossible, partly because of bias and partly because of a lack of systematic records. I then asked permission to examine local registry offices to compile data on the executed, but was denied access.[6] At this point, I decided to direct my attention to the Greek Army, where I expected to find a more tangible answer to the question of figures. Research at the military archives shows that the Government Army had approximately 1,760 recorded cases of the 'disappeared' (Army History Directorate, forthcoming).[7] Yet as an interview with the lieutenant colonel who compiled the data indicated, this figure may underestimate the number, since the calculation is based on counting the soldiers who were missing from the daily turnout of the battalions, without taking into account all other cases (i.e. missing soldiers, executed/missing non-combatant locals etc.) (Interview no. 80).[8] Nor do we know much about the treatment (and the execution) of Government Army captives by the DSE (Marantzides 2010: 148). In other words, little systematic empirical evidence is available.[9]

Still, if 1,760 is the estimated number of 'missing' from the National Army, which has a detailed code of conduct for the dead (identification and burial), we might expect that the number of rebels not properly buried/identified is even greater. If we take into account the proportion of the missing to the total population in the two countries, then Greece may not be so different from Spain. Even if numbers matter, it remains puzzling why the grave in Florina – one of the largest in Europe – is unopened and the demand for truth is minimal.

A second and overlapping explanation offered by several participants over the course of my fieldwork points to the different death rituals in Spain and Greece. That is, compared to the Catholic tradition, where proper burial of the dead constitutes an important ritual, in Greece this issue is not vital. However, this is only partly true. First, since the early 2000s, the Greek Army has followed a policy to unearth, identify and repatriate the approximately 8,000 dead soldiers left buried in unmarked graves in Albania since World War II (Konstantopoulos 2006: 15). Second, one of the most urgent and persistent humanitarian demands of the Greek Ministry of Foreign Affairs to international organizations since 1974 is the return of the remains of the missing persons in Cyprus. Finally, as Paul Sant Cassia shows, the symbolic value of bones in the Greek-Orthodox tradition is of paramount importance (2005). An illustrative example is found in the first verses of the Greek national anthem (ibid.); based on the poem 'Hymn to Liberty', by Dionysios Solomos, the anthem glorifies the bravery of the ancestors in securing liberty: 'From the sacred bones, of the Hellenes arisen, and strengthened by your antique bravery, hail, o hail, Liberty!' In other words, as the path-breaking work of Lorring Danforth has showed, proper burial of human remains constitutes an important ritual in the Greek tradition (1982). This leaves a critical question unanswered: why has the demand for the recovery of the victims of the civil war remained minimal?

The Greek path to reconciliation

It would have been impossible to expect the successful accommodation of past human rights abuses until democratic consolidation in Greece in the mid-1970s. The quality of the Greek democracy following the civil war was uneven (1949–1967), and this semi-democratic regime was overthrown by a military dictatorship (1967–1974) that employed a strongly anti-communist discourse. The collapse of the military junta in the summer of 1974 – over the defeat in Cyprus – completely delegitimized the actors representing the *ancien regime* (in sharp contrast to Spain, where Francoist elements played a vital role in the transition) and allowed the defeated to become legitimate political actors. In addition, soon after 1981, parties representing the defeated (left and centre-left) came to power. Thus, we might have expected an early accommodation of protracted human rights problems pending from the civil war, but this did not happen.

Although a number of laws dealing with issues from the civil war were enacted in the 1980s, certain inconvenient issues were left unaddressed, even once a fully-fledged democratic regime had been consolidated and there was no tangible threat to the stability of democracy. The Greek experience becomes even more puzzling when juxtaposed with the recent grassroots initiatives to address neglected issues of human rights in Spain, a country commonly seen as a paradigmatic case of 'silence'. How can we account for this paradox?

It seems that although there was a clean break with the authoritarian past, the topic of the Greek Civil War remained taboo to all parties involved. It is clear from the study of parliamentary speeches and interviews with politicians that, at least in the first years after the restoration of democracy, elite framing of the memory of the civil war was based on selective silences.

Before proceeding, I should mention the differences in how the memory of the civil war is managed in both Greece and Spain. For one thing, the central cleavages are different. The Spanish Civil War was waged by the defenders of the legitimate (Republican) government and the rebel Nationalist/Francoist forces; the latter won and established a dictatorship lasting nearly 40 years. In Greece, the combatants were a legitimate (yet not entirely democratic) government and the DSE (controlled by the Greek Communist Party), who challenged but did not defeat the state in the aftermath of the liberation of Greece from the Nazi occupation (Kalyvas 2008).

This difference helps explain why Greek political elites drew so selectively on the memory of the civil war. For the defeated that had been repressed and persecuted, the primary objective in the period following the end of the civil war was their successful reintegration into mainstream party politics. Despite the uneven democracy, leftist parties were allowed to participate in parliamentary life, securing breathing space for the left until 1967. Hence, the defeated had to address the urgent political, economic and social problems of their constituents (leftists), thereby relegating issues of justice/human rights problems to some point in the future. As Leonidas Kyrkos says: 'The persistent demand of EDA was based on three principles: Peace – Democracy – Amnesty' (Interview no. 66).[10] This echoes Carillo's calls for reconciliation and the reintegration of the Spanish Communist Party in national politics in the 1970s.

Briefly stated, Greek parties representing the defeated preferred to remain silent and pursue more pragmatic objectives, such as reintegration to parliamentary democracy. But parties representing both sides preferred to avoid using the past as a political instrument. Although the political right preferred anti-communist discourse, its adherents downplayed the civil war, which was perceived to be a 'shameful' period. Even leading figures with personal involvement in the civil war, such as Alexandros Papagos or Konstantinos Karamanlis, preferred to play the card of the past only selectively (Interview no. 60, 81).[11] A prominent member of SYRIZA – the new left in Greece – clearly remembers that silence was both socially and politically constructed until the 1970s:

> For someone like me, growing up in Greece it was impossible to think that a civil war had taken place in the country [...] we were three friends and it was impossible to imagine that the father of one of my best friends was the

torturer of the other. There was a mutual silence both from winners and the defeated.

(Interview no. 72)

The study of elite framing post-1974 shows that silence meant neither a common understanding of the root causes of the civil war, nor obliteration of the past. Rather, it was a mutual unspoken agreement to abstain from using certain inconvenient aspects of the past in political debates in an effort to facilitate democratic consolidation. Thus, contentious issues that might have derailed the democratization processes, such as exhuming graves, were precluded from public debates.[12] Only in the early 1980s did the civil war gradually enter the elite framing, as part of the effort of the Socialist Party, PASOK, to recognize national resistance to the Nazi occupation in World War II. Its leader, Andreas Papandreou, played out the memory of the 1940s by passing a law for the 'Recognition of Resistance of the Greek People against the Occupation Troops 1941–1944' (Law No. 1285/1982). The provisions of the law included: (1) recognition of a number of leftist resistance groups, like EAM; (2) commemoration of the destruction of Gorgopotamos bridge and the declaration of that day as a day of national resistance; and (3) annulment of preceding decrees that offered material benefits to those who collaborated with occupying forces in the period from 1941 to 1944. In follow-up laws (Law No. 1543/1985), pensions and other benefits were offered to those who had participated in, or remained handicapped as a result of their involvement in, resistance organizations. More significantly, it enabled thousands of Greek political refugees who left the country in the aftermath of the war to return to Greece after several decades in neighbouring socialist countries. Of this law, Andreas Papandreou said: 'We are not here today to judge or to divide our people. The primary objective of the law is to reinforce national unity' (17/8/1982: 635).

Although PASOK attempted to delink World War II resistance from the civil war,[13] the law triggered a vehement reaction from the conservative New Democracy (henceforth, ND), whose leader Averoff-Tositsas stressed: 'In reality today a pardon is given to the Communist Party [...] our target is not to reopen wounds, because we really want oblivion', thereby implying that PASOK's policy broke the unofficial silence (17/8/1982: 638). Charilaos Florakis, leader of the Communist Party, responded: '[I]t is ND that should ask for pardon, and the camp it represents. They were either absent or collaborating with the occupying forces' (ibid.: 649).

Both PASOK and the Communist Party decoupled World War II from the civil war and emphasized the need to address that period to achieve national unity. However, this delinkage was unacceptable to the right. In the right's diagnostic framing, the civil war was a response to the efforts of the Communist Party to seize power by recourse to violence during the period of occupation/ resistance. Hence, the right gained legitimacy by drawing on the legacy of the civil war (i.e. averting the threat of communism). In addition, the period of the resistance was the most glorious page in the narrative of the left, while the right was largely absent; hence, the latter had no motivation to acknowledge the resistance out of the context of the civil war.

PASOK's decision to deal with the traumatic period of the 1940s was guided by electoral calculations; essentially, the Socialist Party was attempting to draw on the symbolic capital of the tradition of resistance (Pashaloudi 2012). PASOK played the card of the past to broaden (and consolidate) the pool of potential voters: permitting the return of thousands of refugees and offering material benefits to leftist victims were thought to be powerful incentives for leftist voters to cast their ballot for PASOK, instead of other parties of the left. In the Greek majoritarian model of democracy, this move was sufficient to secure better prospects for a long-term PASOK Government. It satisfied the material demands of the leftists, but at the same time these benefits were not framed as accommodating calls for 'justice', as this would have alienated potential voters in the centre, who remained reluctant to open up debates about the past. Hence, PASOK framed its initiatives as putting a 'full stop' to the traumatic past, enabling society to move forward – a strategy also followed by PSOE in the past. It is not coincidental that none of the provisions were framed as accommodating calls for justice/human rights. In fact, all measures were either material or symbolic and were linked to the spendthrift policies of PASOK in the 1980s. PASOK's material-oriented policies failed to accommodate a number of pending human rights issues, including the return of a sizeable number of DSE political refugees of Slav-Macedonian origin or opening the military archives, not to mention dealing with the missing. I will return to these points in greater detail below.

These questions become more acute if we consider that in 1989 – 40 years after the conclusion of the war – the left, for the first time united in a single party, participated in a coalition government with the conservative ND. Apart from symbolically closing the civil war, an objective of that government was to promote a comprehensive policy of reconciliation. To that end, a new law was passed that, for the first time, addressed issues related to the civil war (Law No. 1863/1989). The primary provisions of the law included the following: (1) it set the period of 1944 to 1949 as the official period of the civil war, thereby ending a lengthy debate about the start date of the war;[14] (2) the official labels '*simmoritopolemos*' (bandit war) and '*simmorites*' (bandits) were changed to 'civil war' and 'combatants of the DSE', respectively (Article 1); (3) judicial decisions against convicted leftists were annulled (Article 2); (4) pensions were given to the DSE fighters (Article 3); and, finally, (5) the personal files of thousands of leftists gathered by the secret police since the 1930s were to be burnt (Rori 2008: 304).

We cannot overstate the importance of the formation of the coalition government: 40 years after the conclusion of the war, the former enemies were sharing power. In the parliamentary debates of the time, both parties celebrate this law as a sign of reconciliation.

Yet despite the inherent promise, the memories of the civil war were not forgotten. One of the pioneers of the rapprochement and the coalition government,

MP Pavlos Bakoyiannis, was assassinated by the terrorist organization 17 November, just days after the legislation passed. For this reason, he was called the 'Greek Moro' – a direct reference to the Italian PM who was executed for his conciliatory political position. His wife, Dora Bakoyiannis, who later became Minister of Foreign Affairs, insists that he was executed because he was one of the pioneers of reconciliation. He was of leftist origins, and his marriage to the daughter of the leader of the conservative ND, Constantinos Mitsotakis, was considered a 'mixed marriage', bridging the left–right divide. His election as an MP of the Conservative Party (ND) and his position on national reconciliation were perceived as betraying the left. Ian Lustick's seminal analysis of deeply divided societies shows that visionary leaders who transcend the divides and promote reconciliation are often assassinated (1993).

Irrespective of the political tensions, Greece passed a number of laws addressing reconciliation and dealing with the legacy of the civil war. If we take these into account, is it too far-fetched to argue that Greece was the first country to implement policies of 'post-transitional justice' in southern Europe? Before replying to this question, remember that the laws focused exclusively on material and symbolic aspects of the civil war, *without direct references to pending human rights abuses* – the distinct feature of transitional justice. Juxtaposing Greece's 1989 law and the 2007 law in Spain (see short timelines) indicates that human rights issues are only marginally addressed in Greece. Although in Spain the 2007 law granted citizenship to all refugees *irrespective of their ethnic status*, in Greece the 1989 law excluded a number of Slav-Macedonian members of the DSE who left the country in the 1940s and were not allowed to return, because the law was confined to 'Greeks by descent'. To this day, there is absolutely no political initiative to deal with the problem of the missing (or exhumations of graves).

To be sure, this is not a normative argument presenting the Spanish experience as a suitable model to emulate. Rather, I argue that in post-transitional settings, even the defeated can be guided by pragmatic considerations (the 'logic of consequence'). The Greek experience illustrates that even when the defeated hold power, they may prefer to silence certain chapters of their past for political, electoral and symbolic reasons. In this respect, the Greek legislation of the 1980s appears more like Spain in the 1970s, when laws were guided by material reparations to victims of the civil war, rather than the 2007 law, which incorporated demands for justice.

In fact, it seems a historical paradox that the Greek Government of 'national reconciliation' is remembered for its exceptional decision to burn millions of personal files of leftists held by the police (Ministerial Decree 8504/7–14668). In a landmark parliamentary speech on 28 August 1989, leaders representing both the defeated and the winners perceived burning these as a prerequisite of reconciliation. After 40 years of discrimination, it was important for the leftists to be freed from the fear of future persecution based on evidence derived from these files – themselves the product of illegal surveillance (Anastassiadis 2009: 23).[15] We cannot avoid drawing analogies, not only with the vocal demand of the autonomous regions in Spain to open up and return military archives to their communities, but also with the management of the German Stasi personal files, which took place, by and large, at the same time and allowed more than 2.7 million persons to see their own files (Pidd 2011). In both cases, the demands were framed in terms of individual rights. Yet the Greek experience is notable, because it came before the 1990s and the domination of liberal peace-building paradigms (Richmond and Franks 2009), shedding light on how societies dealt with these issues in the past.

All in all, reconciliation initiatives in Greece were based on a common decision to 'selectively' silence certain inconvenient aspects of the past, thereby precluding the possibility of truth recovery (including opening graves), even by the defeated. Consider the response of Leonidas Kyrkos, a prominent and moderate leader of the left and a pioneer of the coalition government, to my question regarding whether it would be a good idea to open the grave in Florina:

> No one would wish to relive the nightmare of the civil war. What would be the purpose of reopening the wounds [...]. Do we need skeletons? We had more than our share of deaths. We are just recovering and the healing is just beginning.
>
> (Interview no. 66)

Interestingly, in a public interview in 2008, Santiago Carillo, a prominent and pragmatic leader of the left who participated in the 'pact of silence' in Spain, took a position in favour of the continuation of the politics of exhumations.[16] Throughout the 1970s and 1980s, Carillo was a vocal supporter of the 'logic of consequences', preaching moderation.

Linkage of truth recovery to a sensitive national issue

The case of Florina enables us to better understand Greece's persistent resistance to a more comprehensive policy addressing past human rights abuses. One of the biggest mass graves in Europe remains closed, arguably because it is inextricably linked to a sensitive 'national issue' – namely, the Macedonian problem.

Although the Greek Civil War was not an ethnic conflict (Kalyvas 2006: 311), the role of ethnic groups/unrecognized minorities in the civil war was downplayed in the post-war period, and the individual rights of those persons were disregarded. There is growing consensus among experts that, especially in the final stages of the civil war, a sizeable number of the DSE combatants were Slav-Macedonians (Close 2003: 323). Some say that by 1949, approximately 14,000 were Slav-Macedonians (Marantzides 2010: 57; Woodhouse 1979); other informed scholars estimate Slav-Macedonians to represent two-thirds of the total number of DSE fighters (Rossos 1997). In 1949, the manpower of the DSE was steadily decreasing. The Communist Party, in an effort to safeguard the continuation of its strife in northern Greece, appealed to Slav-Macedonians (5th Plenum), implying that in the event of a successful outcome to the war,

Macedonia would secede to form an independent (or federate) state (Close 2003: 324; Rossos 2008: 207–212). Slav-Macedonians who had been persecuted by the preceding authoritarian regime of Metaxas perceived this to be a unique opportunity (Rossos 2008), but the decision alienated the vast majority of Greek Macedonians, who only 30 years before had launched a bloody war to liberate Macedonia and annex it to Greece. So the final stages of the civil war became a struggle for self-determination for Slav-Macedonians and a bid to protect the national sovereignty of the Greek state by the Government Army.

The Macedonian question has always had symbolic salience in Greek nationalism, so it is hardly surprising that in the early 1990s the Greek state entered into a symbolic conflict with the nascent neighbouring Republic of Macedonia/ FYROM over the decision of the latter to use the name 'Macedonia' (Loizides 2007a). Although not posing a direct threat to Greek territorial integrity, the Macedonian problem captured the 'hearts and minds' of Greeks, setting the stage for mass rallies in all major Greek cities and becoming one of the most sensitive issues in Greece's foreign policy in the post-1990s period.

Slav-Macedonians constituted a significant part of the manpower of DSE in the battle of Florina. Interviews with local experts indicate that the grave holds the remains of many Slav-Macedonians, as well as a number of forcibly recruited Greek youths from the neighbouring town of Naousa (Interview no. 83, 63, 74). In the absence of exhumations and proper DNA identification, it is impossible to estimate the number or the individual features of the victims (i.e. ethnic origin). Yet rigorous collaborative research conducted by postgraduate students at the University of West Macedonia in Florina, including interviews with eyewitnesses coupled with the study of documents from the local registry office, indicates that many victims were from Slavic-speaking villages of Macedonia (Aspasios *et al.* 2007). Hence, the prospect of exhuming and identifying the bodies of those buried in the grave has the potential to open Pandora's Box (so to speak), with all sorts of inconvenient questions arising, including questions about the Greek state and the Communist Party's management of the human rights of this ethnic group.

In legal terms, the individuals buried in the grave are 'disappeared'. Article 32 of Additional Protocol I to the Geneva Convention recognizes that families have the right to know the whereabouts of their relatives (Scovazzi and Citroni 2007).[17] Although these persons are dead, their relatives have the 'right to an effective investigation'. In this case, the Greek state would find itself in the awkward position of being obliged to investigate, unearth and identify the dead bodies of its Slav-Macedonian citizens, possibly leading to a finding of violation of fundamental human rights by competent international bodies and courts. As this aspect of the civil war is highly politicized, the other party in the conflict may opt to invest symbolic capital in this 'forensic evidence' to initiate another contentious chapter of the 'Macedonian question' and place the blame on Greece.

As the crime of 'disappearance' is not subject to statute of limitations, the families have the right to file a lawsuit today, even after the passage of several decades. In a similar case, the ECtHR acknowledged the right of the relatives of the victims of the 'Katyn massacre' to an effective investigation and exhumations.[18] Despite the passage of 70 years since the massacre and the fact that the court has no retrospective jurisdiction on crimes committed before its inception, the ECtHR ruled that the Russian state was obliged to carry out an effective investigation and condemned its previous position as preventing the right of the relatives to know the truth (Articles 2 and 3).[19] The Greek state has no motivation to open the Florina grave, precisely because this would be followed by a complex and highly politicized legal and symbolic battle with its northern neighbour.

The study of the grave in Florina is analytically important, because it sheds light on post-conflict silences and the obstacles to the accommodation of human rights issues in post-transitional settings. To fully grasp the problems involved, we should explore another overlapping, unaddressed issue of the violent legacy of the Greek Civil War – namely, the management of Slav-Macedonian refugees. In the aftermath of the civil war, an estimated 35,000–40,000 Macedonians fled to Yugoslavia and other countries in Eastern Europe (Danforth 1993: 4; Kofos 1989: 250). The Greek state deprived them of their citizenship and enacted a new law saying that the property of those who lost their citizenship (and fought in the civil war with the communists) could be confiscated without compensation (Danforth 1993).[20] To do so, the Greek state drew on a 1927 presidential decree stipulating that 'individuals who were not ethnically Greek' (αλλογενείς) who left the country without a clear intention to return could be deprived of their citizenship (Anagnostou 2005: 338). Under this decree, similar provisions were applied to refugees of 'Greek nationality' until the early 1960s, for 'actions against the nation' (αντεθνικώς δρώντες) (Baltsiotis 2004: 85).

As mentioned above, socialist PASOK passed a law that enabled thousands of refugees to return to the country in the mid-1980s. However, the provision of the law was confined to 'Greeks by descent' (Έλληνες το γένος'), thereby excluding many Slav-Macedonian refugees (Close 2003; Mazower 1995). It is estimated that in the early 1990s, approximately 8,000 of the 30,000 Greek Slav-Macedonians living in Skopje and the former Yugoslav Macedonia sought permission to return to their homes in Greece (Karakasidou 1993).

Returning to our comparative context, it is worth juxtaposing this policy with the 2007 Spanish law that enabled the return of this country's civil war refugees and granted citizenship, *irrespective of their ethnic origins*. Why did the parties representing the defeated not address this issue in Greece? Again, we should look to the Macedonian problem. As Loizides' study of elite framing of the Macedonian conflict in Greece shows, an early consensus was reached among all parties in parliament to securitize the issue of the return of Slav-Macedonians (2007a), thereby precluding the possibility of implementing a post-transitional justice policy similar to the one in Spain. An analysis of parliamentary speeches shows that, even in the late 1970s, the return of the refugees of non-Greek nationality and the granting of citizenship were framed as a security issue. The Minister of Interior, and later President of the Greek Republic, Konstantinos

Stefanopoulos repeatedly argued that the prospect of the return of the Slav-Macedonians was 'in the jurisdiction of the Ministry of Public Order' (not Interior) (p. 902, 20/2/1975). The securitization of the problem is also clear in his statement that 'the return of elements that could pursue objectives that could dissolve national solidarity would not be in our national interests' (p. 1149, 28/11/1975). Essentially, political elites were afraid that a resettlement of the refugees *en masse* would be a major national threat to the relatively homogeneous Greek Macedonia (Loizides 2007a).

Even the Communist Party remained reluctant to bring significant political pressure to bear on this problem. Until the mid-1990s, it felt bound by the early elite consensus on the Macedonian issue and adopted an equally nationalist discourse on mobilization in the early 1990s. In the aftermath of the democratic consolidation in Greece and the Turkish invasion of Cyprus, the legitimization of KKE was followed by a subtle agreement that the Communist Party should remain loyal to the national foreign policy, thereby precluding the possibility of raising the issue of the Slav-Macedonian refugees. So in the period following 1974, the party was very careful not to play up this issue. As Loizides puts it: '[T]he Greek communists implicitly dropped any reference to ethnic Slavs in "exchange" for their own participation in normal democratic politics' (2007a: 6).

This goes a long way towards explaining the reluctance of the left in general and the Communist Party in particular to opening the Florina grave. A decision by KKE to initiate a process of comprehensive acknowledgement of past human rights abuses (of Slav-Macedonians) would clearly represent a break with the national pact over the Macedonian issue, making the party 'twice a traitor'. The decision of the 5th Plenum in 1949 enabled the future secession/self-determination of Macedonia, making the party susceptible to accusations of betraying the nation. Thousands of leftists were executed based on this allegation (Baltsiotis 2004).

In other words, after decades of persecution and consistent efforts to be reintegrated into party politics, this would have been a suicide mission for the Communist Party and would cost them dearly in electoral terms. In any event, the Greek communists were 'incompatible allies' with the Slav-Macedonians (Rossos 1997). Ultimately, in the post-1949 period, the relationship between KKE and the Slav-Macedonians soured, and KKE could not count on their votes (Interview no. 78).

However, this is not the only reason for the Communist Party's reluctance to unearth the remains. Unlike the Spanish experience, where the 'Republican' memory of the civil war was silenced until the mid-1990s in Greece, the series of laws passed in the 1980s enabled the winners of the resistance and the defeated of the civil war to retain the public discourse of the 1940s (Antoniou and Marantzides 2008). As in Spain, those groups whose discourse was sidelined had a vested interest in opening the graves. The Greek Communist Party, until the late 1980s, did not invest on the military or 'heroic' aspect of its struggle, therefore its victims remain without political representation. However, this picture changed in the early 1990s. As PASOK had 'monopolized' the legacy of the national resistance that attracted a significant part of potential voters of KKE, the Communist Party built a strategy of investing symbolic capital on the memory of the civil war. Since the early 1990s, KKE institutionalized a number of commemorations and events that reaffirmed the hegemonic role of the party in representing the 'defeated' of the civil war and, subsequently, lacked a powerful incentive to proceed to exhumations.

Unearthing bodies and gathering forensic evidence may overturn this discourse. If it is verified that a number of the unearthed graves hold youths from the neighbouring town of Naousa, the dominant leftist discourse on the composition and the activities of DSE will suffer a critical blow. A heated debate has emerged over the past few years, challenging the official discourse that DSE was composed primarily of pure idealists; a growing number of scholars argue that violent conscription was part of its recruitment strategies (Marantzides 2010). The Communist Party vehemently resists this emerging version of the truth and thus has no reason to open the grave. The decision to unearth graves may also set in motion an unstoppable series of exhumations, with far-right groups seeking to praise the victims of the 'red violence' of the 1940s (Interview no. 78). In fact, the far-right group Golden Dawn, which secured almost 7 per cent of the votes in the 2012 national elections and won 18 seats in parliament, has been active in organizing commemorations of alleged massacres committed by communists in the 1940s (Antoniou 2013).

Given the tense political context, after the civil war it became very difficult for any civil society group or relatives group to demand the opening of the Florina grave. Greek civil society is described as 'formally weak' (Sotiropoulos 2004: 25; Sotiropoulos and Karamagioli 2005) and extremely dependent on the Greek state and its agents (i.e. political parties). As the case of Cyprus shows, it is hard for any NGO to challenge the official national line in foreign policy. New opportunities for grassroots/truth recovery actors to enter public debates emerge only when political elites slightly change their discourse. In addition, the idiosyncratic conditions in the region of Florina preclude the prospect of establishing a local initiative to demand either the opening of the grave or to address broader issues of the human rights of Slav-Macedonians.

During my short field visit to Florina, it became clear that even today, more than 60 years after the conclusion of the war, people are reluctant to talk about the battle of Florina (Interviews no. 64, 56). In the aftermath of the war, local political and religious authorities imposed a robust nationalist-oriented (and anticommunist) discourse, through the ritualization of the battle of Florina, including parades celebrating the defeat of the 'communist/Slavic threat'. As Antoniou shows in his fascinating study of annual commemorations of the civil war in the region, local political elites of the right organized annual commemoration days where they delivered passionate speeches about the 'communist thugs' (2013). The so-called 'hate speeches' indicate that although silence may have been imposed at the national level, in the local contexts this might not have been the case. For example, those participating in these events sang 'not in oblivion, it's a fairytale' ('οχι στη λήθη είναι παραμύθι') (Antoniou 2007: 176). Even today, many locals believe that the dead lying in the field deserve this treatment, because of the harm they inflicted on the country (Interview no. 73).

Gradually, anti-communism became an entrenched feature of Florina, cultivated by the electoral and material interests of the local political and religious elites (Marantzides 2001; Gounaris 2002). To cite one example, Avgoustinos Kantiotis, one of the most conservative-minded bishops in the country, exerted considerable influence over local politics until the 1990s. In the early 1990s, he excommunicated the prominent director Theo Aggelopoulo for shooting a movie that allegedly insulted Florina's religious beliefs. It is hardly surprising that Kantiotis did not like the idea of exhuming the grave in Florina, even though proper burial is paramount to the Christian Orthodox tradition.

Local politicians are equally hesitant to talk about the grave. For example, my interview with the Mayor of Florina lasted five minutes – by far the shortest interview for this project – revealing his reluctance to talk about this contentious issue (Interview no. 83). Even one of the most popular socialist MPs, a man with Slav-Macedonian origins who has been in office since the 1980s, largely due to the support of the Slav-Macedonians, was reluctant to talk.

Clearly, the silence that prevailed in the post-war period was reproduced by local religious and political elites and dealing with sensitive questions of human rights had the potential to delegitimize this *modus vivendi*. Exhuming the grave in Florina would cause a reaction (Interview no. 57), as the memory of the civil war still remains fresh (Interview no. 84). In fact, in the mid-2000s, the Communist Party put a small marble commemorative stone (see Figure 7.2) in the field; since then, it has been destroyed twice (Interview no. 84). In September 2012, black paint was thrown onto another monument located at the entrance to the town; this particular monument commemorates the dead members of the gendarmerie.

While it seems that civil society and the local community face insurmountable obstacles, this alone cannot explain the continued silence, since local communities and critical constituents (religious or relatives associations) in both Cyprus and Spain adopted far more intransigent positions and yet overcame obstacles by effectively using international human rights tools. This leads to the final puzzling question: why did the Greek political parties representing the defeated (or relatives) not use these tools?

Party ideology: limited socialization to human rights norms

In all three cases examined in this book, the role of political parties is key to explaining why certain societies adopt policies of (delayed)/post-transitional justice, while others resist them. It is clear that political parties are the principal mediators of political demands in post-transitional societies, so examining their framing strategies makes sense.

The absence of policies of post-transitional justice in Greece can be attributed to the limited socialization of the political parties – especially those representing the defeated – to emerging human rights norms. As an MP (and prominent member of the SYRIZA Party) argued in a personal interview: 'The Left never believed in individual rights. This is a cruel subjugation of the individual to the collective' (Interview no. 72). In the long term, he said, this strategy backfired and inhibited the struggle to address the rights of thousands of leftists who were persecuted from the 1950s until the early 1970s. This position became an 'obstacle in protecting the rights of the leftists [when persecuted]. The left hurt its own objectives' (ibid.). Another member of the left added: 'Up to this day the official line of the communist party is that minority issues are instruments used by imperialist forces' (Interview no. 85). In fact, for many leftists, the position adopted by the Greek Communist Party in the wars in the Balkans in the 1990s was an eye-opener. Guided by anti-American/anti-imperialist discourse, the Communist Party was one of the few parties of the left in Europe to vocally support the nationalist offensive of Milosevic against the Muslim Bosnians.

Although I was politely denied access to interviews with MPs in the Greek Communist Party and to party documents for archival research, I did manage to interview two members of the local branch in Florina. These interviews were revealing. After explaining that there are insurmountable obstacles associated with the conservative profile of the local community in opening the grave, I asked whether they had considered the possibility of framing their demands in human rights terms to be directed to international bodies, as their Spanish counterparts did. Both members replied that they (and the party) did not perceive this to be an issue of human rights (Interview nos 62, 63). One said: 'No, we are not following this logic. We argue that this is a political issue, and therefore it can only be resolved through political means' (ibid.). Strangely, an effective tool in the hands of the Spanish left is almost absent in Greece.

However, it is not only the parties of the left that are not socialized into the use of international human rights norms. As illustrated above, all Greek political parties have the tendency to 'securitize' issues of human rights, such as minority issues. Therefore, it is hardly surprising that Greece has a poor record compared to other countries in the same 'wave of democratization' of the 1970s. Scholars studying minority issues in Greece say that the recognition of 'otherness' is framed in security, not human rights, terms (Tsitselikis 2008). Within this kaleidoscopic view of human rights, minority protection and civil society groups mobilized around this subject matter are perceived to be the Trojan Horse of foreign powers (Turkey, Macedonians, etc.). This explains the management of the human rights of Slav-Macedonians[21] and the grave in Florina; so long as political parties frame it as a 'national issue', any grassroots organization challenging this framing will be treated as a traitor (Danforth 1993). In fact, interviews with members of 'Rainbow' (Ουράνιο Τόξο), a local NGO pushing for the rights of Slav-Macedonians, revealed that they have been denounced by close relatives for being members of this NGO (Interview nos 74, 75).

In other words, Greek political parties have only 'selectively' been socialized to use international human rights norms. Political parties' recourse to human rights is non-negotiable when Greece is in a position of moral advantage, such as supporting Greek-Cypriot demands for the accommodation of human rights problems related to the Cyprus problem, but at the same time, they ignore the human rights of other minorities in Greece. A concrete example comes from the early 1990s. The US State Department's annual report explicitly refers to the Slav-Macedonian minority in Greece and criticizes the treatment of minorities (Anagnostou 2005: 343). It is interesting that the reaction of all parties was fierce, irrespective of ideological background (ibid.). Even the left objected, perceiving the report to be an American/imperialist intervention into domestic affairs (Empirikos and Skoulariki 2009: 149). Although concerted efforts were made by a group of experts on minority issues at the Ministry of Foreign Affairs to change the policy, political elites remained reluctant to abandon their position (Anagnostou 2005). While the Greek citizenship code that deprived thousands of political refugees of their citizenship was finally revoked in 2010 (Law No. 2910/2010), it did not have retroactive power. Thousands of Slav-Macedonians cannot reclaim their citizenship or their property rights in Greece (Christopoulos 2012).

It is worth noting that in Spain, it was an external 'stimulus' – namely, the UN WGEID's decision to include Spain in the list of countries with missing persons – that convinced the intransigent Aznar administration to adopt a more accommodating position on the problem of the disappeared. Despite frequent deployment of human rights discourse to support the official line on the Cyprus problem, bilateral relations with Turkey and other national issues, Greek political elites have *resisted external influences*. This can partly be attributed to party politics and the prevalence of majoritarian norms in the post-1974 Greek democracy. Within a majoritarian model, mainstream political parties engage in constant outbidding in an effort to secure their electoral base; at the same time, they seek to attract those who vote for smaller parties, thus enabling them to form a majority government. Any political party deviating from the official line on national issues will pay a high electoral cost. Yet, in Spain, after 40 years of power-sharing, the issue of minorities – although still sensitive – has been gradually 'de-securitized', partly because the pragmatic need to form a coalition government urges parties to adopt more flexible agendas, cooperate with other parties and make concessions.

The position of the Communist Party on the management of the grave in Florina is also guided by electoral considerations. It is interesting that, as Nikos Marantzides notes, the Communist Party has adopted an instrumental use of memory of the civil war; it fluctuates to suit electoral objectives (see Marantzides 2010). Although the 1989 coalition government adopted silence and reconciliation as top priorities, with the break-up of the Greek left into two parties (Synaspismos and KKE), the necessity to activate a new intra-left cleavage that would secure a safe electoral base for the Communist Party became reality with the strategic deployment of the memory of the civil war (ibid.).

This instrumental and top–bottom approach to memory is evident in the management of the grave in Florina. A member of the local branch indicated to me that decisions on how to proceed came directly from the central committee of the Communist Party (Interview no. 64). When I asked why KKE had not done something before, he replied that it was only in 1996 that the central committee decided to recover the memory of the grave, and that this coincided within the broader ideological shift of KKE toward the civil war (ibid.).

The grave in Florina is analytically important if we are to get a better grasp of the ideological and political shift of KKE. Representing a place with high symbolic capital, the grave was selected to be the first place to be visited by party leader Charilaos Florakis in 1996; since then, annual commemorations have been held in Florina (Rizospastis 2009). In the mid-2000s, a local initiative composed primarily of intellectuals and local members of SYRIZA challenged KKE's monopoly of the discourse on the grave, creating an online petition for the erection of a national museum of national memory. In an interview with the leader of the initiative, I realized that, once again, human rights and exhumations were not a consideration (Interview no. 71). Even so, the group's first moves alarmed the central committee of the KKE, and it decided to buy the field where the mass grave is located (Interview no. 56). This peculiar sense of ownership of the grave the individuals buried there reflects KKE's top–bottom approach to memory and human rights and excludes local ownership of the management of memory. This is an unprecedented example of 'privatization of memory' employed by a Communist party. This stands in sharp contrast to Spain, where local ownership is visible: whole villages attend and actively participate, not only in exhumations, but also in the management of the place after the exhumations have taken place (Ferrándiz 2008).

Conclusion

All three countries have established consolidated liberal democracies and become members of the most prestigious international clubs. Yet a closer look reveals that Greece was the only country to adopt a form of retributive justice – in this case, holding the military dictators accountable. If we follow the argumentation of scholars supporting the 'logic of appropriateness', Greece had better prospects than Spain to address the violent legacy of the civil war, as retributive models of justice educate citizens into human rights norms. However, Spain adopted post-transitional justice policies, while Greece continues to maintain a selective silence about the civil war.

As this chapter shows, this ostensibly paradoxical outcome can be attributed to the limited socialization of both political elites and the society at large to international human rights norms. A tool skilfully wielded in Spain by actors representing the defeated was almost absent in Greece. Moreover, the path to reconciliation in Greece was based on political consensus to silence the divisive past – a tacit agreement dictated by electoral considerations. Finally, as the illustrative study of the unopened grave in Florina shows, Greek reluctance to address some of the victims' demands is predicated on the fact that this is linked to a sensitive national issue – namely, the Macedonian question. Ultimately, the limited socialization to human rights norms did not permit the depoliticization that was needed if independent, domestic, truth-seeking groups were to emerge.

Notes

1. Since this chapter focuses on the politics of reconciliation/memory of the Greek Civil War, it will not discuss the causes of the civil war. For a detailed historical account, see Close (1993); Mazower (2000); Nikolakopoulos et al. (2002); Carabott and Sfikas (2004); and Margaritis (2002). For more in relation to the human rights abuses and the long-term impact of the civil war, see Panourgia (2009); Voglis (2002); Vervenioti (2000); and Voutyra et al. (2005).
2. There is growing interest in this aspect of the Greek Civil War. Apart from interesting scholarly work, a number of individuals who were children during the war have started writing about their experiences (see Atzakas 2008).
3. It should be mentioned that different ethnic groups, such as the Slav-Macedonians, Arvanites and Vlachs, were persecuted in the post-civil war period.
4. By early 2013, the International Commission for Missing Persons (ICMP) had identified 16,289 people who were missing from the conflicts out of a total of approximately 29,000 missing persons.
5. An example is the 'Chronicle of Action Democratic Army', published by the DSE during the civil war; it narrates the developments on the military front.
6. Access to Greek archives is often restricted by anachronistic laws or by civil servants serving as 'gatekeepers' of the truth. This structural problem faced by most scholars working on the Greek Civil War partly explains the lack of systematic empirical evidence on several topics of contemporary Greek history and inhibits truth recovery.
7. Another account of the casualties of the Greek Army during the period of the 1940s presents a different picture, according to which an estimated 5,260 persons went missing (Zafiropoulos 1956: 670–671).
8. For the purposes of this study, the category of missing includes combatants or civilians who were abducted or executed, but whose remains were not recovered. This clarification is significant, since the term was used to describe the frequent defection of soldiers to the 'other' camp, thus creating an additional analytical problem.
9. Marantzides refers to a case in Mourgana (Macedonia) where almost 120 of the 180 captures were executed in 1948 (2010: 148).
10. EDA (United Democratic Left) was the main political party of the left in the period following the civil war.
11. As in Spain, despite the silence, there was discursive space for the trauma of the civil war to be exposed in poetry, literature and personal memories (Antoniou and Marantzides 2008; Liakos 2003).
12. In the post-1974 period, even indirect references to the civil war ignited heated debates. Until the late 1970s, members of the conservative New Democracy Party referred to members of the DSE as 'bandits' (*simmorites*) – a scornful term dating back to the civil war.
13. It is worth noting that this delinkage was limited, yet important. By 1980s, resistance and the civil war were inextricably linked in mainstream political discourse; hence, PASOK's decision to skilfully delink the two events was of paramount importance, precisely because it invested in the 'national' aspect of the resistance and subsequently did not challenge one of the main tenets of the right discourse during the period from 1949 to 1974.
14. Even today, there is a heated academic debate on whether the beginning of the civil war should be traced to the last stages of Nazi occupation (1943) or if it was an independent period commencing after the liberation of the country (1946).
15. Some professional historians protested the destruction of unique historical material (Liakos 1991).
16. I am grateful to Kostis Kornetis for bringing this to my attention. *59 Segundos*, TVE1, available online at: www.rtve.es/alacarta/videos/59-segundos/59-segundos-fraga-carrillo-frente-frente-59-segundos/354152/ (accessed 20 January 2014).

17 I am grateful to Nikolas Kyriakou for bringing up this point.
18 Application no. 55508/07 and 29520/09, *Case of Janowiec versus Russia*, 16 April 2012. However, the decision was finally overturned by the Grand Chamber: Application no. 55508/07 and 29520/09, *Case of Janowiec versus Russia*, 21 October 2013. See: http://hudoc.echr.coe.int/sites/eng/pages/search.aspx?i=001-127684 (accessed 28 January 2014)
19 For a relevant precedent on the right to truth, see the ECtHR judgement on *El-Masri versus The Former Yugoslav Republic of Macedonia* (Application no. 39630/09), 13 December 2012. For precedents on the duty to investigate, see Kyriakou (2012) and Scovazzi and Citroni (2007).
20 It is interesting that the confiscated properties were often given to settlers who were nationally minded (*ethnikofrones*), further limiting the prospect of return.
21 Other groups faced similar problems in the post-civil war period, including the Vlachs and Pontians.

8 Cases compared

Belated truth-seekers and post-transitional justice

The literature on transitional justice shows a clear preference for *causes celebres*: South Africa, the former Yugoslavia and Rwanda, to name only a few. However, such a biased sample fails to provide sufficient empirical evidence for even general hypotheses about transitional justice (Brahm 2007; Hamber 2006: 208; Mendeloff 2004; Vinjamuri and Snyder 2004). In addition, by focusing on processes occurring during or immediately after the implementation of a mechanism intended to deal with the past, these studies thwart the evaluation of their impact in the long term.[1] Yet this type of evaluation is (or should be) a central objective of transitional justice literature. We should be asking whether different approaches to dealing with the past produce different results over time. More specifically, if several policies are combined, such as an amnesty and a truth commission, how can we evaluate which is the causal determinant of final 'success'? Could both play a part?

Amnesties and oblivion were the two most obvious trends in the period preceding what has been called the 'third wave' of democratization (Vinjamuri and Boesenecker 2007).[2] In both Cyprus and Spain, for example, amnesties (de facto or *de jure*) and top–bottom policies of selective 'silences' were implemented several decades previously. Yet both countries broke the pattern of silence by developing what has been called a 'politics of exhumations' (exhuming the bodies of the missing) (Kovras 2008). It therefore makes sense to use these two societies to comprehensively test the central arguments of transitional justice literature and shed light on the growing phenomenon of post-transitional justice. In fact, studying these two countries fails to verify one of the literature's central tenets – namely, that a mechanism to comprehensively address past human rights violations should be set up either during or immediately following the transition to peace and democracy (Hayner 2002; Huyse 1995; IDEA 2003; Mani 2005; O'Donnell and Schmitter 1986). Rather, the decades-long developments in the politics of exhumations in Cyprus and Spain illustrate that truth recovery can take place many years after the commission of the events under scrutiny. Paloma Aguilar has coined the term 'post-transitional justice' to describe the situation in Spain (Aguilar 2008), and this is also applicable to Cyprus. Cath Collins's research has focused on similar processes in Chile and El Salvador (2010), and, more recently, two emerging powers in international politics, Brazil and Turkey, have also established fact-finding commissions to look into events of the traumatic past, with a focus on the problem of disappearances.

Post-transitional justice: overcoming the 'linkage trap'

Although Cyprus and Spain are EU member states, only through their politics of exhumation have they taken steps towards truth recovery. Given the slow progress in these otherwise well-developed EU societies, it can be inferred that attempting narrow and/or broader truth recovery would be a Herculean task in societies with less advantageous opportunity structures. An illustrative example is Brazil, where former President Inácio Lula Da Silva signed a decree calling for a truth commission to investigate human rights abuses, including political disappearances, taking place between 1964 and 1985. Although almost three decades had passed, the military's vehement reaction forced Lula to withdraw his plans (The Economist 2010). His successor, Dilma Rousseff, eventually managed to set up a truth commission in 2011, but only after significant political struggles (BBC 2011).

Given the logic of consequences, even political parties representing or affiliated with victims' groups often remain reluctant to deal with past human rights violations, even if they assume power and threats to democracy have vanished. The consecutive socialist governments (1981–1989 and 1993–2004) in Greece, while representing a significant number of those defeated in the Greek Civil War, have abstained from 'touching' the past. This is also the case in Chile. In the aftermath of the 1998 referendum that ousted Augusto Pinochet, the centre–left *Concertación* coalition governed for four consecutive terms, but made only marginal moves towards official acknowledgement of the past (Sandbu 2010).

All cases mentioned above show that political parties representing the defeated or past victims may prefer to disappoint their electoral constituents than to trigger instability and put in danger overarching objectives, including democratic consolidation, economic development or the reconstruction of state infrastructures. By the same token, victims' groups are often silenced, either because of the fragile political balance of power or because 'they have skeletons in their closet' (Nalepa 2010). As time passes, a linkage trap is constructed. Most frequently, during the transition to peace and democracy, a subtle agreement is reached between previous parties in conflict to link the non-instrumental use of the past with the imminent need for political stability in the nascent democracy. Over time, selective silence becomes an entrenched feature of the political discourse and democratic institutions, acquiring a hegemonic status and prolonging the silencing of violence. In this way, silence or selective memories become ingrained into the political discourse, either to establish a culture of victimhood (Cyprus) or achieve other political objectives, such as democratic consolidation (Spain and Greece). As shown in the preceding chapters, in the long term, such elite framing becomes institutionalized and eventually acquires a hegemonic status. Paradoxically, this linkage may constitute the most efficient path toward peace, stability and democratic consolidation. In Spain, Greece and Cyprus, as

150 *Post-transitional justice*

well as the other examples mentioned above, the decision not to unearth the past culminated in full-blown democratic regimes.

However, this is merely one part of the story; at different post-transition periods, these same parties may decide to break the silence and campaign in the interests of victims' groups. For example, during his presidency in Argentina (2003–2007), Néstor Kirchner introduced measures calling for greater scrutiny of the past, declaring the 'full-stop' and 'due obedience' laws as null and void and reopening trials for human rights abuses, including disappearances (The Economist 2003). Similarly, in Uruguay, despite two referendums that rejected the annulment of the amnesty law that protected the military from accountability for human rights abuses committed from 1973 to 1985, President Vázquez campaigned to abolish it, arguing that it violated Uruguay's obligations under international human rights treaties (*The Economist* 2010).

Hence, although a political decision to bury certain issues during a transition may initially silence truth-seekers or victims' groups, it may ultimately be an effective route to truth recovery by providing the institutional tools that allow domestic truth-seekers to carry out a comprehensive truth recovery. More precisely, full-blown democratic institutions, the withdrawal of the military from public life, a functional political party system and, most importantly, the development of a civil society in Spain supplied the tools necessary for a vibrant grassroots movement to challenge the long-standing hegemonic silence. Similarly, in Cyprus, the consolidation of democracy provided the institutional and political backing for domestic groups to put forward – previously unacceptable – policies (i.e. unilateral exhumations) and/or challenge the politicization of human rights issues. In essence, a minimum threshold of democratic consolidation provides the necessary institutional instruments for domestic truth-seeking actors, whenever they decide to initiate the process, not the reverse. To paraphrase Snyder and Vinjamuri, truth 'follows; [it] does not lead' (2003: 6).

Patterns of post-transitional justice

This study's central objective is the exploration of mechanisms that bring about the breaking of prolonged silences, paving the way for the phenomenon of post-transitional justice. As Marie Breen-Smyth notes: 'There is no magic moment of "readiness" for truth recovery ... rather the conditions are constructed rather than spontaneously occurring' (Breen-Smyth 2007: 3). A policy of reviewing the past cannot be implemented without some prior form of agency on the part of social actors willing to use contentious politics to deal with the traumatic past, even with a significant delay. This section highlights the societal and political conditions that facilitated the emergence of a minimum consensus upon which a policy of exhumations was built in Cyprus and Spain and looks at the mechanisms used to break the silence.

The study has argued that *similar causes* but *alternative causal mechanisms* paved the way to the emergence of the post-transitional justice in Cyprus and Spain. Although not a causal determinant, the *passage of time* facilitates several processes. In both countries, the *normative context within which players acted* changed over time. With time, the cards are reshuffled and new opportunities arise that can be used by domestic actors to promote policies that challenge the previous hegemony. People everywhere struggle to construct stories that provide an explanatory framework for complex, confusing and traumatic events. Temporal distance from these events provides the opportunity for stories to be narrated in different ways and by different actors – or to be told at all, for that matter. In this respect, the passage of time enabled three causal processes in Spain and Cyprus: the application of political learning, the creation of a new normative framework within which political decisions were made and the use of forensic science (see Figure 8.1).

Political learning

The most obvious impact of the passage of time is the re-evaluation of the efficiency of policies pursued in the past. As previous chapters have shown, the effectiveness of the decades-long policy of linkage had gradually been challenged by the late 1990s and early 2000s, with challengers labelling it either unproductive or irrelevant. At crucial historical junctures – such EU accession in Cyprus and Turkey and the completion of 30 years of democracy in Spain – societies (re)assess certain fundamental policies. The political strategy of the Republic of Cyprus to deploy human rights violations as a legal instrument in European judicial and political bodies had failed to provide a solution to the humanitarian needs of the victims or to marginalize Turkey in the European forums. Reassessment allowed a group of top bureaucrats to see the need to redraw the policy. For its part, Turkey took a radically new direction in foreign policy on the Cyprus issue, abandoning the previous official thesis that the problem was solved in 1974. And in Spain, a new generation of political leaders with no personal memories of the transition had no need to respect the *pacto de silencio* as the founding tenet of political life, seeing no threat to the regime's stability. As will be argued below, these processes were dictated, to a significant extent, by European institutions.

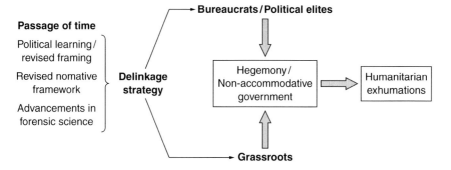

Figure 8.1 Schematic presentation of the emergence of the politics of exhumations.

As previous chapters have indicated, the revision of the elite framing facilitated these processes. The institutionalization of frames – or the devaluation of previous institutions – changed the normative context within which players interacted and their priorities were transformed. In Cyprus, the slightly revised elite framing – encompassing, for the first time, the Turkish-Cypriot missing – convinced even the most reluctant actors that unilateral exhumations would not weaken the political strategy of the Republic of Cyprus. In fact, the publication of the list of the Turkish-Cypriots missing in the *Gazette* and the de facto recognition of these crimes delegitimized particular discourses. The Spanish case is even more revealing. The parties of the centre–left disengaged from the spirit of the transition (*spíritu de la transición*), which prioritized the security of the regime from potential military intervention, especially after the failed coup of 1981. They gradually subscribed to a new framing of human rights, demanding delinkage of these issues from the political legacy of the transition. This new framing has strengthened the institutional role of domestic actors, including the proactive judiciary, who pushed for the politics of exhumations.

Revised international normative framework

Over the last three decades, the practice of enforced disappearances has intensified. The UN Working Group on Enforced and Involuntary Disappearances (henceforth, Working Group) has processed more than 40,000 cases taking place in more than 90 countries (UN 2008a).[3] This, in turn, has amplified calls from around the world for the use of radical legal measures to end the problem. I argue that these expectations were of tremendous political importance in breaking the silence over the missing in Cyprus and Spain, because they transformed the normative context within which political decisions were taken: first, they legitimized the actors already socialized into these norms; second, they convinced domestic political leaders to strategically adapt.

One of the most significant legal steps was taken in 1992, when the UN General Assembly signed the Declaration on the Protection of All Persons from Enforced Disappearance (UN Resolution 47/133). At the same time, various regional bodies fortified the relatives' legal recourse with landmark case law decisions,[4] and the Parliamentary Assembly of the Council of Europe adopted a resolution defining enforced disappearances as a crime against humanity (Citroni and Scovazzi 2009: 92; Council of Europe 828/1984). In 1998, the Statute of Rome established the International Criminal Court, which affirmed that, under certain circumstances, the phenomenon of enforced disappearances constitutes a crime against humanity.

Arguably the most important of these legal norms was the International Convention for the Protection of All Persons from Enforced Disappearance (henceforth, Convention) in 2007 (Scovazzi and Citroni 2007). The Convention represents a breakthrough; it verifies the continuous character of the crime (Article 8) and ascribes the inalienable right of both the relatives and society at large to 'know the truth' (Article 24, para. 2) about the fate of the disappeared and the conditions of their disappearance. The crucial element is that the relatives do not carry the burden of proof; rather, the state has a duty to investigate and, in the case of death, to locate, identify and return the remains to the relatives (Article 24, para. 3). The Convention has been an effective legal instrument; this legal instrument resulted from political pressure mounted by associations of relatives from around the globe, united under the International Coalition against Enforced Disappearance.[5]

The above-mentioned developments indicate the establishment of a new normative context within which the problem of disappearances as a result of political violence can be managed. For one thing, international institutions subscribe to a new diagnosis of the phenomenon of disappearances, identifying *impunity* as the reason for the rapid diffusion of the practice globally (Anderson 2006). Because of this diagnosis, amnesty provisions cannot cover the crime of enforced disappearances; they are considered crimes against humanity and thus can no longer be committed with impunity. In addition, a *legal delinkage of the management of cases of disappearances from political agreements* was achieved, strengthening the ability of domestic actors to shed light on the past. On the one hand, new obligations devolved upon the states involved; on the other hand, domestic actors who had absorbed these norms into their practices were legitimized.

Strategic adaptation guided Turkey to comply – at least partly – with a number of new obligations in the form of several ECtHR decisions, which required it to conduct effective investigations into the 1974 Greek-Cypriot missing (Hoffmeister 2002: 449).[6] By the same token, the knowledge that relatives of the Turkish-Cypriot missing might lodge applications with the ECtHR in the near future (some have already done so) caused the Republic of Cyprus to design a more proactive agenda. In the case of Spain, the hot debate over the competence of Judge Baltazar Garzón in investigating cases of disappearances covered by the amnesty law of 1977 epitomizes this changed normative context. In fact, the latest report of the Working Group lends credence to Judge Garzón's argument; it states that disappearances are not 'political crimes' and thus 'amnesty is not applicable' (UN 2008b: 141). The inclusion of Spain in the list of countries with 'disappeared' triggered the moderation of the previously intransigent Aznar administration and let to the adoption of a precedent-setting parliamentary resolution in 2002. In all these instances, the states involved made some sort of strategic adaptation.

However, the new norms have facilitated the emergence of the politics of exhumations in other ways as well. Perhaps their most important function is the legitimization of the demands of domestic actors. In Spain, the civil society groups involved in the recovery of historical memory have framed their demands in human rights terms, made comparisons with the successful absorption of these norms in other societies with similar experiences and legitimized their cause when the UN Working Group adopted their views in 2002. Equally, the group of bureaucrats in Cyprus and certain branches of the judiciary in Spain who pushed for a policy of unearthing the truth legitimized their proposals by referring to these norms. Specific branches of the bureaucracy have been socialized into these norms and are convinced that delinkage is the appropriate way to deal with the problem. Tellingly, the Ministry of Foreign Affairs in Turkey – considered one of the most pro-EU branches of government – has deployed the progress reports of the European Commission since the early 2000s, as well as the ECtHR judgements, to convince intransigent domestic actors that reform is necessary to reach the higher goal of EU accession.

In the period of the Cold War, the overarching priorities of maintaining global order and stability made amnesties and silence constitutive ingredients of peace agreements (Newman *et al.* 2009). Since then, the global diffusion of human rights norms has increasingly dictated the inclusion of human rights provisions into peace settlements (Risse and Sikkink 1999). As Christine Bell's systematic study of more than 600 peace agreements since 1990 has shown, the emerging normative consensus perceives amnesties as an exception to the norm of accountability (2008: 243). New normative requirements of peace settlements are explained by the proactive role of influential international institutions in combination with the emergence of vocal transnational advocacy networks, which exert pressure for their implementation (ibid.). These external normative pressures have rendered blanket amnesties obsolete, changing the nature and content of elite bargaining in peace processes and democratic transitions (Lutz and Sikkink 2001). The growing deployment of normative tools to address the past in peace agreements is also evident in the decision of an increasing number of countries undergoing negotiated transitions to deal with their violent past – a phenomenon reflected in the burgeoning of truth commissions (Hirsch 2007).

This revised normative framework not only informs the content of pact-making, but as the experience of several South American societies has indicated, it legitimizes domestic truth-seeking actors to exert bottom-up pressure in a way that overturns outdated amnesty laws and challenges decades-long silences (Collins 2010). In other words, the agenda of international politics and law has considerably changed since the historical examples of Cyprus and Spain. The new norms prevent silence from being institutionalized and bring an end to oblivion and denial in societies with well-entrenched cultures of silence. In the period preceding the normative turn of 1990s, it would have been unimaginable for any Spanish government to enact a law that would address several (post-) transitional justice measures or challenge the legitimacy of the amnesty law of 1977 – perceived as the founding tenet of the post-Francoist Spanish democracy.

Advancements in forensic science

Another significant development that facilitated the ability of domestic actors to advance the politics of exhumations occurred in forensic science. The use of forensic tools to identify human remains traces its origins – as legal tools – to the early 1980s, when associations of relatives in several Latin American countries sought to locate the remains of their disappeared relatives. In 1984, the pioneers of contemporary forensic anthropology, Clyde Snow and Eric Stover, were invited to Argentina to search for the *desaparecidos*. In Argentina, they helped a group of local forensic scientists to establish the Argentine Forensic Anthropology Team (EAAF). This team has since been called into neighbouring countries, including Guatemala (1991) and Chile, where they have provided rigorous training to local experts and organized local forensic teams to investigate the fate of the *desaparecidos* (Simmons and Haglund 2005). The knowledge was then rapidly disseminated: by 2003, approximately 100 forensic experts were active in more than 35 countries (Stover et al. 2003: 664).

The turning point for the adoption of forensic tools as a mainstream instrument in the search for the disappeared came in the mid-1990s, as new techniques of identification became available and were used by international tribunals. At that time, two ad hoc international tribunals, the International Criminal Tribunal for the former Yugoslavia (ICTY) and the International Criminal Tribunal for Rwanda (ICTR), decided to use forensic exhumations for 'incriminatory evidence' (ethnicity, cause of death) to substantiate cases of ethnic cleansing (Stover and Shigekane 2002: 354). The major breakthrough, though, came with the use of DNA tests to identify human remains.

The incorporation of DNA testing into standard operating procedures in forensic exhumations explains the timing of the exhumations in Cyprus and Spain. For the first time in human history, science offered a credible way of delinking the process of identification of human remains from human testimony (i.e. truth recovery). Previously, human testimony was the only means by which to locate and identify victims buried in common graves. The findings from such exhumations constituted a *corpus delicti* (body of crime), deterring many witnesses from collaborating, since their participation would have initiated legal proceedings and made them targets for reprisal.

The overall policy of delinkage became possible – or was significantly facilitated – by the ability to perform exhumations for humanitarian purposes. In 'humanitarian exhumations' the objective is merely to unearth and return the remains to relatives. There is no attribution of blame: cause of death is not mentioned, and there are no criminal proceedings. The cases of Spain and Cyprus verify this assumption. In Cyprus, a decision by the Attorney General states that all persons providing information to the CMP will be immune from prosecution; the same provision exists in the terms of engagement of the CMP. Thus, perpetrators of heinous crimes are appeased, while witnesses have incentives for providing information. Similarly, in Spain, the objective of exhumations is not the attribution of responsibility, but to 'dignify' the memory of the missing person. In short, the possibility of establishing certain aspects of the past in a scientific way have *enhanced the credibility of delinkage*. Because it is possible to conduct exhumations for purposes of historical documentation (Juhl 2005), political exhumations are frequently used as a tool by truth commissions.

Needless to say, this development alone cannot explain a successful outcome. In other cases where an equal framework has been applied, the results have been poor. For example, the Independent Commission for the Location of Victims Remains in Northern Ireland was established as a part of the Good Friday

Agreement; its primary objective was the recovery of the bodies of 16 persons who disappeared as a result of the Troubles.[7] Although the principle of confidentiality governs the body, by September 2010, only six had been recovered. Other cases have had better results. In 1996, the International Commission on Missing Persons (henceforth, ICMP) was established as a result of the strenuous efforts of relatives' associations; it also benefitted from being allocated abundant resources by the international community. Its mandate was to assist in the identification of approximately 30,000 persons who went missing during the war in the former Yugoslavia. Since then, more than half of those missing have been identified.[8]

DNA analysis has caused a revolution in political exhumations by challenging the logic of disappearances. The political violence employed by Nationalist forces during the Spanish Civil War, including disappearances, had dual and overlapping objectives: first, to instil terror in the population and, second, to eliminate the evidence (i.e. bodies). Franco could never have imagined that, 70 years after their execution, it would be possible to identify these people, bringing them back into existence, in effect, as they have been ascribed new agency by groups striving for their 'ownership' (McEvoy and Conway 2004).

In Cyprus and Spain, exhumations have been used by different groups to justify their versions of the past. In Spain, some groups see this as a process of belated exculpation of familial legacies; others have politicized the events. Similarly, in Cyprus, exhumations have come to represent the Cyprus problem, this time within both communities. Those taking uncompromising stances blame the 'other' for ongoing suffering, and pro-rapprochement groups deploy exhumations as a means of dealing with the past and paving the way to reconciliation. But with DNA testing, dead bodies carrying significant symbolic capital have become depoliticized.

Resisting post-transitional justice

The comparative analysis of Greece – a country that abstained from implementing policies of post-transitional justice – helps refine the arguments stated above. Why were such policies established in some countries, but not others? Simply stated, despite comparable background conditions, Greece has resisted the norms of post-transitional justice because of three overlapping factors: the Greek path to reconciliation, the securitization of the problem of the missing and the non-socialization of political parties into human rights norms.

Greece's political elites faced a far less important security threat from its small ethnic minorities than did their counterparts in Spain, but they were still framed as a security threat. Consequently, Spanish political elites have effectively accommodated human rights issues pending from the civil war, but in Greece the linkage of human rights with sensitive national issues impedes truth recovery.

Nor is Greek civil society socialized to international human rights norms; although it has access to the tools needed to achieve change, it seems unaware of these instruments, let alone how to use them. For example, in my interview with members of the local branch of Rainbow – a group mobilized around the promotion of minority protection of Slav-Macedonians – participants acknowledged that they had never considered the possibility of raising the issue in international forums or the ECtHR (Interview nos 74, 75). Of course, the group may have other more pressing demands. Nevertheless, it is interesting that some civil society groups are not familiar with international human rights tools. They are not alone in this. Consider the relatives of missing persons in Northern Ireland; despite their decades-long struggle to find their relatives, they never used the tools offered by international legal norms.

More importantly, consensus institutional designs have better prospects of addressing pending human rights issues in the long term. For one thing, in non-majoritarian systems, the definition of 'national interest' is framed in more inclusive terms. In Spain, the political system combines elements of both majoritarian and consensus democracy; despite being politicized gradually, after 40 years of democracy, issues of national minorities are not seen as a national issue posing an imminent threat to the stability of the democratic regime in Spain. For another, in non-majoritarian democracies parties are more willing to participate in coalition governments, thereby facilitating concessions and the adoption of policies that delink human rights from national issues (Lijphart 2012). In majoritarian systems, such as Greece, however, the constant outbidding over national issues requires maximalist and exclusionary definition of national interest, minimizing the possibility of delinking national from humanitarian issues. Thus, external influences may be resisted by local elites out of political and electoral expediency.

Once truth recovery is coupled with national issues, it is hard to delink the problem and initiate exhumations. To achieve this, either the policymakers must convince the political elites of the need to change the framing/policy because of the political cost to the international profile of the country (as the bureaucrats at the Ministry of Foreign Affairs in Cyprus did) or domestic grassroots actors must direct their claims to international legal bodies that will convince domestic leaders to change their course of action. As the case of Greece illustrates, if none of the two conditions applies, then it is impossible to overcome the problem and adopt policies of post-transitional justice.

Delinkage lessons for transitional justice

What lessons can be drawn from the story of the Cypriot Committee for Missing Persons and the transformation of the relatives of the missing into a proactive bi-communal group promoting reconciliation? I argue that in the case of sensitive human rights issues, especially when open wounds preoccupy a sizeable segment of society, such as the problem of the disappeared and missing, delinkage from political settlement constitutes an effective policy alternative (Kovras 2012). Using this strategy, enforced disappearances could be effectively managed elsewhere, becoming a building block of reconciliation in such places as Azerbaijan (Nagorno-Karabakh), Georgia (Abkhazia), Kashmir and Lebanon. The literature does not consider the conditions under which it is better to tie victims' rights to an overall settlement or to treat human rights issues separately. As emotional, symbolic and identity issues, such as the problem of missing persons, are often hijacked by hardliners who drag their feet and prevent solutions, untying human rights issues from political negotiations – or even transitional justice policies – can depoliticize debates and pave the way for the mobilization of vocal domestic pro-truth-seeking actors.

In cases of disappeared/missing persons, official delinkage could benefit from a concomitant decoupling of humanitarian exhumations from the quest for truth recovery. This solution has the potential to assist in other frozen conflicts facing the problem of missing persons, such as Kashmir and Lebanon (Jaquemet 2009).

The delinkage strategy has the potential to provide an early solution to human rights problems and to legitimize the democratization of memory, both of which constitute essential elements of reconciliation. The experiences of societies with prolonged legacies of disappeared/missing persons (Cyprus, Georgia, Abkhazia and Lebanon, for example) reveal that an early solution might promote trust in the 'other', avoid unnecessary poisoning of (inter)communal relations and, under certain circumstances, become a confidence-building measure to facilitate an overall political solution. In post-conflict settings, early accommodation of the most significant human rights problems – even if this means amnesty or impunity for the perpetrators – diminishes the possibility of societal mobilization that might inhibit the achievement of other pressing objectives (economic development, reconstruction, democratic consolidation) and promotes trust in the nascent regime.[9] Similarly, an early solution pulls the rug out from under Nationalist politicians who usurp sensitive humanitarian issues to bolster nationalism and promote a culture of victimhood.

Last, but definitely not least, a delinkage policy implemented by the political elites creates a unique opportunity for civil society actors to play a vital role in overcoming a central human rights problem in post-conflict societies – namely, a lack of communication when the 'other' is not officially recognized and/or the in-group claims to have a monopoly on suffering. In Georgia (Abkhazia), for example, 'each side has a missing persons commission, but [they are] beholden to their governments' and they never communicate (International Committee of the Red Cross 2007: 13). A prolonged lack of contact exacerbates negative stereotypes that prevent genuine dialogue. Establishing and maintaining channels of communication is critical to success, even in the absence of a political settlement. With open lines of communication, hardliners cannot control information or frame the problem according to their own interests, as in Cyprus, where, for several decades, the official RoC organizations of the relatives of the missing dominated public discourse, pursuing an agenda that silenced the relatives of missing persons in the other community.

Notes

1 These mechanisms usually include criminal trials, truth commissions, policies of lustration and public apologies or reparations.
2 On the compatibility of amnesties with international justice, see Mallinder (2007).
3 This figure concerns *only* cases submitted to the Working Group. According to other estimations, in the period from 1970 to 2000, approximately 100,000 people went missing in Latin America alone; if cases from Africa and Europe are added, this figure fluctuates between 300,000 and 500,000 (Scovazzi and Citroni 2007: 6).
4 For example, see one of the first judgements on the *desaparecidos* by the Inter-American Court of Human Rights in 1989 (*Velásquez Rodriguez versus Honduras, Godínez Cruz versus Honduras, Fairın Garbi and Solís Corrales versus Honduras*).
5 For more information on the activities of the group, see online at: www.icaed.org/ (accessed 21 January 2014).
6 In the decision of the fourth Interstate application of Cyprus versus Turkey (27581/94), 10 May 2001, the ECHR adopted the same approach as other international bodies on this issue and set a new precedent (Hoffmeister 2002: 450). This duty is reaffirmed in the latest decision of the ECHR on the case of Varnava and Others versus Turkey, Application no. 16064/90, 16065/90, 16066/90, 16068/90, 16069/90, 16070/90, 16071/90, 16072/90 and 16073/90, decision 10 January 2008.
7 For more information, see online at: www.iclvr.ie (accessed 1 September 2010).
8 The total figure of the missing was 29,030, while 15,675 had been identified by September 2010. For more information, see online at: www.ic-mp.org/about-icmp/ (accessed 1 September 2010).
9 This is valid elsewhere; the bilateral relations of Japan and North Korea have been poisoned because of the intransigence of North Korea in returning 17 Japanese citizens abducted/disappeared during the 1970s and 1980s.

9 Conclusion
'Unearthing the truth'

Since the 1970s, the phenomenon of enforced disappearances and the ensuing demands from relatives to acknowledge the truth have become central features of societies emerging from periods of conflict or authoritarianism. Although in the 1970s the practice was primarily restricted to Latin American countries, over the last few decades it has 'spilled over' into many parts of the world to become an endemic experience following conflict or repressive regimes.

Previous chapters revealed a complex relationship between politically motivated disappearances, human rights violations and the processes of transition and truth recovery. These findings could be read by advocates of transitional justice as an indication of the need for a comprehensive evaluation of the past or by sceptics as an explanation of the pitfalls of transitional justice. In fact, these were the two broad readings that I endorsed at different stages of my research. Originally, I was convinced that as long as societies proceed to exhume mass graves, even up to 70 years after the deaths, then this constitutes proof of a need for justice and truth that was suppressed during the transition; otherwise, the democratic regime remains 'handicapped'. By the end of my research, I endorsed a different explanation – namely, that processes of truth recovery in general and exhumations of disappeared/missing persons in particular have become possible because contextual conditions, such as the consolidation of democratic institutions, enabled the emergence and successful accommodation of these issues. In essence, it is the quality of the emerging (democratic) regime that paves the way for truth recovery and not the reverse.

This concluding chapter presents findings derived from this book and their implications for researchers in the disciplines of transitional justice, international relations and comparative politics, as well as some policy-relevant conclusions. First, the major findings will be presented, focusing primarily on the causal mechanism that constructs, maintains and perpetuates silence. Additionally, the processes that break these decades-long silences and promote truth recovery will be unveiled. Finally, several conclusions related to policymaking, as well as financial, moral and technical issues related to truth recovery, will be discussed.

Overview of findings

As Michael Ignatieff remarked some years ago: 'All nations depend on forgetting: on forging myths of unity, an identity that allows a society to forget its founding crimes, its hidden injuries and divisions, its unhealed wounds' (1998: 170). The examination of Cyprus, Greece and Spain confirms this statement, although the study revealed that it is not 'forgetting' per se, but a deliberate (elite and societal) decision to *silence* specific issues or periods in national history that are traumatic. It is only recently, in the post-Cold War period of international politics with the prevalence of liberal peace (Richmond 2005a) that a comprehensive screening of the violent past of societies in transition, either through retributive or restorative measures, has become imperative.

However, this has not always been the case. In fact, world history is abundant with cases of silence. In ancient Athens, silence was institutionalized in the aftermath of bloody civil wars as a means of reuniting warring factions (Wolpert 2001: 77). In situations where amnesties were the only way of ending conflict – what we could label today as negotiated settlement – then the principle of '*μνησικακείν*' (*mnesikakein* – to recall a past wrong against another) was employed to avoid the past being used as a weapon in the post-conflict period, thereby institutionalizing silence. More recently, France's liberation in the aftermath of World War II was followed by a fratricidal civil war between the supporters of Vichy and the liberation forces. Still, the French refused to confront the truth, and this period is omitted in the official national narrative, since it is superseded by discourse of united resistance of the nation to the Vichy regime (Gildea 1996: 56). Irish independence from British rule (1921) was also followed by a fratricidal civil war between Nationalists, supporting the Anglo-Irish Treaty, and Republicans, who strongly objected to the creation of the terms of the treaty (Bew 2007: 440–443). Although the civil war was more costly in lives than the war of independence itself, it has been silenced in public memory.

Even the central (historical) point of reference for transitional justice advocates – namely, the Nuremberg trials and the remarkable transformation of (West) Germany through a process of critical contemplation and acknowledgement of the past that contributed to the Holocaust – was an endeavour that did not immediately follow the end of the war. In fact, it was only in the late 1950s and most significantly in the 1960s that Germans (gradually) set central policies for a comprehensive screening of the past and the restoration of broken relations with former enemies (Israel, France) (Lind 2008).

It is worth noting that societies do not 'forget'; they merely make a decision to remain silent. However, this process of silence is not an irreversible feature of national identities and collective memories. At some point, societies decide to break this prolonged silence. In order to explain this process of change, though, it is important first to provide the mechanism for the construction of silence.

Constructing and maintaining silence

The primary finding of this study reveals the mechanism that institutionalizes silence or, even better, selective memory. During transitions, the primary tenets of what will be remembered and what will be excluded from public discourse are set. Subsequently, the study of transitions can provide useful insights in explaining the (non-)solution of humanitarian problems and the politics of memory more generally. Societies that undergo (negotiated) transitions frequently face the 'amnesty paradox'. Justice is most necessary in situations where human suffering has reached high levels. However, it is precisely the gravity of human rights abuses and the fragility of transition that makes the search for justice impossible and most frequently evaded, leading to amnesties and silence. In negotiated transitions, the need to encompass groups who are responsible for these crimes in a comprehensive settlement that sets the stage for establishing a new polity frequently excludes the possibility of addressing the past. Subsequently, a subtle agreement is achieved among former enemies – now co-entrepreneurs in the new regime – to avoid the instrumental use of the past for political purposes, while a (consensual) version of the past is adopted that will not be perceived as scapegoating by the groups involved. Sometimes, this invented unity is further reinforced by an external threat, which acts as a unifying force in the adoption of a specific discourse.

The study also identified two interesting findings regarding the study of political learning and framing. First, although the literature on political learning focuses primarily on 'positive' or 'negative' aspects of learning, the experience of Cyprus indicates that learning can also be 'partial'. The traumatic experience of the Turkish invasion became a painful lesson for the Greek-Cypriot political elites, but, at the same time, precisely because framing is directed towards a wide audience, it should be simple (or even Manichean). Therefore, political learning remained 'partial' precisely because it abstained from highlighting issues of the moral, political and legal responsibilities of the state agents of the Republic of Cyprus or the historical responsibilities of the Greek-Cypriot community. Finally, an inherent paradox was identified in the framing process. On the one hand, the objective of any nascent frame is to become hegemonic and be widely accepted as the sole universal truth. On the other hand, by the time a frame becomes hegemonic and institutionalized, the context of the problem may have changed so radically that the frame, originally constructed to promote certain interests and policies, now obstructs, contradicts and entraps the promotion of these same interests. Alternatively put, elite consensus narrows down the options of policymakers, preventing adaptation to new conditions, even when elites realize the need for a policy shift (Loizides 2009).

Delinkage and breaking prolonged silences

This early elite pact to construct an invented unity and silence certain aspects of the past is ingrained in political discourse, political institutions, the electoral

Conclusion: 'unearthing the truth' 163

system and the political culture of the nascent regime and ultimately acquires a hegemonic status. As soon as this framing becomes a hegemonic belief, dissenting voices that subscribe to a different perception of the past are silenced, while it narrows the conception of the national interest and inhibits the solution to human rights issues, even when new windows of opportunity appear. At first sight, this situation leads to a deadlock.

However, as the hypothesis of 'linkage paradox' shows, the linkage of (i.e. the silence on) human rights issues to the elite pact that serves as the founding tenet of transition, in the long term, becomes the most efficient way to unearth the truth. More precisely, this silence enables the consolidation of strong democratic institutions, which, in turn, provide the institutional tools for (domestic) truth-seekers to put forward a comprehensive truth recovery, when such a societal demand emerges. Usually, this demand is most likely to arise when the political opportunity structure is propitious, the rule of law is established, respect for human rights and a functional political party system are available and threats to the regime's stability have disappeared.

In fact, the process of truth recovery can be likened to the efforts of two hostile neighbours trying to build a common house. There is a need to deploy instruments previously used to cause harm (sticks) as the foundations of a new common house. Any attempt to withdraw the sticks from the infrastructure to use them as a means of threatening the other would result in the collapse of the joint venture. However, if consensual agreement to abstain from instrumental use of the sticks as a means of threat is observed, in the long term the foundations of the new house become well entrenched, it can accommodate both neighbours and, subsequently, they have minimal incentives to use the past/sticks as a means of threat. As the study of Cyprus and Spain showed, even if they do decide to use it, the harm that could be inflicted to the 'other' would be minimal, especially since the past will no longer pose any threat to the stability of the democratic venture.

Therefore, it remains a paradox that linking the legacy of human rights abuses to (negotiated) transition most frequently results in silencing the past, but at the same time this silence, in the long term, is a very efficient way to unearth the past. It is also worth noting that this explanation unveils a hidden aspect of transitional justice. Although the *raison d'être* of the literature is the accommodation of calls from society to provide a solution to human rights problems, literature has abstained from defining *when* society demands truth. Hence, this analysis, by focusing on the timing of the emergence of societal demand, argues that if this is done prematurely, either due to pressure from international institutions or because of the complete victory of either of side in the conflict, this would result again in an 'imposed' version of truth. Of course, this mechanism should not be perceived as a universally applicable model. The (conducive) political, judicial and institutional conditions that circumscribed the transition in the two societies may not be available in other cases with less advantageous political opportunity structures. Hence, this causal mechanism should also be critically tested in cases outside the EU or in advanced industrialized states.

164   Conclusion: 'unearthing the truth'

After unveiling the process of constructing hegemonic framing which perpetuates silence, analysis provided the causal mechanism that explains the eventual break of these prolonged silences. The fact that societies at certain historical junctures decide to remember or forget certain events of their past does not necessarily mean that this will be an irreversible feature of their collective identities. In fact, engagement with the past is like a kaleidoscopic view. Frequently, the need to address current or future challenges dictates a change in position by the viewer of the kaleidoscope, which results in revealing previously hidden aspects of the past. Thus, it is equally important to understand when societies are ready to face certain aspects of their past that were previously forgotten, and this is unavoidably related to available opportunities.

More specifically, the study of elite framing on the disappeared shows that this takes place when, at discourse level, a decoupling of human rights issues from (the legacy of) transition revises the previous (hegemonic) framing. The juxtaposition of Cyprus and Spain revealed that the passage of time, although not a causal determinant, facilitated this transformation. The most obvious function of the passage of time is that it *may* lead to a change in the normative context within which (pro-truth-seeking) players make decisions. The recent normative turn, for example, provides fertile ground for normative considerations in societies emerging from conflict, where, previously, international institutions, transnational advocacy networks and even specific venues utilized to address the past such as trials and truth commissions were absent. Borrowing a metaphor from Ian Lustick, every now and then history is throwing the dice, and every new throw *may* create new opportunities that strengthen the negotiating position of certain (previously disadvantaged) actors that have adopted a truth-seeking agenda. More precisely, this study has identified three ways in which time facilitated the delinkage leading to the break in silence. First, it enables some degree of political learning from the failures and pitfalls of the pursued (linkage) policy – as well as 'horizontal learning' from countries that implement a delinkage policy abroad – which convinces several domestic actors of the need for policy change. Second, human rights have become central to the agenda of international institutions since the 1990s, which legitimizes the truth-seeking demands of domestic actors. Finally, technical advancements in forensic science have facilitated the process of delinkage by making the identification of human remains possible (forensic truth) in criminal proceedings.

The study of Cyprus and Spain also highlights the power of international norms. More precisely, this normative wave has the potential to initiate truth recovery on certain hidden historical legacies of repression, even in developed industrialized countries. For example, Canada has recently undergone a process of acknowledgement of abuse carried out by the state against indigenous people (Indian Residential Schools) throughout the late nineteenth and most of the twentieth centuries (Miller 1996). An equivalent process is underway in Australia, acknowledging the abuse of the human rights of indigenous Aboriginal people.

However, even when a policy of dealing with the past is implemented, the process of truth recovery is not linear. In fact, some sort of acknowledgement of the past, such as exhumations and identification of the disappeared, does not necessarily mean the end of the process, since these are usually followed by maximalist demands, such as prosecution of the perpetrators. In fact, in certain cases, those responsible for the crimes remain powerful, which means that demands should be formulated in such a way as to achieve a delicate balance between the need to avoid threatening these people, but at the same time paving the way for societal alliances that support the truth-seeking agenda.

The analysis found that even when early steps towards truth recovery are taken immediately following transition, this is not a linear process, but rather a gradual progression with frequent ruptures and steps backwards. For example, the end of the dictatorship in Argentina led to the instatement of a truth commission in 1983, with its primary focus on the acknowledgement of the truth regarding disappeared persons. Still, in 1990, a step backwards was taken when a pardon was issued to the perpetrators; this was later ruled unconstitutional in 2003 and prosecutions for the torturers were initiated. Equally, in Uruguay in 2009, 24 years after the end of dictatorship, the majority of Uruguayans decided in a referendum *not* to overturn the amnesty law and therefore opted for 'oblivion'. Finally, Brazil verifies this logic, since 25 years after the end of the dictatorship, the proposal of President Lula to establish a truth commission on the disappeared triggered a fierce reaction from the leadership of the military and subsequently was withdrawn.

The role of ideas in transitional justice

An equally interesting aspect of this study focuses on the important causal role of ideas in perpetuating hegemony. The literature accepts as given the existence of an outcome (forgetting), without providing an analytical framework of how this is generated. This book revealed the central role of ideas in this process. National interests are not exogenously given, but constructed. The study of elite framing adopted by this study illustrates how ideas shape the way in which people learn lessons from the past and subsequently how other frames/interests are excluded or sidelined. Ideas are often incorporated into public narratives during transitions at a time when collective memories are constructed, thus acting as 'legitimizing moments' for the new regime. Therefore, the role of ideas is central in understanding the reasons for, and the process through, which societies decide (not) to engage with their painful past. Moreover, the ideational aspect is important in shedding light on the role of political leaders. For example, the framing of post-apartheid South Africa as a 'rainbow nation' was clearly influenced by the ideological inclinations of Nelson Mandela.

Furthermore, the study identified an internal logic that guides policy change. Apart from a specific group of policymakers, a change in ideas and policymaking occurs while politicians or society at large may not realize the need for a change. As the case of Cyprus indicates, even policymakers may initially pretend that change in the management of a specific problem (i.e. the missing) constitutes an exception to the hegemonic framing, which remains intact. It is only later that the results of the management of the specific issue convince political elites and society of the need for change in policy.

The study also offers some insights into framing. In fact, although the literature of framing focuses on continuities or the importance of discourse strategies in explaining specific outcomes (mobilization of social movements, adoption of policy measures, etc.), the literature has abstained from tracing an analytically clear framework that explains change. Although the approach of framing offers interesting analytical tools to explain policy outcomes, it remains vague as to how and why a change in discourse takes place in the first place. The analysis of Cyprus and Spain showed that polarization in the political domain has the potential to realign framing and create windows of opportunity for political leaders to revise the (previously hegemonic) discourse. In the cases under examination, polarization came as a result of an external stimulus – namely, the referendums for the Annan (Reunification) Plan in 2004 and the decision of the Aznar administration to join the 'Coalition of the Willing' in Iraq. In both cases, polarization led to societal mobilization and the resumption of old cleavages that had been swept under the carpet for decades. Hence, electoral and symbolic considerations before major decisions frequently explain decisions of certain groups of political elites to change the proffered frame, which leads to revision of the previously hegemonic frame or the emergence of a counter-frame.

Policy considerations

In the case of human rights issues, especially when these are related to 'open wounds' that preoccupy a significant segment of society, such as the problem of the disappeared/missing, delinkage from any political consideration and an early solution constitutes an efficient policy alternative. It is not only normative considerations that lend credence to this view, though. The experience of societies with disappeared/missing persons (Cyprus, Georgia, Abkhazia or Lebanon) reveals that an early solution might promote trust for the 'Other', avoid unnecessary poisoning of (inter-)communal relations and, under certain circumstances, become a confidence-building measure that facilitates an overall political solution (Crettol and La Rosa 2006). In post-authoritarian settings, early accommodation of the most significant human rights problems, even if this means amnesty/impunity for the perpetrators, not only diminishes the possibility of societal mobilization that inhibits the achievement of other pressing objectives (economic development, reconstruction, etc.), but also promotes trust in the nascent democratic regime. This is also valid in international politics. For example, the bilateral relations of Japan and North Korea have been poisoned because of the intransigence of North Korea in returning 17 Japanese citizens abducted or 'disappeared' during the 1970s and 1980s (French 2002).

Also, the study shows that the sustainability of agreements accommodating human rights issues is significantly enhanced when actors from different political backgrounds are included. In this way, domestic players who could otherwise have deviated for ideological or electoral reasons are committed to the

Conclusion: 'unearthing the truth' 167

process. For example, a policymaker in the Ministry of Foreign Affairs of the Republic of Cyprus became a close aide of President Papadopoulos (who had hitherto taken an uncompromising stance), thereby helping to convince the president to change his approach on this specific issue. And the 1997 Denktas Agreement, although officially a dead letter, was later used by Talat to reactivate the CMP, without him being labelled a traitor. In other words, the sustainability of a peace agreement or resolution of human rights issues presupposes participation of a wide variety of actors and, if possible, the engagement of 'hawks', sceptics and doves (Stedman 1997). The more inclusive a settlement, the more possible it becomes to be sustainable, explained not only by the support of divergent influential actors, but most significantly because in the long term it becomes difficult for ensuing governments to deviate from this specific course of action.

The soft power of Europe

Paradoxically, although the 'incentives' structure' offered by the EU to set the stage for a comprehensive solution to the Cyprus problem failed (Demetriou 2004; Heraclides 2006; Richmond 2005b), the soft power of European institutions are better suited to address and resolve humanitarian issues. In essence, its influence was more important when not direct. The EU set the normative context within which (human rights) issues should be resolved, while by legitimizing the (pro-truth-seeking) agenda of domestic actors they opened a window of opportunity for tackling the past. Hence, the EU may be more efficient in providing the general context for the solution of humanitarian problems, rather than providing political 'carrots' and 'sticks'. In other intractable conflicts, such as in Georgia or Chechnya, the role of European institutions could be more efficient if they deploy soft power to 'delink' and eventually resolve humanitarian issues, which could ultimately pave the way for a political settlement.

Victims' groups: good intentions, positive outcomes?

After spending six months in Cyprus and Spain interviewing several members of (victims') groups involved in the truth recovery project, a paradoxical process unfolded. The original good intentions of addressing a humanitarian issue that was the driving force behind the establishment of these associations sometimes produced contentious outcomes. As soon as the work of these groups became a 'success story', attracting material resources, publicity and political support, the leaders of these associations developed a sense of 'ownership' of the (successful) process, which has ultimately led to the adoption of competing agendas – frequently explained by the effort to secure financial aid. These agendas, at the end of the day, produced outcomes that were not always positive for victims. Although at times the split in victims' associations constitutes an indication of democratic culture, it frequently reflects competing political agendas (adopting an instrumental view of victims), struggles over material resources or even conflicting personal ambitions of leaders. This is of crucial importance, for the policymaking resulting from victims' demands (represented by victims' groups) constitutes the basis for legitimizing diverse forms of intervention, such as transitional justice and humanitarian intervention (Newman *et al.* 2009). Besides, victims' associations have become the focal point through which to invest resources in post-conflict settings by the international society. However, a closer scrutiny of the activities of these associations reveals a thornier picture. This is not to argue that these groups are 'spoilers', but only that the allocation of financial aid *may* sometimes (paradoxically) empower the most vocal groups – deemed the most representative – in ways not originally intended.

Da Capo

In conclusion, it is safe to assume that Lorca's quote that 'in Spain dead people are more alive than any other part of the world', presented in the introduction, holds true for every country in the world facing the problem of disappeared/ missing persons. As illustrated throughout the analysis, the dead/missing have a vibrant political life in all societies with enforced disappearances, precisely because 'the dead body is a mark of good political symbol: it has legitimating effects not because everyone agrees on its meaning but because it compels interest despite divergent views of what it means' (Verdery 1999: 31). As McEvoy and Conway have remarked: 'The question who "owns" the dead I [...] inextricably linked to the notion of who "owns" the past' (2004: 593). Visiting the (Greek-Cypriot) military cemetery of Makedonitisa in Nicosia, one will find a part of the cemetery that has been recently extended with new, empty graves waiting to welcome the recently identified Greek-Cypriot soldiers (previously missing). Their identification brings them back to the national community, bringing closure and possibly an opening for reconciliation and the reunification of the island?

Appendix: short timelines

Table A The Spain experience

Date	Event	Short description
1940	First exhumations following the civil war	• The nascent Francoist regime legislated laws/decrees that safeguarded the places where those had fallen for 'the God and Spain' and ensured proper reburial according to Catholic rituals.
1977	(Amnesty) Law 46/1977	• Institutionalization of silence for the civil war.
1977–1980	Early unofficial exhumations (of Republican victims)	• A popular magazine of the time, (*Interviú*) featured detailed coverage of the efforts of the relatives of *desaparecidos* to exhume the graves and provide their loved ones with a decent burial. These exhumations took place throughout Spain, including La Rioja, Casas de don Pedro (Badajoz), Granada, Navarra and Galicia.
23 February 1981	Failed military coup (23-F)	• A group of soliders and officers of the Civil Guard seizes the parliament; the attempted *coup* fails after the intervention of King Juan Carlos.
1997–2003	Repatriation of Blue Division	• PP Government repatriated the remains of 1,162 individuals–members of *Division Azul* (Blue Division), who fought alongside the Nazis on the Eastern Front during World War II.
2000	First DNA identification	• The first 'disappeared' of the civil war is identified in the region of *El Bierzo* (Leon).
2002	First resolution that condemns the Francoist regime	• For the first time in Spanish history, the coup of Franco is deemed illegitimate (unanimous vote).
June 2004	Inter-ministerial Commission for the study of the situation concerning the victims of the civil war and Francoism	• Establishment of the Inter-ministerial Commission to investigate the situation of victims of Francoism and promote measures to regulate rectification of this problem, which would be enshrined in law.

Date	Event	Short description
October 2007	'Law of Historical Memory' (Law 52/2007)	(a) Annulment of decisions of military tribunals; (b) state-sponsoring of exhumations/identification of *desaparecidos*; (c) banning public symbols/removing names of streets that commemorate Franco; (d) granting citizenship to all refugees (*irrespective of their ethnic status*).
2010–	The 'super judge' (Garzón debate)	• Judge Garzón attempted to characterize disappearances as crimes against humanity (i.e. ongoing crime) and as therefore not subject to the prohibition of retroactive application of criminal law. • Far-right political groups charged Garzón for breaching the 1977 amnesty law, which provides that political crimes committed before 1976 cannot be prosecuted. This incident triggered a global debate about the quality of Spanish democracy that preserves a (amnesty) law which contravenes fundamental international laws.

Table B The Greek experience

Date	Event	Short description
February 1949	Florina battle	• Mass grave of 700–800 persons.
1949	(Law 971/1949) 'Moral Award to the National Rebel Groups and National Organizations of Resistance'	• Resistance organizations representing the defeated of the civil war were excluded.
April 1982	(Law 1285/1982) 'Law for the Recognition of the Resistance of the Greek People Against the Occupation Troops 1941–1944'	• Recognition of all resistance organizations (including EAM). • Annual commemoration of the destruction of Gorgopotamos bridge. • Annulment of laws passed during dictatorship providing benefits to collaborators to the Nazis. • Provisions for pensions to all those who participated in the resistance. • Repatriation of political refugees ('Greeks by Descent', exclusion of Slavic-speaking Greeks).
August 1989	(Law 863/1989) «Άρση των συνεπειών του εμφυλίου 1944–1949»	(a) Officially rehabilitating the defeated Left in the civil war (annulment of decision of trials); (b) officially referred to no longer as 'bandit war', but as 'civil war'; (c) provision for pensions to its disabled veterans of the national side.

continued

172 *Appendix*

Table B Continued

Date	Event	Short description
2009	Florina grave 'bought' by the Greek Communist Party	
2009	The puzzle of Lesvos	• Unofficial exhumations of the remains of members of DSE carried out in the island of Lesvos.

Table C The Cypriot experience

Date	Event	Short description
1963–1967	Inter-communal violence	• 228 Turkish-Cypriot missing persons.
July–August 1974	Military coup and Turkish invasion	• 1,493 Greek-Cypriot missing persons and 274 Turkish-Cypriot missing persons.
April 1981	Establishment of the Committee on Missing Persons (CMP)	• Three-Members: Greek-Cypriot, Turkish-Cypriot and a third member appointed by the UN Secretary General. • Attribution of responsibility for deaths, excluded from the mandate. • Decisions taken by consensus.
31 July 1997	Clerides–Denktas Agreement	• Delinkage from the political negotiations. • Exchange of information about burial sites. • Return of the bodies to the relatives of the missing of both communities.
June 1999	Unilateral exhumations in two cemeteries in the Republic of Cyprus	• A number of persons perceived to be missing were dead and buried within the jurisdiction of the RoC since 1974. • First official apology of the RoC to its (G/C) citizens. • A number of lawsuits filed by relatives against the state for negligence.
2000–2003	Delinkage policy	(a) Official lists with the names and details of both the Greek-Cypriot and Turkish-Cypriot missing persons were published in the Gazette; (b) coordinated efforts to collect blood and genetic samples from the relatives of Turkish-Cypriot missing – both in Cyprus and abroad – to establish a genetic material bank.
May 2001	ECtHR: Fourth Inter-State Application	• Turkey's non-cooperation on the fate of the missing constitutes a continuous deprivation of the relatives' right to 'know the truth' about their relatives.

Date	Event	Short description
2003	Open checkpoints	• The emergence of a new (grassroots) actor: 'relatives across the divide'.
August 2004	Resumption of the CMP	• No enquiry over the 'cause of death'. • 'De facto immunity' for those providing information.

List of interviews

Personal Interview no. 1, 28 July 2008, Nicosia.
Personal Interview no. 2, 21 July 2008, Nicosia.
Personal Interview no. 3, 15 July 2008, Nicosia.
Personal Interview no. 4, 10 July 2008, Nicosia.
Personal Interview no. 5, 16 July 2008, Nicosia.
Personal Interview no. 6, 3 July 2008, Nicosia.
Personal Interview no. 7, 22 July 2008, Nicosia.
Personal Interview no. 8, 22 July 2008, Nicosia.
Personal Interview no. 9, 16 July 2008, Nicosia.
Personal Interview no. 10, 30 July 2008, Nicosia.
Personal Interview no. 11, 23 July 2008, Famagusta.
Personal Interview no. 12, 9 July 2008, Nicosia.
Personal Interview no. 13, 16 July 2008, Nicosia.
Personal Interview no. 14, 21 July 2008, Nicosia.
Personal Interview no. 15, 3 July 2008, Nicosia.
Personal Interview no. 16, 26 July 2008, Nicosia.
Personal Interview no. 17, 25 July 2008, Nicosia.
Personal Interview no. 18, 17 July 2008, Nicosia.
Personal Interview no. 19, 18 July 2008, Nicosia.
Personal Interview no. 20, 16 July 2008, Nicosia.
Personal Interview no. 21, 30 July 2008, Nicosia.
Personal Interview no. 22, 30 July 2008, Nicosia.
Personal Interview no. 23, 10 July 2008, Nicosia.
Personal Interview no. 24, 30 July 2008, Nicosia.
Personal Interview no. 25, 15 July 2008.
Personal Interview no. 26, 30 January 2009, Nicosia.
Personal Interview no. 27, 3 February 2009, Nicosia.
Personal Interview no. 28, 11 February 2009, Nicosia.
Personal Interview no. 29, 10 February 2009, Nicosia.
Personal Interview no 30, 3 February 2009, Nicosia.
Personal Interview no. 31, 2 February 2009, Nicosia.
Personal Interview no. 32, 2 February 2009, Nicosia.
Personal Interview no. 33, 7 February 2009, Nicosia.
Personal Interview no. 34, 9 February 2009, Nicosia.
Personal Interview no. 35, 12 February 2009, Nicosia.
Personal Interview no. 36, 11 February 2009, Nicosia.

List of interviews 175

Personal Interview no. 37, 6 May 2009, Madrid.
Personal Interview no. 38, 12 May 2009, Barcelona.
Personal Interview no. 39, 18 May 2009, Madrid.
Personal Interview no. 40, 8 May 2009, Madrid.
Personal Interview no. 41, 13 May 2009, Barcelona.
Personal Interview no. 42, 15 May 2009, Granada.
Personal Interview no. 43, 25 March 2009, Madrid.
Personal Interview no. 44, 20 March 2009, Madrid.
Personal Interview no. 45, 24 March 2009, Madrid.
Personal Interview no. 46, 25 March 2009, Madrid.
Personal Interview no. 47, 26 March 2009, Madrid.
Personal Interview no. 48, 6 May 2009, Madrid.
Personal Interview no. 49, 16 May 2009, Madrid.
Personal Interview no. 50, 28 April 2009, Madrid.
Personal Interview no. 51, 18 May 2009, Madrid.
Personal Interview no. 52, 21 June 2010, (via telephone).
Personal Interview no. 53, 20 July 2010, (via telephone).
Personal Interview no. 54, 4 February 2010, Nicosia.
Personal Interview no. 55, 5 February 2010, Nicosia.
Personal Interview no. 56, 11 June 2012, Florina.
Personal Interview no. 57, 13 June 2012, Florina.
Personal Interview no. 58, 26 April 2012, Mytilene.
Personal Interview no. 59, 30 April 2010, Mytilene.
Personal Interview no. 60, 28 June 2012, Athens.
Personal Interview no. 61, 29 March 2010, Athens.
Personal Interview no. 62, 12 June 2012, Florina.
Personal Interview no. 63, 12 June 2012, Florina.
Personal Interview no. 64, 12 June 2012, Florina.
Personal Interview no. 65, 12 June 2012, Florina.
Personal Interview no. 66, 5 April, 2010, Athens.
Personal Interview no. 67, 13 June 2012, Florina.
Personal Interview no. 68, 1 May 2012, Mytilene.
Personal Interview no. 69, 21 May, 2010, Athens.
Personal Interview no. 70, 29 March 2010, Athens.
Personal Interview no. 71, 12 June 2012, Florina.
Personal Interview no. 72, 7 July 2012, Athens.
Personal Interview no. 73, 12 June 2012, Florina.
Personal Interview no. 74, 11 June 2012, Florina.
Personal Interview no. 75, 11 June 2012, Florina.
Personal Interview no. 76, 25 June 2012, Mytilene.
Personal Interview no. 78, 5 May 2012, Mytilene.
Personal Interview no. 79, 15 June 2012, Salonica.
Personal Interview no. 80, 17 June 2012, Athens.
Personal Interview no. 81, 18 June 2012, Athens.
Personal Interview no. 82, 11 June 2012, (via telephone).
Personal Interview no. 83, 11 June 2012, Florina.
Personal Interview no. 84, 12 June 2012, Florina.
Personal Interview no. 85, 5 April 2010, Athens.
Personal Interview no. 86, 18 April 2013, New Jersey.

Bibliography

Aguilar, Paloma (1999) 'Agents of Memory: Spanish Civil War Veterans and Disabled Soldiers', in Jay Winter and Emmanuel Sivan (eds), *War and Remembrance in the Twentieth Century*, New York, NY: Cambridge University Press, pp. 84–103.
Aguilar, Paloma (2002) *Memory and Amnesia. The Role of the Spanish Civil War in the Transition to Democracy*, London: Berghahn Books.
Aguilar, Paloma (2008) 'Transitional or Post-Transitional Justice? Recent Developments in the Spanish Case', *South European Society and Politics*, vol. 13(4), pp. 417–433.
Aguilar, Paloma (2009) 'Whatever Happened to Francoist Socialization? Spaniards' Values and Patterns of Cultural Consumption in the Post-Dictatorial Period', *Democratization*, vol. 16(3), pp. 455–484.
Aguilar, Paloma Fernandez and Carsten Humlebaek (2002) 'Collective Memory and National Identity in the Spanish Democracy: The Legacies of Francoism and the Civil War', *History and Memory*, vol. 14(1/2), pp. 121–164.
AKEL (1975) *Chronicle of the Contemporary Tragedy of Cyprus: July–August 1974*, Nicosia: AKEL.
Ali, Saleem H. (2008) 'Water Politics in South Asia: Technocratic Cooperation and Lasting Security in the Indus Basin and Beyond', *Journal of International Affairs*, vol. 61(2), pp. 167–182.
Alitheia (1999) '*Ταπεινά συγγνώμη ζήτησε χθές η Πολιτεία απο τους συγγνείς νεκρών*', 7 November 1999, p. 1.
Anagnostou, Dia (2005) 'Deepening Democracy or Defending the Nation? The Europeanisation of Minority Rights and Greek Citizenship', *West European Politics*, vol. 28(2), pp. 336–358.
Anastasiou, Harry (2008) *The Broken Olive Branch (Nationalism, Ethnic Conflict and the Quest for Peace in Cyprus)*, Syracuse, NY: Syracuse University Press.
Anastassiadis, Anastassios (2009) ' "El Pueblo no Olvida…", el estado si. La destruccion de los archivos de la seguridad interior en Grecia, entre la instrumentacion politica, la historia y el rechazo de la violencia en demoracia', in S. Baby, O. Campagnon and E. Gonzalez Calleja (eds), *Violencia y Transiciones Politicas a finales del Siglo XX*, Madrid: Casa de Velazquez, pp. 15–29.
Anderson, Benedict (1991) *Imagined Communities*, London: Verso.
Anderson, Kristen (2006) 'How Effective is the International Convention for the Protection of all Persons from Enforced Disappearance Likely to be in Holding Individuals Criminally Responsible for Acts of Enforced Disappearance?', *Melbourne Journal of International Law*, vol. 7(2), pp. 245–277.

Antoniou, Giorgos (2007) *Memory and Historiography of the Greek Civil War 1943–1949*, unpublished PhD thesis, European University Institute, Florence.

Antoniou, Giorgos (2013) '"Οι 'Γιορτές Μίσους" και οι πόλεμοι της δημόσιας μνήμης στην περίοδο της Μεταπολίτευσης (1974–2000). Από το τραύμα των ηττημένων στο τραύμα των νικητών', in Nikos Demertzis, Elenis Pashaloudi and Giorgos Antoniou (eds), *Civil War: Cultural Trauma [Εμφύλιος Πόλεμος, Πολιτισμικό Τραύμα]*, Athens: Alexandria, pp. 174–191.

Antoniou, Giorgos and Marantzides (2008) *Η Εποχή της Σύγχυσης. Η Δεκαετία του '40 και η Ιστοριογραφία [Time of Confusion. 1940s in Historiography]*, Athens: Estia.

Army History Directorate (forthcoming) *Struggles and the Dead of the Hellenic Army 1941–1993 [Αγώνες και Νεκροί του Ελληνικού Στρατού 1941–1993]*, Athens: Hellenic Army General Staff.

Asmal, Kader, Louise Asmal and Ronals Suresh Roberts (1996) *Reconciliation through Truth: Reckoning of Apartheid's Criminal Governance*, Cape Town: David Philips Publishers.

Aspasios, D., D. Dagdemverenis, G. Borovas, N. Orfanos, Z. Papaioannou, E. Skideri and O. Tzagli (2007) *The Battle of Florina as a Field of Conflict and the Post-Conflict Battle over Memory [Η Μάχη της Φλώρινας ως πεδίο Συγκρουσης και η Μετεμφυλιακή μάχη της Μνήμης]*, Joint MA dissertation, University of Western Macedonia, Department of Balkan Studies.

Assefa, Hizkias (2001) 'Reconciliation', in L. Reychler and T. Paffenholz (eds), *Peacebuilding: A Field Guide*, Boulder, CO: Lynne Reiner Publishers, pp. 336–343.

Attalides, Michalis A. (1979) *Cyprus: Nationalism and International Politics*, Edinburgh: Q Press.

Atzakas, Yiannis (2008) *Tholos Vythos*, Athens: Agra.

Backer, David (2009) 'Cross-National Comparative Analysis', in Hugo Van Der Merwe, Victoria Baxter and Audrey Chapman (eds), *Assessing the Impact of Transitional Justice*, Washington, DC: United States Institute of Peace Press, pp. 23–89.

Balcells, Laia (2010) 'Rivalry and Revenge. Violence against Civilians in Conventional Civil Wars', *International Studies Quarterly*, vol. 54(2), pp. 291–313.

Baltsiotis, Lambros (2004) 'Citizenship in the Cold War', in Michalis Tsapogas (ed.), *Civic Rights in Greece: From the Cold War to the End of Metapolitefsi [Τα Δικαιώματα στην Ελλάδα: από τον Ψυχρό Πόλεμο στο τέλος της Μεταπολίτευσης]*, Athens: Kastaniotis, pp. 81–98.

Barnett, Michael and Jack Snyder (2008) 'The Grand Strategies of Humanitarianism', in Michael Barnett and Thomas Weiss (eds), *Humanitarianism in Question: Politics, Power, Ethics*, Ithaca, NY: Cornell University Press, pp. 143–171.

Barreiro, Belén and Ignacio Sánchez-Cuenca (1998) 'Análisis del Cambio de Voto Hacia el PSOE en las Elecciones de 1993', *REIS*, vol. 82, pp. 191–211.

Barrero, Alzac (2007) 'Los Fusilamientos del 15 Mayo de 1939 en Casas de Don Pedro (Badajoz)', *Todos Los Nombres*. Available online at: www.todoslosnombres.org/doc/investigaciones/investigacion34.pdf (accessed 30 October 2010).

Barton, Charles (2000) 'Empowerment and Retribution in Criminal and Restorative Justice', in Heather Strang and John Braithwaite (eds), *Restorative Justice: From Philosophy to Practice*, Aldershot: Dartmouth, pp. 55–76.

Bazerman, Max and Margaret Neale (1993) *Negotiating Rationally*, London: Free Press.

British Broadcasting Corporation (BBC) (2008) 'Court Halts Franco-Era Exhumation', 8 November 2008.

British Broadcasting Corporation (BBC) (2011) 'Brazil's Dilma Rousseff Approves Truth

Commission Law', 18 November 2011. Available online at: www.bbc.co.uk/news/world-latin-america-15799705 (accessed 23 January 2014).

Bell, Christine (2008) *On the Law of Peace: Peace Agreements and Lex Pacificatoria*, Oxford: Oxford University Press.

Belloni, Roberto (2007) 'The Trouble with Humanitarianism', *Review of International Studies*, vol. 33, pp. 451–474.

Benford, Robert D. (1997) 'An Insider's Critique of the Social Movement Framing Perspective', *Social Inquiry*, vol. 67(4), pp. 409–430.

Benford, Robert and David Snow (2000) 'Framing Processes and Social Movements: An Overview and Assessment', *Annual Review of Sociology*, vol. 26, pp. 611–639.

Bermeo, Nancy (1992) 'Democracy and the Lessons from Dictatorship', *Comparative Politics*, vol. 24(3), pp. 273–291.

Bermeo, Nancy (1999) 'Myths of Moderation: Confrontation and Conflict during Democratic Transitions', in Lisa Anderson (ed.), *Transitions to Democracy*, New York, NY: Columbia University Press, pp. 120–139.

Bermeo, Nancy (2003) 'What the Democratization Literature Say – or Doesn't Say – About Postwar Democratization', *Global Governance*, vol. 9, pp. 159–177.

Bew, Paul (2007) *Ireland. The Politics of Enmity 1789–2006*, Oxford: Oxford University Press.

Biggar, Nigel (2003) 'Making Peace or Doing Justice: Must we Choose?', in N. Biggar (ed.), *Burying the Past. Making Peace and Doing Justice after Civil Conflict*, Washington, DC: Georgetown University Press, pp. 3–24.

Blaaw, Magriet and Virpi Lähteenmäki (2002) '"Denial and Silence" or "Acknowledgement and Disclosure"', *International Review of the Red Cross*, vol. 848, pp. 767–784.

Black, Jeremy (2008) 'Contesting the Past', *History*, vol. 93(310), pp. 224–254.

Blakeley, Georgina (2005) 'Digging up Spain's Past: Consequences of Truth and Reconciliation', *Democratization*, vol. 12(1), pp. 44–59.

Blakeley, Georgina (2008) 'Politics as Usual? The Trials and Tribulations of the Law of Historical Memory in Spain', *Entelequia, Revista Interdisciplinaria*, vol. 7, pp. 315–330.

Blau, Soren and Mark Skinner (2005) 'The Use of Forensic Archaeology in the Investigation of Human Rights Abuse: Unearthing the Past in East Timor', *Journal of Human Rights*, vol. 9(4), pp. 449–463.

Boraine, Alex (2000*) A Country Unmasked: Inside South Africa's Truth and Reconciliation Commission*, Oxford: Oxford University Press.

Borer, Anne Tristan (2006) 'Truth Telling as a Peace-Building Activity: A Theoretical Overview', in Anne Tristan Borer (ed.), *Telling the Truths. Truth-Telling and Peace Building in Post-Conflict Societies*, Notre Dame, IN: University of Notre Dame Press, pp. 1–58.

Boyd, Carolyn (2006) 'De la Memoria Oficial y la Memoria Histórica. La Guerra Civil Y La Dictadura en los Textos Escolares de 1939 al Presente', in Santos Juliá (ed.), *Memoria de la Guerra Civil y el Franquismo*, Madrid: Taurus, pp. 79–99.

Boyd, Caroline (2008) 'The Politics of History and Memory in Democratic Spain', *The Annals of the American Academy of Political and Social Science*, vol. 617, pp. 133–148.

Bouris, Erica (2007) *Complex Political Victims*, Boulder, CO: Kumarian Press.

Brahm, Eric (2007) 'Uncovering the Truth: Examining Truth Commission Successes and Impact', *International Studies Perspectives*, vol. 8, pp. 16–35.

Breen-Smyth, Marie (2007) *Truth Recovery and Justice after Conflict: Managing Violent Pasts*, London: Routledge.

Brewer, John (2004) 'Justice in the Context of Racial and Religious Conflict', *Logos*, vol. 41, pp. 80–103.
Brewer, John (2006) 'Memory, Truth and Victimhood in Post-Trauma Societies', in G. Delanty and K. Kumar (eds), *The Sage Handbook of Nations and Nationalism*, London: Sage, pp. 214–224.
Brewer, Paul R., Joseph Graf and Lars Willnat (2003) 'Priming or Framing. Media Influence on Attitudes toward Foreign Countries', *Gazette: The International Journal for Communication Studies*, vol. 65(6), pp. 493–508.
Bumiller, Elisabeth (2009) 'Seizing a Last Chance to Find Lost G.I.'s as WWII Memories Fade', *New York Times*, 6 September 2009, pp. 1, 8.
Burton, Michael and John Higley (1987) 'Elite Settlements', *American Sociological Review*, vol. 52(3), pp. 295–307.
Burton, Michael, Richard Gunther and John Higley (1992) 'Introduction: Elite Transformations and Democratic Regime', in John Higley and Richard Gunther (eds), *Elites and Democratic Consolidation in Latin America and South Europe*, Cambridge: Cambridge University Press, pp. 1–37.
Camino, Mercedes (2007) 'War, Wounds and Women: The Spanish Civil War in Victor Erice's El Espíritu de la Colmena and David Trueba's Soldados de Salamina', *International Journal of Iberian Studies*, vol. 20(2), pp. 91–104.
Carabott, Philip and D. Sfikas Thanasis (eds) (2004) *The Greek Civil War. Essays on a Conflict of Exceptionalism and Silences*, Hampshire: Ashgate.
Carillo, Santiago (2009) *La Crispación En España*, Madrid: Ediciones Planeta.
Casanova, Julián (2002) 'Una Dictadura de Cuarenta Años', in Julian Casanova (ed.), *Morir, Matar, Sobrevivir. La Violencia en la Dictadura del Franco*, Barcelona: Crítica, pp. 3–50.
Casanova, Julián (2010) *The Spanish Republic and Civil War*, Cambridge: Cambridge University Press.
Cazorla-Sánchez, Antonio (2005) 'Beyond They Shall Not Pass. How the Experience of Violence Reshaped Political Value's in Franco's Spain', *Journal of Contemporary History*, vol. 40(3), pp. 503–520.
Cenarro, Ángela (2003) 'La Institucionalización del Universo Penitenciario Franquista', in C. Molinero, M. Sala and J. Sobrequés (eds), *Una Inmensa Prisión. Los Campos de Concentración y las Prisiones durante la Guerra Civil y el Franquismo*, Barcelona: Crítica, pp. 133–154.
Centro de Investigaciones Sociológicas (CIS) (1994) 'Constitución e Instituciones', *Research Study Number 2124*, 19 November 1994. Available online at: www.cis.es/cis/opencm/EN/1_encuestas/estudios/ver.jsp?estudio=1115 (accessed 23 January 2014).
Centro de Investigaciones Sociológicas (CIS) (1995a) *Barómetro, Diciembre 1995, Research Study Number 2201*, 9 December 1995. Available online at: www.cis.es/cis/opencm/EN/1_encuestas/estudios/ver.jsp?estudio=1191&cuestionario=1336&muestra=4233 (accessed 23 January 2013).
Centro de Investigaciones Sociológicas (CIS) (1995b) *Cultura Politica III, Research Study Number 2154*, 4 April 1995. Available online at: www.cis.es/cis/opencm/EN/1_encuestas/estudios/ver.jsp?estudio=1144 (accessed 23 January 2014).
Centro de Investigaciones Sociológicas (CIS) (1998) *Constitución e Instituciones (iii). 20 Aniversario de la Constitución, Research Study Number 2309*, 10 December 1998. Available online at: www.cis.es/cis/opencm/EN/1_encuestas/estudios/ver.jsp?estudio=1298 (accessed 23 January 2014).
Cercas, Javier (2009) *The Anatomy of a Moment. Thirty-five Minutes in History and Imagination*, New York, NY: Bloomsbury.

Chambers, Simone and Jeffrey Kopstein (2001) 'Bad Civil Society', *Political Theory*, vol. 29(6), pp. 837–865.
Charalambous, Loucas (2004) 'Does the President Have Memory Problems?', *Cyprus Mail*, 12 September 2004.
Chari, Raj and Paul Heywood (2008), 'Institutions, European Integration, and the Policy Process in Contemporary Spain', in B. Field and K. Hamann (eds), *Democracy and Institutional Development*, London: Palgrave MacMillan, pp. 26–54.
Christoforou, Christoforos (2009) 'The Evolution of Greek-Cypriot Party Politics', in James Ker-Lindsay and Hubert Faustman (eds), *The Government and Politics of Cyprus*, Oxford: Peter Lang, pp. 83–106.
Christopoulos, Dimitris (2012) *Ποιος είναι Έλληνας Πολίτης; Το καθεστώς Ιθαγένειας από την ίδρυση του ελληνικού Κράτους ως τις αρχές του 21ου Αιώνα* [*Who is a Greek Citizen?*], Athens: Vivliorama.
Christou, Jean (2004) 'Annan Urges Both Sides to Identify Remains of Missing Persons', *Cyprus Mail*, 5 August 2004.
Citroni, Gabriela and Tullio Scovazzi (2009) 'Recent Developments in the International Law to Combat Enforced Disappearances', *Revista Internacional de Dereito e Ciudadania*, vol. 3, pp. 89–111.
CIVICUS (2005) 'An Assessment of Civil Society in Cyprus'. Available online at: www.civicus.org/csi/csi-publications?07c23fc490fb56da28db023ad7e04d9d=cc04e930ab737905634ff8dfb6382cc2 (accessed 23 January 2014).
Clark, Janine Natalya (2010) 'Missing Persons, Reconciliation and the View from Below: A Case-Study of Bosnia-Hercegovina', *Southeast European and Black Sea Studies*, vol. 10(4), pp. 425–442.
Clerides, Glafkos (2007) *Γλαύκος Κληρίδης. Η πορεία μιας Χώρας*, in Niyazi Kizilyurek (ed.), Athens: Ellinika Grammata.
Close, David (1993) *The Greek Civil War: Studies of Polarization, 1943–1950*, London: Routledge.
Close, David (2003) *The Roots of the Greek Civil War in Greece* [*Οι Ρίζες του Εμφυλίου Πολέμου στην Ελλάδα*], Athens: Filistor.
Cohen, David (2001) 'The Rhetoric of Justice: Strategies of Reconciliation and Revenge in the Restoration of Athenian Democracy in 403 BC', *Arch. Europ. Sociol.*, vol. XLII(2), pp. 335–356.
Collins, Cath (2010) *Post-Transitional Justice: Human Rights Trials in Chile and El Salvador*, University Park, PA: Penn State University Press.
Colomer, Josep M. (2004) 'The General Election in Spain, March 2004', *Electoral Studies*, vol. 24(1), pp. 149–156.
Committee on Missing Persons (CMP) (2013) 'Fact Sheet, December 2013', *Committee on Missing Persons in Cyprus*. Available online at: www.cmp-cyprus.org/nqcontent.cfm?a_id=1 (accessed 23 January 2014).
Congram, Derek and Dawnie Wolfe Steadman (2009) 'Distinguished Guests or Agents of Ingerénce: Foreign Participation in Spanish Civil War Grave Excavations', *Complutum*, vol. 19(2), pp. 161–173.
Constantinou, Costas and Yannis Papadakis (2001) 'The Cypriot State(s) in Situ: Cross-Ethnic Contact and the Discourse of Recognition', *Global Society*, vol. 15(2), pp. 125–148.
Council of Europe (1978) *European Commission on Human Rights Resolution*, 17(XXXIV), 7 March 1978.
Council of Europe (1984) *Parliamentary Assembly, Resolution 828 on Enforced Disappearances*, 26 September 1984.

Council of Europe (1987) *European Commission on Human Rights Resolution*, 1987/50, 11 March 1987.
Council of Europe (1992) *Committee of Ministers of the Council of Europe Resolution*, DH(92)12, 2 April 1992.
Council of Europe (2003a) *Committee of Ministers of the Council of Europe*, CM/inf(2003a)14, 26 November 2003.
Council of Europe (2004) *Committee of Ministers of the Council of Europe*, CM/Inf/DH(2004)4/1, 26 November 2004.
Council of Europe (2005a) *Committee of Ministers of the Council of Europe, Interim Resolution ResDH(2005)44 Concerning the Judgement of the European Court of Human Rights of 10 May 2001 in the Case of Cyprus against Turkey*, 7 June 2005.
Council of Europe (2005b) *Committee of Ministers of the Council of Europe*, CM/Inf/(2005)6/1, 23 November 2005.
Council of Europe (2006), 'Need for International Condemnation of the Franco Regime', *Recommendation 1736 (2006)*, M/AS(2006)Rec1736 final, 5 May 2006.
Crawford, L. (2007) 'What Lies Beneath', *FT Magazine, Financial Times*, 10 November 2007, p. 26.
Crawshaw, Nancy (1978) *The Cyprus Revolt. An Account of the Struggle for Union with Greece*, London: George Allen and Unwin.
Crettol, Monique and Anne-Marie La Rosa (2006) 'The Missing and Transitional Justice: The Right to Know and the Fight against Impunity', *International Review of the Red Cross*, vol. 862, pp. 355–362.
Cuesta, Josefina (2008) *La Odisea de la Memoria. Historia de la Memoria en España*, Madrid: Alianza Editorial.
Danforth, Loring (1982) *The Death Rituals of Rural Greece*, Princeton, NJ: Princeton University Press.
Danforth, Loring (1993) 'Claims to Macedonian Identity: The Macedonian Question and the Breakup of Yugoslavia', *Anthropology Today*, vol. 9(4), pp. 3–10.
De Brito, Alexandra Barahona, Paloma Aguilar and Carmen Gonzalez-Enriquez (2001) 'Introduction', in Alexandra Barahona De Brito, Paloma Aguilar and Carmen Gonzalex-Enriquez (eds), *The Politics of Memory. Transitional Justice in Democratizing Societies*, Oxford, Oxford University Press, pp. 1–39.
De la Cueva, Julio (1998) 'Religious Persecution, Anticlerical Tradition and Revolution: On Atrocities against the Clergy during the Spanish Civil War', *Journal of Contemporary History*, vol. 33(3), pp. 355–369.
Demetriou, Olga (2004), 'EU and the Cyprus Conflict. Review of the Literature', *Working Papers Series in EU Border Conflict Studies No. 5*, January 2004.
Diamond, Larry (1999) *Developing Democracy. Toward Consolidation*, Baltimore, MD: The Johns Hopkins University Press.
Drousiotis, Makarios (2000) *1,619 Ενοχές – Τα λαθη, τα Ψέμματα και οι Σκοπιμότητες*, Nicosia: Alfadi.
Drousiotis, Makarios (2005) '*Γιατί ήταν πολιτικές Δολοφονίες των ΑΚΕΛικών. Όλοι οι Ελληνοκύπριοι που Εκτέλεσε η ΕΟΚΑ*', *Politis*, 10 April 2005.
Druliolle, Vincent (2008) 'Democracy Captured by its Imaginary: The Transition as Memory and Discourses of Constitutionalism in Spain', *Social Legal Studies*, vol. 17, pp. 75–92.
Dyzenhaus, David (2000) 'Justifying the Truth and Reconciliation Commission', *The Journal of Political Philosophy*, vol. 8(4), pp. 470–496.
Economist, The (2003) 'A Full Stop Removed', *The Economist*, vol. 368(8340), p. 33.

182 Bibliography

Economist, The (2010) 'Lula and the Generals. The Army Blocks a Truth Commission', *The Economist*, 7 January 2010.

Edkins, Jenny (2003) *Trauma and the Memory of Politics*, Cambridge: Cambridge University Press.

Edles Desfor, Laura (1998) *Symbol and Ritual in the New Spain*, Cambridge: Cambridge University Press.

Elkin, Mike (2006) 'Opening Franco's Graves. The Victims of Spain's Past are Beginning to Tell their Stories', *Archaeology*, September/October 2006, pp. 38–43.

Elster, Jon (2004) *Closing the Books: Transitional Justice in Historical Perspective*, Cambridge: Cambridge University Press.

Empirikos, Leonidas and Athina Skoulariki (2009) '*Το Μακεδονικό από τη Μεταπολίτευση ως την κρίση της δεκαετίας του 90'* ['The Macedonian Question from the Transition to the Crisis of 1990s'], *Archeiotaxeio*, vol. 11, pp. 144–160.

Encarnación, Omar (2001) 'Civil Society and the Consolidation of Democracy in Spain', *Political Science Quarterly*, vol. 116(1), pp. 53–79.

Encarnación, Omar G. (2003) 'The Legacy of Transitions: Pact-Making and Democratic Consolidation in Spain', *Estudio/Working Paper 2003/193*. Available online at: www.google.com/url?q=http://www.march.es/ceacs/publicaciones/working/archivos/2003_193.pdf&sa=U&ei=MojjUqSQPOiG0AWWxIG4Ag&ved=0CAUQFjAA&client=internal-uds-cse&usg=AFQjCNGrnV0NRlsACvhScjeyvgagvZESGQ (accessed 23 January 2014).

Encarnación, Omar (2007) 'Pinochet's Revenge: Spain Revisits its Civil War', *World Policy Journal*, Winter 2007/2008, pp. 39–50.

Encarnación, Omar G. (2009) 'Spain's New Left Turn: Society Driven or Party Instigated?', *South European Society and Politics*, vol. 14(4), pp. 399–415.

Entman, Robert (1993) 'Framing: Toward Clarification of a Fractured Paradigm', *Journal of Communication*, vol. 43(4), pp. 51–58.

Esteban, Jorge and Luis Lopez Guerra (1985) 'Electoral Rules and Candidate Selection', in Penniman Howard and Mujan-Leon Eusebio (eds), *Spain at Polls. 1977, 1979, and 1982*, North Carolina, NC: Duke University Press, pp. 48–72.

Faustman, Hubert (2009) 'Aspects of Political Culture in Cyprus', in James Ker-Lindsay and Hubert Faustman (eds), *The Government and Politics of Cyprus*, Oxford: Peter Lang, pp. 17–44.

Feher, Michael (1999) 'Terms of Reconciliation', in Carla Hesse and Robert Post (eds), *Human Rights in Political Transitions: Gettysburg to Bosnia*, New York, NY: Zone Books, pp. 325–338.

Ferrándiz, Francisco (2006) 'The Return of Civil War Ghosts. The Ethnography of Exhumations in Contemporary Spain', *Anthropology Today*, vol. 22(3), pp. 7–12.

Ferrándiz, Francisco (2008) 'Cries and Whispers. Exhuming and Narrating Defeat in Spain Today', *Journal of Spanish Cultural Studies*, vol. 9(2), pp. 177–192.

Ferrándiz, Francisco (2009) 'Fosas Comunes, Paisajes del Terror', *Revista de Dialectologia y Tradiciones Populares*, vol. LXIV(1), pp. 61–94.

Ferrándiz, Francisco and Alejandro Baer (2008) 'Digital Memory: The Visual Recording of Mass Grave Exhumations in Contemporary Spain', *Forum: Qualitative Social Research*, vol. 9(3), pp. 1–23.

Field, Bonnie N. (2005) 'De-Thawing Democracy: The Decline of Political Party Collaboration in Spain (1977 to 2004)', *Comparative Political Studies*, vol. 38, pp. 1079–1103.

Field, Bonnie N. (2008) 'Interparty Politics in Spain: The Role of Informal Institutions', in

Bonnie N. Field and Kerstin Hamann (eds), *Democracy and Institutional Development. Spain in Comparative Theoretical Perspective*, London: Palgrave Macmillan, pp. 44–67.

Field, Bonnie N. (2009) 'A "Second Transition" in Spain? Policy, Institutions and Interparty Politics under Zapatero', *South European Society and Politics*, vol. 14(4), pp. 379–397.

Field, Bonnie and Kerstin Hamann (2008a) 'Introduction; The Institutionalization of Democracy in Spain', in Bonnie N. Field and Kerstin Hamann (eds), *Democracy and Institutional Development. Spain in Comparative Theoretical Perspective*, Basingstoke: Palgrave, pp. 1–22.

Field, Bonnie and Kerstin Hamann (2008b) 'Conclusion: The Spanish Case and Comparative Lessons on Institutions, Representations and Democracy', in Bonnie N. Field and Kerstin Hamann (eds), *Democracy and Institutional Development. Spain in Comparative Theoretical Perspective*, Basingstoke: Palgrave, pp. 203–216.

Finnemore, Martha and Kathryn Sikkink (1998) 'International Norm Dynamics and Political Change', *International Organization*, vol. 52(4), pp. 887–917.

Fontana, Josep (2003) 'Prologo', in C. Molinero, M. Sala and J. Sobrequés (eds), *Una Inmensa Prisión. Los Campos de Concentración y las Prisiones durante la Guerra Civil y el Franquismo*, Barcelona: Crítica, pp. xi–xvi.

Frazer, Ronald (1994) *Blood of Spain. An Oral History of the Spanish Civil War*, London: Pimlico.

French, Howard W. (2002) 'Korean Kidnappings: The South's Wound', *New York Times*, 18 November 2002. Available online at: www.nytimes.com/2002/11/18/world/korean-kidnappings-the-south-s-wound.html (23 January 2014).

Fundación Alternativas (2007) 'The Strategy of Confrontation', *Report on Democracy in Spain*. Available online at: www.falternativas.org/ (accessed 23 January 2014).

Fundación Alternativas (2009) 'Alliances for a New Spanish Prosperity. Towards a New Global Deal', *Report on Democracy in Spain*. Available online at: www.falternativas.org/ (accessed 23 January 2014).

Galanter, Mark (2002) 'Righting Old Wrongs', in Martha Minow (ed.), *Breaking the Cycles of Hatred. Memory, Law and Repair*, Princeton, NJ: Princeton University Press, pp. 107–123.

Gálvez-Biesca, Sergio (2006) 'El Proceso de la Recuperación de la Memoria Histórica en España: Una Aproximación a los Movimientos Sociales por la Memoria', *International Journal of Iberian Studies*, vol. 19(1), pp. 25–51.

Gamson, William (1992) *Talking Politics*, Cambridge: Cambridge University Press.

Gamson, William and David S. Meyer (1996) 'Framing Political Opportunity', in Doug McAdam, John McCarthy and Zald Mayer (eds), *Comparative Perspectives on Social Movements. Political Opportunities, Mobilizing Structures, and Cultural Framing*, Cambridge: Cambridge University Press, pp. 259–270.

Garton, Timothy Ash (2004) 'Is this Europe's 9/11?', *Guardian*, 13 March 2004.

George, Alexander L. and Andrew Bennett (2005) *Case Studies and Theory-Development in Social Sciences*, Cambridge, MA: MIT Press.

Gibbons, John (1999) *Spanish Politics Today*, Manchester: Manchester University Press.

Gibson, Ian (1979) *The Assassination of Federico García Lorca*, London: W.H. Allen.

Gibson, James L. (2006) 'The Contributions of Truth to Reconciliation: Lessons from South Africa', *Journal of Conflict Resolution*, vol. 50(3), pp. 409–432.

Gildea, Robert (1996) *France since 1945*, Oxford: Oxford University Press.

Goffman, Erving (1974) *Frame Analysis: An Essay on the Organization of the Experience*, New York, NY: Harper Colophon.

Bibliography

Gounaris, Vasilis (2002) *Εγνωσμένων Κοινωνικών Φρονημάτων. Κοινωνικές και αλλες όψεις του Αντικομμουνισμου στη Μακεδονια του Εμφυλίου Πολέμου*, Salonica: Paratiritis.

Graham, Helen (2004) 'The Spanish Civil War, 1936–2003: The Return of the Republican Memory', *Science and Society*, vol. 68(3), pp. 313–328.

Greer, Steven (2006) *The European Convention on Human Rights. Achievements, Problems and Prospects*, Cambridge: Cambridge University Press.

Grekos, Costas (1991) *Κυπριακή Ιστορία [Cyprus History]*, Nicosia: Printco.

Grigoriadis, Ioannis (2009) *The Trials of Europeanization. Turkish Political Culture and the European Union*, Basingstoke: Palgrave.

Guardian (2008) 'Spanish Judge Orders Poet Garcia Lorca's Grave to be Opened', *Guardian*, 16 October 2008. Available online at: www.guardian.co.uk/world/2008/oct/16/lorca-grave-spain (23 January 2014).

Gunther, Richard (1992) 'Spain, the Very Model of the Modern Elite Settlement', in John Higley and Richard Gunther (eds), *Elites and Democratic Consolidation in Latin America and South Europe*, Cambridge: Cambridge University Press, pp. 38–80.

Gunther, Richard and Jonathan Hopkin (2002) 'A Crisis of Institutionalization: The Collapse of UCD in Spain', in Richard Gunther, Jose Ramon Montero and Juan Linz (eds), *Political Parties. Old Concepts and New Challenges*, Oxford: Oxford University Press, pp. 191–230.

Gunther, Richard and Jose Ramon Montero (2009) *The Politics of Spain*, Cambridge: Cambridge University Press.

Gunther, Richard, Giacomo Sani and Goldie Shabad (1988) *Spain after Franco. The Making of a Comparative Party System*, Berkeley, CA: University of California Press.

Hadjikiriakou, Andreas (1999) '*Ο Κασουλίδης σημερα στο Σημειο των Εκταφών. Εκταφές ΕΛΔΥΚαριων του 1974'*, *Πολίτης*, 2 June 1999.

Hadjipavlou, Maria (2007a) 'The Cyprus Conflict: Root Causes and Implications for Peacebuilding', *Journal of Peace Research*, vol. 44(3), pp. 349–365.

Hadjipavlou, Maria (2007b) 'The "Crossings" as Part of Citizens' Reconciliation Efforts in Cyprus?', *Innovation*, vol. 20(1), pp. 53–73.

Haklai, Oded (2007) 'Religious – Nationalist Mobilization and State Penetration: Lessons from Jewish Settlers' Activism in Israel and the West Bank', *Comparative Political Studies*, vol. 40, pp. 713–739.

Hall, Peter A. (1993) 'Policy Paradigms, Social Learning and the State. The Case of Economic Policy-Making in Britain', *Comparative Politics*, vol. 25(3), pp. 275–296.

Halperin, Morton and Arnold Kanter (1991) 'Leaders and Bureaucrats: The Bureaucratic Perspective', in Art Robert and Jervis Robert (eds), *International Politics: Enduring Concepts and Contemporary Issues*, 3rd edn, New York, NY: Longman Higher Education, pp. 397–450.

Hamber, Brandon (2006) '"Nunca Mas" and the Politics of Person. Can Truth Telling Prevent the Recurrence of Violence?', in Tristan Ann Borer (ed.), *Truth Telling and Peace-Building in Post-Conflict Societies*, Notre Dame, IN: University of Notre Dame Press, pp. 207–230.

Hamber, Brandon and Richard Wilson (2002) 'Symbolic Closure through Memory, Reparation and Revenge in Post-Conflict Societies', *Journal of Human Rights*, vol. 1(1), pp. 35–53.

Haravgi (2009) '*Ελληνοκύπριοι δολοφονούσαν αθώους Τουρκοκυπρίους το 1963–64*', *Haravgi*, 29 January 2009, p. 8.

Harris, Fredrick (2002) 'Collective Memory, Collective Action and Black Activism in the 1960s', in Martha Minow (ed.), *Breaking the Cycles of Hatred. Memory, Law and Repair*, Princeton, NJ: Princeton University Press, pp. 154–168.

Hartzell, Caroline (1999) 'Explaining the Stability of Negotiated Settlements to Intrastate Wars', *The Journal of Conflict Resolution*, vol. 43(1), pp. 3–22.

Hayner, Priscilla B. (1996) 'Commissioning the Truth: Further Research Questions', *Third World Quarterly*, vol. 17(1), pp. 19–22.

Hayner, Priscilla (2002) *Unspeakable Truths. Facing the Challenges of Truth Commissions*, London: Routledge.

Helfer, Laurence (2008) 'Redesigning the European Court of Human Rights: Embeddedness as a Deep Structural Principle of the European Human Rights Regime', *European Journal of International Law*, vol. 19(1), pp. 1–30.

Heraclides, Alexis (2001) I Ellada ke o Ex Anatolon Kindynos [*Greece and the Eastern Threat*], Athens: Polis Publishers.

Heraclides, Alexis (2006) *Το Κυπριακό Πρόβλημα 1974–2000. Απο την 'Ενωση στη Διχοτόμηση*; [*The Cyprus Problem 1947–2004. From Union to Partition?*], Athens: Sideris Publishing.

Heraclides, Alexis (2010) 'The Cyprus Gordian Knot: An Intractable Ethnic Conflict', *Nationalism and Ethnic Conflict*, vol. 17(2), pp. 117–139.

Hesse, Carla and Robert Post (1999) 'Introduction', in Carla Hesse and Robert Post (eds), *Human Rights in Political Transitions: Gettysburg to Bosnia*, New York, NY: Zone Books, pp. 13–38.

Heywood, Paul (1995) *The Government and Politics of Spain*, Basingstoke: Macmillan Press.

Higley, John and Michael Burton (1989) 'The Elite Variable in Democratic Transitions and Breakdowns', *American Sociological Review*, vol. 54(1), pp. 17–32.

Hirsch, Michal Ben-Josef (2007) 'Agents of Truth and Justice. Truth Commissions and the Transitional Justice Epistemic Community', in David Chandler and Volker Heins (eds), *Rethinking Ethical Foreign Policy. Pitfalls, Possibilities and Paradoxes*, London: Routledge, pp. 184–205.

Hoffmeister, Frank (2002) 'Cyprus v. Turkey App. No. 25781/94', *The American Journal of International Law*, vol. 96(2), pp. 445–452.

Humphrey, Michael (2003) 'From Victim to Victimhood: Truth Commissions and Trials as Rituals of Political Transition and Individual Healing', *The Australian Journal of Anthropology*, vol. 14(2), pp. 171–187.

Huntington, Samuel (1968) *Political Order in Changing Societies*, New Haven, CT: Yale University Press.

Huntington, Samuel (1991) *The Third Wave. Democratization in the Late 20th Century*, Norman, OK: University of Oklahoma Press.

Huyse, Luc (1995) 'Justice after Transition: On the Choices Successors Elites Make in Dealing with the Past', *Law and Social Inquiry*, vol. 20(1), pp. 51–78.

Huyse, Luc (2003) 'Victims', in David Bloomfield, Teresa Barnes and Luc Huyse (eds), *Reconciliation after Violent Conflict. A Handbook*, Stockholm: IDEA, pp. 54–65. Available online at: www.idea.int/publications/reconciliation/ (accessed 23 January 2014).

International Commission on Missing Persons (ICMP) (2010) 'Fact Sheet on South East Europe', *International Commission on Missing Persons*. Available online at: www.ic-mp.org/icmp-worldwide/southeast-europe/ (accessed 23 January 2014).

Institute for Democracy and Electoral Assistance (IDEA) (2003) *Reconciliation after*

Violent Conflict. A Handbook, David Bloomfield, Teresa Barnes and Luc Huyse (eds), Stockholm: IDEA. Available online at: www.idea.int/publications/reconciliation/ (accessed 23 January 2014).

Ignatieff, Michael (1998) *The Warrior's Honor: Ethnic War and the Modern Conscience*, New York, NY: Holt Paperbacks.

Iguarta, Juanjo and Dario Paez (1997) 'Art and Remembering Traumatic Collective Events: The Case of the Spanish Civil War', in James W. Pennebaker, Dario Paez and Bernard Rime (eds), *Collective Memory of Political Events. Social Psychological Perspectives*, New Jersey, NJ: Lawrence Erlbaum Publishers, pp. 79–102.

Inglehart, Ronald and Christian Welzel (2005) *Modernization, Cultural Change, and Democracy*, Cambridge: Cambridge University Press.

International Committee of the Red Cross (ICRC) (2007) 'Missing Persons: A Hidden Tragedy', *ICRC Resource Centre*, Policy Briefing 0929. Available online at: www.icrc.org/eng/resources/documents/publication/p0929.htm (accessed 23 January 2014).

Ioannou, Fifis (2005) *Έτσι άρχισε το Κυπριακό*, Athens: Philistor, Paralos.

Ireton, Kathleen and Iosif Kovras (2012) 'Non-Apologies and Prolonged Silences in Post-Conflict Settings: The Case of Post-Colonial Cyprus', *Time & Society*, vol. 21(1), pp. 71–88.

Jackson, Gabriel (1965) *The Spanish Republic at War 1931–1939*, Princeton, NJ: Princeton University Press.

Jaquemet, Iolanda (2009) 'Fighting Amnesia: Ways to Uncover the Truth about Lebanon's Missing', *International Journal of Transitional Justice*, vol. 3(1), pp. 69–90.

Joyce, Christopher and Eric Stover (1991) *Witnesses from the Grave: The Stories Bones Tell*, London: Little Brown.

Juhl, Kirsten (2005) *The Contribution by (Forensic) Archaeologists to Human Rights Investigations of Mass Graves*, AmS-NETT, Number 5, Stavanger.

Juliá, Santos (1999) 'De "Guerra Contra el Invasor" a "Guerra Fratricida"', in Santos Juliá (ed.), *Las Víctimas de la Guerra Civil*, Madrid: Temas de Hoy, pp. 11–57.

Juliá, Santos (2006) 'Memoria, Historia y Política de un Pasado de Guerra y Dictadura', in Santos Juliá (ed.), *Memoria de la Guerra y del Franquismo*, Madrid: Taurus, pp. 27–77.

Juliá, Santos (2008) 'Amnistía como Triunfo de la Memoria', *El País*, 24 November 2008. Available online at: http://reggio.wordpress.com/2008/11/24/amnistia-como-triunfo-de-la-memoria-de-santos-julia-en-el-pais/ (accessed 23 January 2014).

Kakoullis, Loucas (1990) *Η Αριστερά και οι Τουρκοκύπριοι. Το Κυπριακό απο μια άλλη Σκοπιά*, Nicosia: Casoulides.

Kalyvas, Stathis N. (2006) *The Logic of Violence in Civil War*, New York, NY: Cambridge University Press.

Kalyvas, Stathis N. (2008) 'How Not to Compare Civil Wars: Greece and Spain, in *"If You Tolerate This"....*', in Martin Baumeister and Stefanie Schuler-Springorum (eds), *The Spanish Civil War in the Age of Total War*, Frankfurt and New York, NY: Campus Verlag, pp. 247–263.

Kalyvas, Stahis N. (2010) '*Ανορθόδοξος Πόλεμος και Εκλογική Συμπεριφορά: Ο Εμφύλιος ως Διαιρετική Τομή*' ['Irregular Warfare and Electoral Behavior: The Cleavage of the Civil War'], in Vasilis Gounaris, Stathis Kalyvas and Ioannis Stefanidis (eds), *Ανορθόδοξοι Πόλεμοι: Μακεδονία, Εμφύλιος, Κύπρος* [*Irregular Wars: Macedonia, Civil War, Cyprus*], Athens: Patakis, pp. 227–241.

Kaminski, Marek M., Monica Nalepa and Barry O'Neill (2006) 'Normative and Strategic Aspects of Transitional Justice', *Journal of Conflict Resolution*, vol. 50(3), pp. 295–302.

Karakasidou, Anastasia (1993) 'Politicizing Culture: Negating Ethnic Identity in Greek Macedonia', *Journal of Modern Greek Studies*, vol. 11(1), pp. 1–28.
Karl, Terry Lynn (1987) 'Petroleum and Political Pacts: The Transition to Democracy in Venezuela', *Latin American Research Review*, vol. 22(1), pp. 63–94.
Karl, Terry Lynn (1990) 'Dilemmas of Democratization in Latin America', *Comparative Politics*, vol. 23(1), pp. 1–21.
Katsiaounis, Rolandos (2008) *Η Διασκεπτική 1946–1949*, Nicosia: Cyprus Centre of Scientific Research.
Kaufman, Stuart J. (2008) 'Symbols, Frames and Violence: Studying Ethnic War in the Philippines', *International Studies Quarterly*, vol. 55(4), pp. 937–958.
Keck, Margaret E. and Kathryn Sikkink (1998) *Activists beyond Borders. Advocacy Networks in International Politics*, Ithaca, NY: Cornell University Press.
Kelman, Herbert C. (1999) 'Building a Sustainable Peace: The Limits of Pragmatism in the Israeli–Palestinian Negotiations', *Peace and Conflict: Journal of Political Psychology*, vol. 5(2), pp. 101–115.
Ker-Lindsay, James (2009a) 'Presidential Power and Authority', in James Ker-Lindsay and Hubert Faustman (eds), *The Government and Politics of Cyprus*, Oxford: Peter Lang, pp. 107–124.
Kim, Hunjoon and Kathryn Sikkink (2010) 'Explaining the Deterrence Effect of Human Rights Prosecutions for Transitional Countries', *International Studies Quarterly*, vol. 54(4), pp. 939–963.
Kiss, Elizabeth (2001) 'Moral Ambition Within and Beyond Political Constraints: Reflections on Restorative Justice', in Robert I. Rotberg and Dennis Thompson (eds), *Truth v. Justice. The Morality of Truth Commissions*, Princeton, NJ: Princeton University Press, pp. 68–98.
Klandermans, Bert (1997) *The Social Psychology of Protest*, Oxford: Blackwell.
Kofos, Evangelos (1989) 'National Heritage and National Identity in Nineteenth- and Twentieth-Century Macedonia', *European History Quarterly*, vol. 19, pp. 229–267.
Kohler, Beate (1982) *Political Forces in Spain, Greece and Portugal*, London: Butterworth Scientific.
Kokkinakis, Kriton (2002) *Οι Αποφάσεις των Ευρωπαϊκών Δικαιοδοτικών Οργάνων Σχετικά με το Κυπριακό*, Athens: Sakkoulas Publishers.
Koliopoulos, John (1999) *Plundered Loyalties: World War II and Civil War in Greek West Macedonia*, New York, NY: New York University Press.
Konstantopoulos, Panagiotis (2006) 'The Dead of the Greek Army during the Greco-Italian War: An Analysis of the Army History Directorate' ['*Οι Νεκροί του Στρατού Ξηράς κατα τη Διάρκεια του Ελληνοϊταλικού Πολέμου μέσα από τα αρχεία της ΔΙΣ*'], *Stratiotiki Epitheorisi*, September–October 2006, pp. 14–33.
Kovras, Iosif (2008) 'Unearthing the Truth: The Politics of Exhumations in Cyprus and Spain', *History and Anthropology*, vol. 19(4), pp. 371–390.
Kovras, Iosif (2012) 'Delinkage Processes and Grassroots Movements in Transitional Justice', (2012) *Cooperation and Conflict*, Vol. 47(1), pp.88–105.
Kovras, Iosif (2013) 'Explaining Prolonged Silences in Transitional Justice: The Disappeared in Cyprus and Spain', *Comparative Political Studies*, vol. 46(6), pp. 730–757.
Kovras, Iosif and Neophytos Loizides (2011) 'Delaying Truth Recovery for Missing Persons', *Nations and Nationalism*, vol. 7(3), pp. 520–539.
Kovras, Iosif and Neophytos Loizides (2012) 'Protracted Peace Processes: Policy (Un)learning and the Cyprus Debacle', *Ethnopolitics*, vol. 11(4), pp. 406–423.

Kriesi, Hanspeter (1995) 'The Political Opportunity Structure of New Social Movements: Its Impact on their Mobilization', in Craig Jenkins and Bert Klandermans (eds), *The Politics of Social Protest. Comparative Perspective on States and Social Movements*, London: UCL Press, pp. 167–197.

Kriesi, Hanspeter (2004) 'Political Context and Opportunity', in David A. Snow, Sara A. Soule and Hanspeter Kriesi (eds), *The Blackwell Companion to Social Movements*, Oxford: Blackwell Press, pp. 67–90.

Kriesi, Hanspeter, Ruud Koopmans, Jan Willem Duyvendak and Marco G. Giugni (1995) *New Social Movements in Western Europe. A Comparative Analysis*, London: University College London Press.

Kritz, Neil (1997) 'Coming to Terms with Atrocities: A Review of Accountability Mechanisms for Mass Violations of Human Rights', *Law and Contemporary Problems*, vol. 59(4), pp. 127–152.

Kyriakou Nikolas (2012) 'An Affront to the Conscience of Humanity. Enforced Disappearance in International Human Rights Law', PhD Dissertation, European University Institute, Florence.

Landsman, Stephan (1997) 'Alternative Responses to Serious Human Rights Abuses: Of Prosecutions and Truth Commissions', *Law and Contemporary Problems*, vol. 59(4), pp. 81–92.

Ledesma, Manuel Pérez (2006) 'La Guerra Civil y Historiografía: No Fue Posible el Acuerdo', in Santos Juliá (ed.), *Memoria de la Guerra Civil y el Franquismo*, Madrid: Taurus, pp. 101–133.

Leebaw, Bronwyn (2011) *Judging State-Sponsored Violence, Imagining Political Change*, New York, NY: Cambridge University Press.

Liakos, Antonis (1991) 'Sigxrona Arxeia. Fakeloi kai Istoriki Ereyna', in S. Asdrahas *et al.*, *Sigxrona Arxeia. Fakeloi kai Istoriki Ereyna*, Athens: Mnimon, pp. 24–32.

Liakos, Antonis (2003) 'Antartes kai Simorites sta Akadimaika amfitheatra', in Hangen Fleischer (ed.), *Ellada '36–'49. Apo ti Diktatoria ston Emfylio. Tomes kai Sinecheies [Greece 1936–1949. From the Dictatorship to the Civil War. Changes and Continuities]*, Athens: Kastaniotis, pp. 25–36.

Licklider, Roy (1995) 'The Consequences of Negotiated Settlements in Civil Wars: 1945–1993', *The American Political Science Review*, vol. 89(3), pp. 681–690.

Lie, Tove Grete, Helga Malmin Binningsbo and Scott Gates (2007) 'Post-Conflict Justice and Sustainable Peace', *Post-Conflict Transitions, Working Paper No. 5, World Bank Policy Research Working Paper 4197*. Available online at: http://elibrary.worldbank.org/doi/book/10.1596/1813-9450-4191 (accessed 25 January 2014).

Lijphart, Arend (2012) *Patterns of Democracy: Government Forms and Performance in Thirty-Six Countries*, 2nd edn, New Haven, CT: Yale University Press.

Lind, Jennifer (2008) *Sorry States. Apologies in International Politics*, New York, NY: Cornell University Press.

Linz, Juan and Alfred Stepan (1996) *Problems of Democratic Transition and Consolidation. Southern Europe, South America, and Post-Communist Europe*, Baltimore, MD: Johns Hopkins University Press.

Lohman, Sussane (1997) 'New Games: Modeling Domestic-International Linkages', *Journal of Conflict Resolution*, vol. 41(1), pp. 38–67.

Loizides, Neophytos G. (2007a) 'Doves against Hawks: Symbolic Politics in Greece and the Macedonian Question'. Paper presented at the International Studies Association annual convention, Chicago, February 2007.

Loizides, Neophytos G. (2007b) 'Ethnic Nationalism and Adaptation in Cyprus', *International Studies Perspectives*, vol. 8(2), pp. 172–189.

Loizides, Neophytos G. (2009) 'Elite Framing and Conflict Transformation in Turkey', *Parliamentary Affairs*. Available online at: doi:10.1093/pa/gsn038 (accessed 25 October 2008).

Loizides, Neophytos G. (2014) *Cyprus: Federal and Consociational Failures and Prospects*, Philadelphia, PA: University of Pennsylvania Press.

Loizides, Neophytos G. and Markos Antoniades (2009) 'Negotiating the Rights of Return', *Journal of Peace Research*, vol. 46(5), pp. 611–622.

Long, William J. and Peter Brecke (2003) *War and Reconciliation: Reasons and Emotion in Conflict Resolution*, Cambridge, MA: MIT Press.

Lustick, Ian (1993) *Unsettled States, Disputed Lands: Britain and Ireland, France and Algeria, Israel and the West Bank*, Ithaca, NY: Cornell University Press.

Lutz, Ellen and Kathryn Sikkink (2001) 'The Justice Cascade: The Evolution and Impact of Foreign Human Rights Trials in Latin America', *Chicago Journal of International Law*, vol. 2(1), pp. 1–34.

Maddox, Richard (1995) 'Revolutionary Anti-Clericalism and Hegemonic Processes in an Andalusian Town: August 1936', *American Ethnologist*, vol. 22(1), pp. 125–143.

Magone, Jose M. (2004) *Contemporary Spanish Politics*, Basingstoke: Palgrave.

Mallinder, Louise (2007) 'Can Amnesties and Transitional Justice be Reconciled?', *International Journal of Transitional Justice*, vol. 1, pp. 208–230.

Mallinder, Louise Maria (2008) *Amnesty, Human Rights, and Political Transitions: Bridging the Peace and Justice Divide*, Oxford: Hart Publishing.

Mani, Rama (2005) 'Rebuilding and Inclusive Political Community after War', *Security Dialogue*, vol. 36(4), pp. 511–526.

Manning, Carrie (2001) 'Competition and Accommodation in Post-Conflict Democracy: The Case of Mozambique', *Democratization*, vol. 8(2), pp. 140–168.

Manning, Carrie (2007a) 'Interim Governments and the Construction of Political Elites', in Karren Guttieri and Jessica Piombo (eds), *Interim Governments: Institutional Bridges to Peace and Stability*, Washington, DC: USIP, pp. 53–72.

Manning, Carrie (2007b) 'Party-Building on the Heels of War: El Salvador, Bosnia, Kosovo, and Mozambique', *Democratization*, vol. 14(2), pp. 253–272.

Marantzides, Nikos (2001) Γιασασίν Μιλέτ, Ζήτω το Έθνος [*Yasasin Millet: Long Live the Nation*], Crete: Crete University Press.

Marantzides, Nikos (2010) *The Democratic Army of Greece 1946–1949* [Δημοκρατικός Στρατός Ελλάδας 1946–1949], Athens: Alexandria Publishers.

Maravall, José (1982) *The Transition to Democracy in Spain*, New York, NY: St Martin's Press.

Maravall, Jose M. (1985) 'The Socialist Alternative: The Policies and Electorate of PSOE', in Howard Penniman and Eusebio Mujan-Leon (eds), *Spain at Polls. 1977, 1979, and 1982*, Durham, NC: Duke University Press, pp. 129–159.

March, James and Johan Olsen (1984) 'The New Institutionalism: Organizational Factors in Political Life', *American Political Science Review*, vol. 78(3), pp. 734–749.

Margaritis, Giorgos (2002) *I Istoria tou Ellinikou Emfyliou Polemou (1946–1949)* [*History of the Greek Civil War (1946–1949)*], vols 1 and 2, Athens: Vivliorama.

Markides, C.K. (1977) *The Rise and the Fall of the Cyprus Republic*, New Haven, CT: Yale University Press.

Martin, Curtis H. (2002) 'Rewarding North Korea: Theoretical Perspectives on the 1994 Agreed Framework', *Journal of Peace Research*, vol. 39(1), pp. 51–68.

Mavratsas, Caesar (2003) *Εθνική Ομοψυχία και Πολιτική Ομοφωνία. Η ατροφία της Ελληνοκυπριακής κοινωνίας των πολιτων στις απαρχες του 21ου αιώνα*, Athens: Katarti.

Mazower, Mark (1995) 'The Cold War and the Appropriation of Memory: Greece After Liberation', *East European Politics and Societies*, vol. 9, pp. 279–294.

Mazower, Mark (2000) *After the War was Over: Reconstructing the Family, Nation and State in Greece, 1943–1960*, Princeton, NJ: Princeton University Press.

McAdam, Douglas, Sidney Tarrow and Charles Tilly (2001) *Dynamics of Contention*, Cambridge: Cambridge University Press.

McCoy, Mary Kay (2002) 'Hidden Past. Search for Graves of Missing Victims of Civil War Atrocities', *The Volunteer, Journal of the Veterans of the Abraham Lincoln Brigade*, vol. XXIV(3), September 2003, pp. 5–22.

McDonald, Henry (2007) 'Churches Plea to IRA over "Disappeared"', *Observer*, 7 January 2007.

McEvoy, Kieran and Heather Conway (2004) 'The Dead, the Law, and the Politics of the Past', *Journal of Law and Society*, vol. 31(4), December 2004, pp. 539–562.

McEvoy, Kieran and Louise Mallinder (2012) 'Amnesties in Transition: Punishment, Restoration, and the Governance of Mercy', *Journal of Law and Society*, vol. 39(3), pp. 410–440.

Meister, Robert (1999) 'Forgiving and Forgetting: Lincoln and the Politics of National Recovery', in Carla Hesse and Robert Post (eds), *Human Rights in Political Transitions: Gettysburg to Bosnia*, New York, NY: Zone Books, pp. 135–176.

Mendeloff, David (2004) 'Truth-Seeking, Truth-Telling, and Post-Conflict Peacebuilding: Curbing the Enthusiasm?', *International Studies Review*, vol. 6, pp. 355–380.

Mendeloff, David (2009) 'Trauma and Vengeance: Assessing the Psychological and Emotional Effects of Post-Conflict Justice', *Human Rights Quarterly*, vol. 31, pp. 592–623.

Méndez, Juan E. (2001) 'National Reconciliation, Transnational Justice, and the International Criminal Court', *Ethics and International Affairs*, vol. 15(1), pp. 25–44.

Miller, J. R. (1996) *Shingwauk's Vision: A History of Native Residential Schools*, Toronto: University of Toronto Press.

Minow, Martha (1998) 'Between Vengeance and Forgiveness. South Africa's Truth and Reconciliation Commission', *Negotiation Journal*, vol. 14(4), pp. 319–355.

Minow, Martha (2002) 'Breaking the Cycles of Hatred', in Martha Minow (ed.), *Breaking the Cycles of Hatred: Memory, Law and Repair*, Princeton, NJ: Princeton University Press, pp. 16–75.

Moravcsik, Andrew (2000) 'The Origins of Human Rights Regimes: Democratic Delegation in Postwar Europe', *International Organization*, vol. 54(2), pp. 217–252.

Moreno, Francisco (1999) 'La Represión en la Posguerra', in Santos Juliá (ed.), *Las Víctimas de la Guerra Civil*, Madrid: Temas de Hoy, pp. 275–407.

Müftüler-Baç, Meltem (2005) 'Turkey's Political Reforms and the Impact of the European Union', *South European Society and Politics*, vol. 10(1), pp. 17–31.

Muro, Diego (2009) 'The Politics of War Memory in Radical Basque Nationalism', *Ethnic and Racial Studies*, vol. 32(4), pp. 659–678.

Nalepa, Monica (2010) 'Captured Commitments: An Analytic Narrative of Transitions with Transitional Justice', *World Politics*, vol. 62(2), pp. 341–380.

Newman, Edward (2002) '"Transitional Justice": The Impact of Transnational Norms and the UN', in Edward Newman and Albrecht Schnabel (eds), *Recovering from Civil Conflict: Reconciliation, Peace and Development*, London: Frank Cass, pp. 31–52.

Newman, Edward and Oliver Richmond (2006) 'Introduction. Obstacles to Peace Processes: Understanding Spoiling', in Edward Newman and Oliver Richmond (eds),

Challenges to Peacebuilding: Managing Spoilers during Conflict Resolution, Tokyo: United Nations University Press, pp. 1–20.

Newman, Edward, Roland Paris and Oliver Richmond (2009) 'Introduction', in Edward Newman, Roland Paris and Oliver Richmond (eds), *New Perspectives on Liberal Peacebuilding*, Tokyo: United Nations University Press, pp. 3–25.

Newsweek (2007) 'Reliving the Past', *Newsweek*, 27 December 2007, p. 32.

Nikolakopoulos, AIlias, Alkis Rigos and Grigoris Psallidas (eds) (2002) *Emfylios Polemos: Apo ti Varkiza sto Grammo, Fevrouarios 1945–Augoustos 1949* [*The Civil War: From Varkiza to Grammos, February 1945–August 1949*], Athens: Themelio.

Norval, Aletta (1998) 'Memory, Identity and the (Im)possibility of Reconciliation: The Work of the Truth and Reconciliation Commission in South Africa', *Constellations*, vol. 5(2), pp. 250–265.

O'Donnell, Guillermo and Philippe C. Schmitter (1986) *Transitions from Authoritarian Rule*, Baltimore, MD: Johns Hopkins University Press.

Olsen, Tricia, Leigh Payne and Andrew Reiter (2010) *Transitional Justice in Balance: Comparing Processes, Weighing Efficacy*, Washington, DC: US Institute of Peace.

Orentlicher, Diane (1991) 'Settling Accounts: The Duty to Prosecute Human Rights Violations of a Prior Regime', *The Yale Law Journal*, vol. 100(8), pp. 2537–2615.

Ortega, Jose Ignacio Wert (1985) 'The Transition from Below: Public Opinion among the Spanish Population from 1977 to 1979', in Howard Penniman and Eusebio Mujan-Leon (eds), *Spain at Polls. 1977, 1979, and 1982*, North Carolina, NC: Duke University Press, pp. 73–87.

Panayiotou, Andreas (1999) *Island Radicals: The Emergence and Consolidation of the Cyprus Left, 1920–1960*, unpublished PhD thesis, University of California, Santa Cruz.

Pan-Cyprian Organization of Missing Persons (2000) '*Αγνοούμενοι της Κύπρου – Προοπτικές Επίλυσης*'. Minutes of seminar organized by the Pan-Cyprian Organization of Missing Persons, 31 May 2000, Nicosia.

Pan-Cyprian Organization of Missing Persons (2006) '*Διακρίβωση της Τύχης των Αγνοουμένων μια νομική και ανθρωπιστική αναγκαιότητα*'. Minutes of seminar organized by the Pan-Cyprian Organization of Missing Persons, 14 April 2006, Nicosia.

Pan-Cyprian Organization of Relatives of Missing Persons (2000) *Πρακτικά Σεμιναρίου: Αγνοούμενοι της Κύπρου-Προοπτικές Επίλυσης*. Seminar presented on 31 May 2000, Nicosia.

Panourgia, Neni (2009) *Dangerous Citizens. The Greek Left and the Terror of the State*, New York, NY: Fordham University Press.

Papadakis, Yiannis (1993) 'The Politics of Memory and Forgetting', *Journal of Mediterranean Studies*, vol. 3(1), pp. 139–154.

Papadakis, Yiannis (1998) 'Greek Cypriot Narratives of History and Collective Identity: Nationalism as a Contested Process', *American Ethnologist*, vol. 25(2), pp. 149–165.

Papadakis, Yiannis (2006) 'Disclosure and Censorship in Divided Cyprus: Toward an Anthropology of Ethnic Autism', in Yiannis Papadaksi, Nicos Peristianis and Gisela Weiz (eds), *Divided Cyprus: Modernity, History and an Island in Conflict*, Bloomington, IN: Indiana University Press, pp. 66–83.

Paraschos, Andreas (2009) '*Μαρτυρας Δολοφονίας Αιχμαλώτων*', *Καθημερινή*, 11 August 2009, p. 3.

Paroutis, Sotiris (1999) '*Υπόθεση Αγνοουμενων:Ανοίγουν οι Τάφοι των «Αγνώστων»*', *Πολίτης*, 3 June 1999, p. 5.

Pashaloudi, Eleni (2013) '*Η δεκαετία του 1940 στον πολιτικό λόγο: από την αμηχανία των νικητών στη «δικαίωση» των ηττημένων*', in Nikos Demertzis, Elenis Pashaloudi and

Bibliography

Giorgos Antoniou (eds), *Civil War: Cultural Trauma [Εμφύλιος Πόλεμος, Πολιτισμικό Τραύμα]*, Athens: Alexandria, pp. 89–124.

Patrick, Richard A. (1976) *Political Geography and the Cyprus Conflict. 1963–1971*, Waterloo: Department of Geography, University of Waterloo.

Payne, Stanley G. (1990) 'Political Violence during the Spanish Second Republic', *Journal of Contemporary History*, vol. 25(2/3), pp. 269–288.

Pennebaker, James and Becky Banasik (1997) 'On the Creation and Maintenance of Collective Memories: History as Social Psychology', in James W. Pennebaker, Dario Paez and Bernard Rime (eds), *Collective Memory of Political Events. Social Psychological Perspectives*, New Jersey, NJ: Lawrence Erlbaum Publishers, pp. 3–19.

Peristianis, Nicos (2006) 'The Rise of the Left and the Intra-Ethnic Cleavage', in Hubert Faustman and Nicos Peristianis (eds), *Colonialism and Post-Colonialism 1878–2006*, Mannheim: Bibliopolis, pp. 233–267.

Philpott, Daniel (2006) 'Beyond Politics as Usual. Is Reconciliation Compatible with Liberalism?', in Daniel Philpott (ed.), *The Politics of Past Evil, Religion, Reconciliation and the Dilemmas of Transitional Justice*, Notre Dame, IN: University of Notre Dame Press, pp. 11–44.

Pidd, Helen (2011) 'Germans Piece Together Millions of Lives Spied on by Stasi', *Guardian*, 13 March 2011.

Poguntke, Thomas (2004) 'Do Parties Respond? Challenges to Political Parties and their Consequences', in Kay Lawson and Thomas Poguntke (eds), *How Political Parties Respond. Interest Aggression Revisited*, London: Routledge, pp. 1–14.

Politis (1999) '*Οξεια Αντιπαραθεση Υπουργων με τον Οικονόμο Χριστοφορο*', *Politis*, 6 November 1999, p. 3.

Politis (2009) '*Εισαγωγικός Οδηγός στο Δόγμα Δεν Ξεχνώ*' ['Introduction to the "Den Ksehno" Doctrine'], *Politis*, 31 May 2009, p. 76.

Popkin, Margaret and Naomi Roht-Arriaza (1995) 'Truth as Justice: Investigatory Commissions in Latin America', *Law & Social Inquiry*, vol. 20(1), Winter, pp. 79–116.

Poumpouris, Michalis (1999) *Μέρες Δοκιμασίας*, Nicosia: Poumpouris Pub.

Preston, Paul (1990) *The Politics of Revenge. Fascism and the Military in the Twentieth-Century Spain*, London: Unwin Hyman.

Pridham, Geoffrey (2000) 'Confirming Conditions and Breaking with the Past: Historical Legacies, Political Learning in Transitions to Democracy', *Democratization*, vol. 7(2), pp. 36–64.

PSOE (2004) 'Merecemos una España Mejor', Programa Electoral, Elecciones Generales 2004. Available online at: www.psoe.es/ambito/comprometidos/pressnotes/index.do?id=49137&action=View (accessed 23 January 2014).

Ramiro, Luis and Laura Morales (2004) 'Latecomers but "Early-Adapters". The Adaptation and Response of Spanish Parties to Social Changes', in Kay Lawson and Thomas Poguntke (eds), *How Political Parties Respond. Interest Aggression Revisited*, London: Routledge, pp. 198–226.

Richards, Michael (1998) *A Time of Silence. Civil War and the Culture of Repression in Franco's Spain, 1936–1945*, Cambridge: Cambridge University Press.

Richards, Michael (2002) 'From War Culture to Civil Society. Francoism, Social Change and Memories of the Spanish Civil War', *History and Memory*, vol. 14(1/2), pp. 93–120.

Richmond, Oliver (2005a) *The Transformation of Peace*, Basingstoke: Palgrave, Macmillan.

Richmond, Oliver (2005b) 'Shared Sovereignty and the Politics of Peace: Evaluating the EU's "Catalytic" Framework in the Eastern Mediterranean', *International Affairs*, vol. 82(1), pp. 149–176.

Richmond, Oliver and Jason Franks (2009) *Liberal Peace Transitions: Between State-building and Peacebuilding*, Edinburgh: Edinburgh University Press.
Rigby, Andrew (2000) 'Amnesty and Amnesia in Spain', *Peace Review*, vol. 12(1), pp. 73–79.
Risse, Thomas and Kathryn Sikkink (1999) 'The Socialization of International Human Rights Norms into Domestic Practices: Introduction', in Thomas Risse, Steven Ropp and Kathryn Sikkink (eds), *The Power of Human Rights: International Norms and Domestic Change*, Cambridge: Cambridge University Press, pp. 1–38.
Rizospastis (2009) '*Εκδήλωση τιμής και μνήμης διοργάνωσε την περασμένη Κυριακή στον ομαδικό τάφο όπου είναι θαμμένοι οι περίπου 850 μαχητές του ΔΣΕ η ΕΠ Δυτικής Μακεδονίας του ΚΚΕ*', *Rizospastis*, 25 March 2009.
Robins, Simon (2013) *Families of the Missing. A Test for Contemporary Approaches to Transitional Justice*, London: Routledge.
Robinson, Darryl (2003) 'Serving the Interests of Justice: Amnesties, Truth Commissions and the International Criminal Court', *EJIL*, vol. 14(3), pp. 481–505.
Roht-Arriaza, Naomi and Javier Mariezcurrena (2006) *Transitional Justice in the Twenty-First Century: Beyond Truth versus Justice*, Cambridge: Cambridge University Press.
Rori, Lambrini (2008) '*Η Μνήμη της Δεκαετίας του '40 στον Πολιτικό Λόγο του ΠΑΣΟΚ*', in Ricky Van Boshouten, Tasoula Vervenioti, Eftychia Voutira, Vasilis Dalkavoukis and Constantina Bada (eds), *Memories and Oblivion of the Greek Civil War* [*Μνημες και Λήθη του Ελληνικού Εμφυλίου*], Athens: Epikentro, pp. 293–309.
Rosenblum, Nancy L. (2002) 'Justice and the Experience of Injustice', in Martha Minow (ed.), *Breaking the Cycles of Hatred: Memory, Law and Repair*, Princeton, NJ: Princeton University Press, pp. 77–106.
Ross, Marc Howard (2007) *Cultural Contestation in Ethnic Conflict*, Cambridge: Cambridge University Press.
Rossos, Andrew (1997) 'Incompatible Allies: Greek Communism and Macedonian Nationalism in the Civil War in Greece, 1943–1949', *The Journal of Modern History*, vol. 69(1), pp. 42–76.
Rossos, Andrew (2008) *Macedonia and the Macedonians: A History*, Stanford, CA: Hoover Institute Press.
Rotberg, Robert I. and Dennis Thompson (2000) 'The Moral Foundations of Truth Commissions', in Robert I. Rotberg and Dennis Thompson (eds), *Truth V. Justice. The Morality of Truth Commissions*, Princeton, NJ: Princeton University Press, pp. 22–44.
Rothschild, Donald (2002) 'Settlement Terms and Post-Agreement Stability', in Stephen J. Stedman, Donald Rothschild and Elizabeth Cousens (eds), *Ending Civil Wars. The Implementation of Peace Agreements*, London: Lynne Rienner Publishers, pp. 117–138.
Ruiz, Julius (2005) 'A Spanish Genocide? Reflections on the Francoist Repression after the Spanish Civil War', *Contemporary European History*, vol. 14(2), pp. 171–191.
Ruiz, Julius (2007) 'Defending the Republic: The Garcia Atadell Brigade in Madrid, 1936', *Journal of Contemporary History*, vol. 42(1), pp. 97–115.
Ryan, Lorraine (2009) 'For Whom the Dominant Bell Tolls: The Suppression and Re-Emergence of Republican Memory and Identity in Spain', in Laura Rorato and Anna Saunders (eds), *The Essence and the Margin. National Identities and Collective Memories in Contemporary European Culture*, Amsterdam: Rodopi, pp. 119–134.
Salvado, Francisco Romero (2005) *The Spanish Civil War. Origins, Course and Outcomes*, Basingstoke: Palgrave.
Sandbu, Martin (2010) 'Chile Six Months since the Earthquake', *Financial Times*, 28 August 2010.

Sant Cassia, Paul (2005) *Bodies of Evidence. Burial, Memory and the Recovery of Missing Persons in Cyprus*, Oxford: Berghahn Books.

Sant Cassia, Paul (2006a) 'Guarding Each Other's Dead, Mourning One's Own: The Problem of Missing Persons and Missing Pasts in Cyprus', *South European, Society & Politics*, vol. 11(1), pp. 111–128.

Sant Cassia, Paul (2006b) 'Recognition and Emotion: Exhumations of Missing Persons in Cyprus', in Yiannis Papadakis, Nicos Peristianis and Gisela Welz (eds), *Divided Cyprus. Modernity, History, and an Island in Conflict*, Indianapolis, IN: Indiana University Press, pp. 194–213.

Scott, Colleen (2000) 'Combating Myth and Building Reality', in Charles Villa-Vicencio and Wilhelm Verwoerd (eds), *Looking Back, Reaching Forward: Reflections on the Truth and Reconciliation Commission of South Africa*, Cape Town; London: Zed Books, pp. 107–113.

Scott, James C. (1987) *Weapons of the Weak: Everyday Forms of Peasant Resistance*, New Haven, CT: Yale University Press.

Scovazzi, Tullio and Gabriela Citroni (2007) *The Struggle Against Enforced Disappearance and the 2007 UN Convention*, Leiden: Martinus Nihoff Publishers.

Shriver, Donald W. (2003) 'Where and When in Political Life is Justice Served by Forgiveness?', in Nigel Biggar (ed.), *Burying the Past. Making Peace and Doing Justice after Civil Conflict*, Washington, DC: Georgetown University Press, pp. 25–44.

Sikkink, Kathryn (2011) *Justice Cascade. How Human Rights Prosecutions Are Changing World Politics*, New York, NY: Norton and Norton.

Silva, Emilio (2000) 'Mi Abuelo También fue un Desaparecido', *Crónica de León*, 8 October 2000.

Silva, Emilio and Santiago Macias (2009) *Las Fosas del Franco. Los Republicanos que el Dictador dejo en las Cunetas*, Madrid: Ediciones temas de hoy.

Simmons, Tal and William Haglund (2005) 'Anthropology in a Forensic Context', in John Hunter and Margaret Cox (eds), *Forensic Archaeology: Advances in Theory and Practice*, New York, NY: Routledge, pp. 151–173.

Snow, David, Steven Worden Rochford and Robert Benford (1986) 'Frame Alignment Processes, Micromobilization, and Movement Participation', *American Sociological Review*, vol. 51(4), pp. 464–481.

Snyder, Jack and Leslie Vinjamuri (2003) 'Trials and Errors. Principle and Pragmatism in Strategies of International Justice', *International Security*, vol. 28(3), pp. 5–44.

Snyder, Jack and Leslie Vinjamuri (2006) 'A Midwife for Peace', *International Herald Tribune*, 27 September 2006.

Solé i Sabaté, Josep M. and Joan Villaroya (1999) 'Mayo de 1937–Abril de 1939', in Santos Juliá (ed.), *Las Víctimas de la Guerra Civil*, Madrid: Temas de Hoy, pp. 57–178.

Solomonidou, Antigoni (2010) '*Ξενοφών Καλλής: Ποτέ Ξανά Αγνοούμενοι – Ποτέ Ξανά Πόλεμος*', *Fileleftheros*, 29 August 2010, p. 10.

Sotiropoulos, Dimitri A. (2004) 'Formal Weakness and Informal Strength: Civil Society in Contemporary Greece', *Discussion Paper No. 16, LSE/Hellenic Observatory Working Papers*. Available online at: www2.lse.ac.uk/europeanInstitute/research/hellenicObservatory/pubs/DP_oldseries.aspx (accessed 10 October 2012).

Sotiropoulos, Dimitri A. (2010) 'The Authoritarian Past and Contemporary Greek Democracy', *Southern European Society and Politics*, vol. 15(3), pp. 449–465.

Sotiropoulos, Dimitri A. and Evika Karmagioli (2005) 'Greek Civil Society: The Long Road to Maturity', *CIVICUS Civil Society Index Short Assessment Tool*. Available

online at: www.civicus.org/new/media/CSI_Greece_Executive_Summary.pdf (accessed 10 October 2012).
Spicer, Keith (2006) 'The King who Saved Democracy', *Ottawa Citizen*, 1 May 2006, p. 10.
Stedman, Stephen John (1997) 'Spoiler Problems in Peace Processes', *International Security*, vol. 22(2), pp. 5–53.
Stepan, Alfred (1997) 'Democratic Opposition and Democratization Theory', *Government and Opposition*, vol. 32(4), pp. 657–678.
Stover, Eric and Rachel Shigekane (2002) 'The Missing in the Aftermath of War: When Do the Needs of Victims' Families and International War Crimes Tribunals Clash?', *IRRC*, vol. 84(848), December, pp. 845–866.
Stover, Eric, William Haglund and Margaret Samuels (2003) 'Exhumation of Mass Graves in Iraq Considerations for Forensic Investigations, Humanitarian Needs, and the Demands of Justice', *JAMA*, vol. 290(5), pp. 663–666.
Subotic, Jelena (2009) *Hijacked Justice: Dealing with the Past in the Balkans*, Ithaca, NY: Cornell University Press.
Taki, Yiouli and David Officer (2009) 'Civil Society and the Public Sphere', in James Ker-Lindsay and Hubert Faustman (eds), *The Government and Politics of Cyprus*, Oxford: Peter Lang, pp. 205–220.
Tansey, Oisin (2007) 'Process Tracing and Elite Interviewing: A Case of Non-Probability Sampling', *Political Science and Politics*, vol. 40(4), pp. 765–772.
Tarrow, Sidney (1998) *Power in Movement. Social Movements and Contentious Politics*, 2nd edn, Cambridge: Cambridge University Press.
Tarrow, Sidney (2001) 'Silence and Voice in the Study of Contentious Politics: Introduction', in Ronald R. Aminzade *et al.* (eds), *Silence and Voice in the Study of Contentious Politics*, Cambridge: Cambridge University Press, pp. 1–13.
Tarrow, Sidney and Charles Tilly (2007) 'Contentious Politics and Social Movements', in Charles Boix and Susan C. Stokes (eds), *The Oxford Handbook of Comparative Politics*, Oxford: Oxford University Press, pp. 435–460.
Tetlock, Philip E. (1998) 'Social Psychology and World Politics', in Daniel T. Gilbert, Susan T. Fiske and Gardner Linzey (eds), *The Handbook of Social Psychology*, 4th edn, vol. 2, New York, NY: Oxford University Press, 1998, pp. 868–914. .
Theissen, Gunar (2004) 'Supporting Co-Existence and Reconciliation after Armed Conflict: Strategies for Dealing with the Past', *Berghof Research Centre for Constructive Conflict Management*. Available online at: www.berghof-handbook.net (accessed 23 January 2014).
Theodoulou, George (2009) '*Ανοίγουν οι γνωστοί ομαδικοί τάφοι αγνώστων*', *Αλήθεια*, 2 February 2009, p. 13.
Thomas, Hugh (1977) *The Spanish Civil War*, London: Hamish Hamilton.
Thoms, Oskar, Ron Jamer and Ronald Paris (2008) 'The Effects of Transitional Justice Mechanisms', *Center for International Policy Studies, Working Paper*, April 2008.
TIME (1974) 'Man with an Olive Tree', *TIME*, 16 December 1974.
Torrance, Alan (2006) 'The Theological Grounds for Advocating Forgiveness and Reconciliation in the Sociopolitical Realm', in Daniel Philpott (ed.), *The Politics of Past Evil, Religion, Reconciliation and the Dilemmas of transitional Justice*, Notre Dame, IN: University of Notre Dame Press, pp. 45–86.
Tremlett, Giles (2006) 'Newspaper Spat over Madrid Bombs "Conspiracy"', *Guardian*, 15 September 2006.
Tremlett, Giles (2008) 'Franco's Repression Ruled as a Crime against Humanity', *Guardian*, 17 October 2008, p. 31.

196 Bibliography

Tremlett, Giles (2012) 'Baltazar Garzón Cleared over his Franco-era Crimes Inquiry', *Guardian*, 27 February 2012.

Trimikliniotis, Nikos (2007) 'Reconciliation and Social Action in Cyprus: Citizens' Inertia and the Protracted State of Limbo', *Cyprus Review*, vol. 19(1), pp. 125–145.

Tsitselikis, Konstantinos (2008) 'Minority Mobilization in Greece and Litigation in Strasbourg', *International Journal of Minority and Group Rights*, vol. 15, pp. 27–48.

United Nations (1975) *General Assembly Resolution 3450(XXX)*, 9 December 1975.

United Nations (1977) *General Assembly Resolution 32/128*, 16 December 1977.

United Nations (1978) *General Assembly Resolution 33/172*, 20 December 1978.

United Nations (1981) *General Assembly Resolution A/RES/34/164*, 16 December 1981.

United Nations (2004) 'The Rule of Law and Transitional Justice in Conflict and Post-Conflict Societies', *UN Security Council*, S/2004/616/23, August 2004.

United Nations (2008a) A/HRC/7/2/ 'Protection and Promotion of all Human Rights, Civil, Political, Economic, Social and Cultural Rights, Including the Right to Development', *Report of the Working Group on Enforced or Involuntary Disappearances*, 10 January 2008.

United Nations (2008b) UN/CCPR/C/ESP/CO/5, 'Consideration of Reports Submitted by States Parties under Article 40 of the Convenant', *Concluding Observations of the Human Rights Committee*, Spain, 13–31 October 2008.

United Nations (2009) CCPR/C/ESP/CO/5 *Concluding Observations of the Human Rights Committee*, Spain, UN Doc. CCPR/C/ESP/CO/5 (2009), 5 January 2009.

UNFICYP (2007) 'The UN in Cyprus. An Inter-Communal Survey of Public Opinion by UNFICYP', *United Nations Peacekeeping Force in Cyprus*. Available online at: www.unficyp.org/nqcontent.cfm?a_id=1324 (accessed 23 January 2014).

United Nations General Assembly (1992) *Declaration on the Protection of All Persons from Enforced Disappearance*, A/RES/47/133, 18 December 1992.

Usher, Rod (1998) 'The Long Life of Lorca. Spain's Most Translated Poet Outlives his Violent Fate', *The Art/Appreciation*, vol. 151(25), 22 June 1998.

Van Biezen, Igrid and Jonathan Hopkin (2005) 'Presidentialization of Spanish Democracy: Sources of Prime Ministerial Power in Post-Franco Spain', in Thomas Poguntke and Paul Webb (eds), *The Presidentialization of Politics. A Comparative Study of Democracies*, Oxford: Oxford University Press, pp. 107–127.

Vasquez, John A. and Brandon Valeriano (2008) 'Territory as a Source of Conflict and a Road to Peace', in J. Bercovitch, V. Kremenyuk and W. Zartman (eds), *Sage Handbook of Conflict Resolution*, London: Sage, pp. 193–209.

Verdery, Katherine (1999) *The Political Lives of Dead Bodies*, New York, NY: Columbia University Press.

Vervenioti, Tasoula (2000) 'Left-Wing Women between Politics and Family', in Mark Mazower (ed.), *After the War was Over: Reconstructing the Family, Nation and State in Greece, 1943–1960*, Princeton, NJ: Princeton University Press, pp. 105–121.

Vinjamuri, Leslie and Aaron Boesenecker (2007) 'Accountability and Peace Agreements. Mapping Trends from 1980 to 2006', *Centre for Humanitarian Dialogue*, September 2007.

Vinjamuri, Leslie and Jack Snyder (2004) 'Advocacy and Scholarship in the Study of International War Crimes Tribunals and Transitional Justice', *Annual Review of Political Science*, vol. 7, pp. 345–362.

Voglis, Polymeris (2002) *Becoming a Subject: Political Prisoners during the Greek Civil War*, New York, NY: Berghahn Books.

Volkan, Vamik (1997) *Blood Lines: From Ethnic Pride to Ethnic Terrorism*, Boulder, CO: Westview Press.
Voutyra, Efi, Vasilis Dalkavoukis, Nikos Marantzidis and Maria Bontila (eds) (2005) *'To oplo para poda'. Oi politikoi prosfyges tou ellinikou emfyliou polemou stin Anatoliki Europi* [*'Ground Arms'. The Political Refugees of the Greek Civil War in Eastern Europe*], Thessaloniki: University of Macedonia Publications.
Wilson, Richard Ashby (2003) 'Anthropological Studies on National Reconciliation Processes', *Anthropological Theory*, vol. 3(3), pp. 367–387.
Wolpert, Andrew (2001) *Remembering Defeat: Civil War and Civic Memory in Ancient Athens*, New York, NY: The Johns Hopkins University Press.
Woodhouse, C.M. (1979) *The Struggle for Greece, 1941–1949*, London: Ivan R. Dee Publisher.
Woodworth, Paddy (2004) 'Spain Changes Course. Aznar's Legacy, Zapatero's Prospects', *World Policy Journal*, vol. 21(2), pp. 7–26.
Yakinthou, Christalla (2008) 'The Quiet Deflation of Den Xehno? Changes in the Greek–Cypriot Communal Narrative on the Missing Persons in Cyprus', *Cyprus Review*, vol. 20(1), pp. 15–33.
Zafiropoulos, Dimitrios (1956) *The Struggle Against Bandits 1945–1949* [*Ο Αντισυμμοριακός Αγών 1945–1949*], Athens: Mavrides.

Parliamentary Documents

(House of Representatives, Cyprus)

Cyprus, House of Representatives. Law No. 77/1979, *Ο Περί Αγνοουμένων. Νόμος Περιέχων Προσωρινάς Διατάξεις εν Σχέση προς τη Διαχείριση Περιουσίας Αγνοουμένων και Ρυθμίζων Ορισμένα Θέματα εν Σχέση προς την Περιουσίαν Ταύτην και των Αγνοουμένων εν Γένει*.
Cyprus, House of Representatives. Law No. 34/1980, *Ο Περί Ωφελημάτων Αφυπηρετήσεως Αγνοουμένων Κρατικών Υπαλλήλων εις την επίσημον εφημερίδων Κυπριακής Δημοκρατίας συμφώνως τω αρθρω 52 του Συντάγματος*.
Cyprus, House of Representatives. Law No. 53(E)/1992, *Ο Περί Επαγγελματικής Αποκατάστασης Αναπήρων και Εξαρτωμένων των Πεσόντων, Αγνοούμενων, Αναπήρων και Εγκλωβισμένων*.
Cyprus, House of Representatives. Law No. 24(I)/1998, *Ο Περί Ρυθμίσεως των Συνταξιοδοτικών Κρατικών Υπαλλήλων και Υπαλλήλων Οργανισμών των Οργανισμών Δημοσίου Δικαίου*.
Cyprus, House of Representatives. Law No. 178(I)/2003, *Ο Περί Ρυθμίσεως Ορισμένων Θεμάτων Σε Σχέση με τις Περιουσίες Αγνοουμένων*.
Cyprus, House of Representatives. Law No. 17(I)/1993, *Ο Περί Άμεσης Εποπτείας απο τον Πρόεδρο της Δημοκρατίας των Θεμάτων των Αγνοουμένων, Εγκλωσιμένων και Παθόντων*.
Gazette of the House of Representatives. *Κατάλογος Αγνοουμένων Προσώπων Συνεπεία της Τουρκικής Εισβολής του 1974*, no. 3418, 20 July 2000.
Gazette of the House of Representatives. *Κατάλογος Τουρκοκυπρίων Αγνοουμένων*, no. 3713, 12 May 2003.

198 *Bibliography*

Debates

Classified Minutes, Cyprus House of Representatives, Committee on Refugees-Enclaved-Missing-Adversely Affected Persons, 11 February 2004.
Classified Minutes, Cyprus House of Representatives, Committee on Refugees-Enclaved-Missing-Adversely Affected Persons, 19 January 2005.
Parliamentary Debates, House of Representatives, 10 January 1974a, pp. 507–523.
Parliamentary Debates, House of Representatives, 17 January 1974b, pp. 526–551.
Parliamentary Debates, House of Representatives, 23 January 1974c, pp. 564–580.
Parliamentary Debates, House of Representatives, 12 December 1974d, p. 155.
Parliamentary Debates, House of Representatives, 15 July 1975a, p. 576.
Parliamentary Debates, House of Representatives, 15 July 1975b, pp. 576–591.
Parliamentary Debates, House of Representatives, 15 July 1975c, p. 581.
Parliamentary Debates, House of Representatives, 14 July 1978, p. 1807.
Parliamentary Debates, House of Representatives, 15 July 1979, p. 1886.
Parliamentary Debates, House of Representatives, 15 July 1980, pp. 2013–2023.
Parliamentary Debates, House of Representatives, 15 July 1981a, pp. 265–277.
Parliamentary Debates, House of Representatives, 15 July 1981b, p. 269.
Parliamentary Debates, House of Representatives, 10 December 1981c, pp. 723–744.
Parliamentary Debates, House of Representatives, 7 January 1982a, pp. 938–980.
Parliamentary Debates, House of Representatives, 14 January 1982b, pp. 1041–1076.
Parliamentary Debates, House of Representatives, 21 January 1982c, pp. 1091–1213.
Parliamentary Debates, House of Representatives, 28 January 1982d, p. 1154.
Parliamentary Debates, House of Representatives, 28 January 1982e, p. 1187.
Parliamentary Debates, House of Representatives, 11 February 1982f, p. 129.
Parliamentary Debates, House of Representatives, 11 February 1982g, pp. 1250–1303.
Parliamentary Debates, House of Representatives, 18 February 1982h, pp. 1358–1402.
Parliamentary Debates, House of Representatives, 15 July 1982i, pp. 2785–2798.
Parliamentary Debates, House of Representatives, 15 July 1983, pp. 1419–1431.
Parliamentary Debates, House of Representatives, 15 July 1985, pp. 2199–2213.
Parliamentary Debates, House of Representatives, 15 July 1987, pp. 2987–2997.
Parliamentary Debates, House of Representatives, 13 July 1989, pp. 2955–2958.
Parliamentary Debates, House of Representatives, 15 July 1991, pp. 279–289.
Parliamentary Debates, House of Representatives, 16 July 1992a, pp. 3581–3592.
Parliamentary Debates, House of Representatives, 16 July 1992b, p. 3607.
Parliamentary Debates, House of Representatives, 15 July 1993, pp. 2455–2465.
Parliamentary Debates, House of Representatives, 15 July 1994a, pp. 2539–2554.
Parliamentary Debates, House of Representatives, 15 July 1994b, p. 2554.
Parliamentary Debates, House of Representatives, 9 January 2001, pp. 94–104.
Parliamentary Debates, House of Representatives, 24 January 2002, p. 300.
Parliamentary Debates, House of Representatives, 10 January 2003, pp. 69–87.

Resolutions

House of Representatives, Resolution 37 (1975a).
House of Representatives, Resolution 75 (1975b).
House of Representatives, Resolution 46 (1978).
House of Representatives, Resolution, 75 (1982).
House of Representatives, Resolution 113 (1992).

House of Representatives, Resolution 17 (2007a) (3 May 2007).
House of Representatives, Resolution 19 (2007b).
House of Representatives, Resolution 25 (2008) (8 May 2008).
House of Representatives, Resolution 18 (2009) (29 January 2009).

Spanish Parliament (Cortes)

Congreso (Lower House)

Diario De Sesiones del Pleno (Congreso), no. 5, 27 July 1977a, pp. 66–72.
Diario De Sesiones del Pleno (Congreso), no. 5, 27 July 1977b, pp. 73–76.
Diario De Sesiones del Pleno (Congreso), no. 5, 27 July 1977c, pp. 82–84.
Diario De Sesiones del Pleno (Congreso), no. 5, 27 July 1977d, pp. 85–94.
Diario De Sesiones del Pleno (Congreso), no. 24, 14 October 1977a, pp. 959–961.
Diario De Sesiones del Pleno (Congreso), no. 24, 14 October 1977b, pp. 961–963.
Diario De Sesiones del Pleno (Congreso), no. 24, 14 October 1977c, pp. 965–968.
Diario De Sesiones del Pleno (Congreso), no. 24, 14 October 1977d, pp. 968–970.
Diario De Sesiones del Pleno (Congreso), no. 24, 14 October 1977e, pp. 970–971.
Diario De Sesiones del Pleno (Congreso), no. 24, 14 October 1977f, pp. 972–973.
Diario De Sesiones del Pleno (Congreso), no. 141, 23 November 1978a, pp. 5575–5576.
Diario De Sesiones del Pleno (Congreso), no. 141, 23 November 1978b, pp. 5576–5578.
Diario De Sesiones del Pleno (Congreso), no. 195, 1 December 1978c, pp. 4199–4201.
Diario De Sesiones del Pleno (Congreso), no. 411, 27 September 2002a, pp. 4–6.
Diario De Sesiones del Pleno (Congreso), no. 411, *Proposición no de Ley por el Grupo Parlamentario Mixto, Sobre la Devolución de la Dignidad a los Familiares de los Fusilados durante el Franquismo*, 27 September 2002b, pp. 4–6.
Diario De Sesiones del Pleno (Congreso), no. 412, *Proposición no de Ley Presentada por el Grupo Parlamentario Socialista, por la que se declara y se Insta a los poderes públicos a reparar moralmente a las víctimas de la Guerra Civil desaparecidas y asesinadas por defender valores republicanos y a reconocer el derecho de familiares y herederos a recuperar sus restos, nombre y dignidad*, 30 September 2002c, pp. 6–8.
Diario De Sesiones del Pleno (Congreso), no. 423, *Proposición no de Ley por el Grupo Parlamentario Federal de la Izquierda Unida, para Proceder a las Exhumaciones de las Fosas Comunes de la Guerra Civil*, 22 October 2002d, pp. 9–11.
Diario De Sesiones del Pleno (Congreso), no. 625 (161/001591), Alcaraz Massats, 20 November 2002e, pp. 20503–20505.
Diario De Sesiones del Pleno (Congreso), no. 625 (161/001636), Valcarce Garcia, 20 November 2002f, pp. 20507–20508.
Diario De Sesiones del Pleno (Congreso), no. 444, *Proposición no de Ley presentada por el Grupo Parlamentario Mixto, sobre la devolución de la dignidad a los familiares de los fusilados durante el franquismo*, 25 November 2002g, pp. 10–11.
Diario De Sesiones del Pleno (Congreso), no. 76 (122/000008), Atencia Robledo, 15 March 2005a, p. 2645.
Diario De Sesiones del Pleno (Congreso), no. 76 (122/000008), Atencia Robledo, 15 March 2005b, p. 3645.
Diario De Sesiones del Pleno (Congreso), no. 625 (161/001591), Atencia Robledo, 20 November 2005c, pp. 20515–20517.

200 Bibliography

Diario De Sesiones del Pleno (Congreso), no. 172 (122/000180), Cerda Argent, 27 April 2006a, p. 8609.
Diario De Sesiones del Pleno (Congreso), no. 172 (122/000180), Cerda Argent, 27 April 2006b, pp. 8609–8611.
Diario De Sesiones del Pleno (Congreso), no. 172 (122/000180), Atencia Robledo, 27 April 2006c, pp. 8613–8615.
Diario De Sesiones del Pleno (Congreso), no. 172 (122/000180), Jauregui Atondo, 27 April 2006d, pp. 8615–8617.
Diario de Sesiones del Pleno (Senado), no. 84, Muñoz Alonso, 23 May 2006e, pp. 4967–4971.
Diario De Sesiones del Pleno (Congreso), no. 187 (122/000180), Atencia Robledo, 22 June 2006f, pp. 9400–9401.
Diario De Sesiones del Pleno (Congreso), no. 222 (121/000099), Atencia Robledo, 14 December 2006g, pp. 11259–11262.
Diario De Sesiones del Pleno (Congreso), no. 222 (121/000099), Tarda i Coma, 14 December 2006h, pp. 11262–11264.
Diario De Sesiones del Pleno (Congreso), no. 222 (121/000099), Torres Mora, 14 December 2006i, pp. 11280–11281.
Diario De Sesiones del Pleno (Congreso), no. 296 (121/000099), Zaplana Henrandez-Soro, 31 October 2007a, pp. 14627–14630.
Diario De Sesiones del Pleno (Congreso), no. 296 (121/000099), 31 October 2007b, p. 14633.

Laws and Royal Decrees

Real Decreto Ley 6/1978(a), *De 6 de marzo, por el que se regula la situación de los militares que tomaron parte en la guerra civil*, no. 69, 14 March 1978, pp. 1253–1254.
Real Decreto Ley 43/1978(b), *Por el que se reconococen beneficios económicos a los que sufrieron lesiones y mutilaciones en la guerra civil española*, no. 221, 23 December 1978, pp. 4718–4721.
Real Decreto Ley 8/1980, no. 39–v, 22 October 1980.
Real Decreto Ley 1891/2004, *Por el que se crea la Comisión Interministerial para el estudio de la situación de las víctimas de la guerra civil y del franquismo*, 10 September 2004.
Ley 5/1979, *De 18 de septiembre, sobre reconocimiento de pensiones, asistencia médico-farmacéutica y asistencia social en favor de las viudas, y demás familiares de los españoles fallecidos como consecuencia o con ocasión de la pasada guerra civil*, 18 September 1979.
Ley 37/1984, *De 22 de octubre, de reconocimiento de derechos y servicios prestados a quienes durante la guerra civil formaron parte de las Fuerzas Armadas, Fuerzas de Orden Público y Cuerpo de Carabineros de la República*. BOE no. 262, 1 November 1984.
Ley 18/1984, *De 8 de junio, sobre reconocimiento como años trabajados a efectos de la Seguridad Social de los períodos de prisión sufridos como consecuencia de los supuestos contemplados en la Ley de Amnistía de 15 de octubre de 1977*. BOE no. 140, 12 June 1984.
Ley 24/2006, de 7 de julio, *Sobre declaración del año 2006 como Año de la Memoria histórica*. BOE no. 162, 8 June 2006.

Ley 52/2007, *Por la que se reconocen y amplían derechos y se establecen medidas a favor de quienes padecieron persecución o violencia durante la guerra civil y la dictadura*. BOE no. 310, 27 December 2007.

Boletín Oficial del Estado (BOE) (Official Bulletin of the State)

Boletin Oficial del Estado (BOE), *Orden de 7 Febrero de 1940 aprobando modelo y Regulando los Derechos de Expedicion de actas de Exhumacion*, 8 February 1940, no. 39, pp. 1015–1016.

Boletin Oficial del Estado (BOE), *Decreto Numero 67*, 11 November 1936, no. 27, p. 154.

Boletin Official del Estado (BOE), *Decreto Numero 174*, 11 January 1937, no. 83, p. 85.

Legal Framework on Missing Persons in the Republic of Cyprus

Law No. 77/1979, *Ο Περί Αγνοουμένων Νόμος*, 19 October 1979.

Law No. 34/1980, *Ο Περί Ωφελημάτων Αφυπηρετήσεως Αγνοουμένων Κρατικών Υπαλλήλων*, 20 June 1980.

Law No. 41/1980, *Ο Περί Κοινωνικών Ασφαλίσεων Νόμος*, 16 July 1980.

Law No. 53(I)/1992, *Ο Περί Επαγγελματικής Αποκατάστασης των Αναπήρων και των Εξαρτωμένων των Πεσόντων, Αγνοουμένων, Αναπήρων και Εγκλωβισμένων*, 10 July 1992.

Law No. 24(I)/1998, *Νόμος που Προβλέπει τον Υπολογισμό και την Καταβολή Συνταξιοδοτικών Ωφελημάτων στους Κρατικούς Υπαλλήλους και στους Υπαλλήλους των Οργανισμών Δημοσίου Δικαίου που είναι Αγνοούμενοι*, 16 April 1998.

Law No. 178(I)/2003, *Νομος Που Περιέχει Διατάξεις σε Σχέση με την Περιουσία Αγνοουμένου και Ρυθμίζει ορισμένα Θεματα σε Σχεση με την Περιουσία του*, 28 November 2003.

Legal Framework in Post-Civil War Greece

Law No. 1543/1985, *On the Pension Rights of National Resistance Fighters, the Rehabilitation of Resistance Fighters who were Prosecuted for their Social Views and the Pension Rights of Fighters against the Dictatorship*.

Law No. 1863/1989, *Lifting the Adverse Consequences of the Civil War, 1944–1949*, 18 September 1989.

Law No. 1285/1992, *On Recognition of the National Resistance of the Greek People against the Occupation Forces, 1941–1944*, 20 September 1982.

Law No. 2910/2010, *Greek Nationality Code*, 24 March 2010.

Ministerial Decree of the Presidency, Ministry of Interior, Justice and Public Order, 28 August 1989.

Archival Research (Interviú Magazine)

Interviú (1977a) 'Galicia: Recuerdos de los Crímenes Fascistas', *Interviú*, no. 103 (4–10 May 1977), pp. 60–64.

Interviú (1977b) 'La otra Historia del Abad Escarré. Monsterrat, Símbolo Antifranquista', *Interviú* (July 1977), pp. 38–41.

202   Bibliography

Interviú (1977c) 'Las Matanzas no se Olvidan. Como García Lorca, Miles de Personas Fueron Asesinadas por los Fascistas', *Interviú*, no. 81 (July 1977), pp. 32–34.

Interviú (1977d) 'Otro valle de los Caídos: La Barrana, Fosa Común para 2000 Riojanos', *Interviú*, no. 74 (13–19 October 1977), Martínez Esteban, pp. 88–90.

Interviú (1978a) 'Navarra 1936 (2) Los Verdugos de la Cruzada', *Interviú*, no. 137 (28 February 1978), pp. 20–22.

Interviú (1978b) 'Mi Vida en Carbanchel', *Interviú* (18 April 1978), pp. 59–61.

Interviú (1978c) 'Un Vendaval de Sangre y Terror. En Galicia, Aquel Verano del 36', *Interviú*, no. 103 (4–10 May 1978), Costa Clavel, Xavier, pp. 60–64.

Interviú (1978d) 'El Pueblo Desentierra a sus Muertos. Casas de Don Pedro, 39 Años Después de la Matanza', *Interviú*, no. 119 (15–21 June 1978), Catalán Deus, José, pp. 86–88.

Interviú (1978e) 'Las Esquelas Franquistas: Una Generación de Tarados', *Interviú* (15 June 1978), pp. 38–41.

Interviú (1978f) 'Navarra 1936 (1) Fusilados por Dios y por España', *Interviú*, no. 136 (21–27 November 1978), Gimenez Plaza, Dionosio, pp. 76–79.

Interviú (1978g) 'Navarra: Fusilados por Dios y por España', *Interviú*, no. 136 (21 December 1978), pp. 76–79; Interviú (1980) '17 Pueblos Recuperan 211 Cadáveres. Legionarios Fusilados por Falangistas', *Interviú*, no. 190 (3 January 1980), pp. 75–77; Interviú (1936) 'NAVARRA 1936 (2) Los verdugos de la Cruzada', *Interviú*.

Interviú (1978h) 'Navarra: Fusilados por Dios y por España', *Interviú*, no. 136 (21 December 1978), pp. 76–79.

Interviú (1979) 'Las Primeras Venganzas Fascistas. Gibraleón, Julio 1936', *Interviú*, Damiano González, Cipriano, no. 142 (1–7 February 1979), pp. 78–81.

Interviú (1980a) '17 Pueblos Recuperan 211 Cadáveres. Legionarios Fusilados por Falangistas', *Interviú*, no. 190 (3 January 1980), pp. 75–77; Interviú (1936) 'NAVARRA 1936 (2) Los Verdugos de la Cruzada', *Interviú*, no. 136, pp. 20–24.

Interviú (1980b) 'La Universidad Antifranquista, Réquiem por el Movimiento Estudiantil (1)', *Interviú* (30 January 1980), pp. 38–40.

Index

accountability 5, 14, 150
amnesty: in Greece 133; law in Spain 25–32, 42n13; paradox 162, 165; in literature 4–6, 17n8, 70–3, 76, 130, 148, 150, 153, 154, 159n2; efforts to circumvent amnesty law in Spain 99–102, 153; policy proposals on amnesties 166
Association for the Recovery of Historical Memory (ARMH) 1, 81, 85, 88–91, 99, 104

Bakoyiannis assassination 136
Baltazar Garzón 35, 153
broader truth *see* truth recovery

Carillo 30, 133, 137
Clerides 65n17, 65n29, 72, 107, 111, 113, 114
Coalition of the Radical Left (SYRIZA) 133, 143, 145
Committee on Missing Persons (CMP) 3, 10, 12, 43, 45, 54, 65n24, 107; critique of CMP's mandate 16n4; exhumations by CMP 44, 64n1, 106 public perception of CMP 106; resumption of its activities 2, 46, 53, 55, 108, 111, 116–24; terms of CMP 155
Cyprus conflict 2, 43, 44, 50, 117, 118, 124, 132; culture of victimhood *see* victimhood; linked to Missing Persons *see* linkage policy; position of the two communities on 44; silence 46–7
delayed justice *see* post-transitional justice
delinkage policy: Cyprus 110–15, 118, 122–4; negotiations 11, 108, 109, 121, 122; Spain 28, 84, 102, 103
Democratic Army of Greece (DSE) 14, 127, 127, 128, 131–41, 146n5, 146n12
Denktaş Rauf 53, 61, 107, 111–14, 117, 120, 124, 167

disappearances *see* enforced disappearances
DNA 26, 48, 113, 116, 121, 138, 155, 156

enforced disappearances: in Cyprus 2, 43–5, 48–53, 62, 106–9, 115, 116, 121, 125; in Greece 14, 130–2, 135, 136, 144; in Northern Ireland 68; forensic science 154–6; legal framework and definitions 5, 9, 10, 17n10, 22, 91, 108, 119, 126n16, 138, 152, 153, 157, 160; post transitional justice and 3, 108, 113, 150; transitional justice and 6–10; truth recovery and 7–9
Enosis 2, 51, 55, 56, 58, 65n20
European Court of Human Rights (ECtHR) 53, 54, 117, 118, 119, 120, 124, 129, 147n19, 153, 154, 157
exhumations: in Cyprus *see* CMP; in Spain during civil war 24, 81; in Spain during transition 25, 34; in Spain since 2000 1, 24, 26, 35, 82, 87–92, 99; post-conflict 7, 8, 33

Florina: battle of 127, 128, 138, 141; grave 14, 127–32, 137, 139–45
forensic science 26, 48, 108, 113, 151, 154, 164
Foro Por La Memoria 16n1, 91
framing 11, 12, 49, 52, 102; diagnostic framing 27, 28, 31, 50, 51, 134; elite framing 11, 12, 15, 25–8, 32, 36, 49, 54, 67, 84 ,100, 105, 133–9, 149, 152, 164, 165; prognostic framing 27, 29, 30, 34, 50, 66n32, 101, 102
Francoism 1, 13, 28–32, 35, 38, 40, 41n5, 42n10, 75, 82, 87, 90, 98, 103, 105n1, 130–3; repression during 21–4, 28, 81, 89, 93, 99

204 Index

frozen conflict 10, 108, 158

González Felipe Márquez 94
Greek Civil War 3, 14, 16, 56, 127, 137, 149; atrocities 127, 129, 139 memory of 12, 40, 127–9, 134, 140–2, 146n2; missing of 14, 130, 133; reconciliation 132–7, 146n1
Greek Communist Party (KKE) 140, 141, 144, 145

hegemony 102, 105, 112, 124, 141, 149, 151, 165; hegemonic framing 102, 114, 162–6

International Committee for Missing Persons (ICMP) 130, 146n4, 156, 159n8
international norms 5, 14, 70, 83, 84, 100, 103–5, 108, 111, 113, 118–20, 124, 145, 152–4, 164; socialization into 11, 15, 83, 84, 100, 105, 111, 113, 118, 131, 142, 145, 156; socialization of Greek parties into 131, 142, 143, 156
Intrerviú: exhumations during transition 25, 27, 34; Interviú magazine 34, 42n18

justice cascade 5
Justice and Development Party (AKP) 117–19, 124

Kallis Xenophon 111–14
Kasoulides Ioannis 112, 114, 115
Küçük Gülden Plümer 123
Kyrkos Leonidas 133, 137

Law of Historical Memory 2, 16, 24, 25, 30, 39, 81, 82, 97–104
linkage policy: in Cyprus 50–1, 53, 108; in Greece 131, 137–42; in Spain 100, 101; linkage trap 14, 67, 69; negotiation and 15, 63, 69, 108
logic of appropriateness 3–5, 17n8, 118, 145
logic of consequences 4, 5, 17n8, 110, 137, 149
Lorca Federico Garcia 1, 81, 99, 169

Macedonian question 138, 145
Makarios 49, 51, 53, 56, 65n20, 65n30
management of the personal files of the secret policy in Greece 130, 135–7
missing persons see enforced dissappearances

narrow truth see Truth Recovery

National Organization of Cypriot Struggle (EOKA) 56, 65n28, 74
negotiated transition see pacted transitions

pact of silence 1, 13, 15, 21, 38, 81–5, 100, 104, 105, 137
pacted transitions 35, 63, 67–9
Pan-Cyprian organization of relatives 60, 62
Panhellenic Socialist Movement (PASOK) 14, 40, 134, 135, 139, 140, 146n13
Papandreou Andreas 134
Popular Party (PP) 38, 40, 42n12, 42n22

political institutions 15, 27, 33, 36, 69, 86, 162; in Cyprus 49, 52, 54, 58; role of institutions in truth recovery 5, 7, 14, 34, 36, 63, 67, 70, 71, 149, 150, 160, 163; in Spain 37, 39, 41, 92
political learning 11, 15, 16, 25, 29, 55, 57, 65n29, 67, 69, 108, 124, 151, 162, 164
political opportunities 11, 85–7, 92
post-transitional justice 3, 10, 12, 14–16, 130, 136, 139, 142, 145, 148–51, 156, 157
Progressive Party for the Working People (AKEL) 40, 51, 52, 55–9, 65n30, 68
prolonged silences 47, 130, 150, 162, 164

realist 5, 8, 13, 17n8
reconciliation 3–14, 17n8, 28–34, 40, 47, 52, 63, 64n10, 69–74, 81; in Cyprus 156–8, 169; in Greece 131–7, 144, 145, 146n1; in Spain 101, 012, 104, 108
Republic of Cyprus (RoC): application to ECtHR 109, 110, 118, 119, 126n18, 153, 159n6; EU accession 112, 120, 126n15, 126n19; House of Representatives 51, 52, 54, 59; institutions in 58, 59, 172; Ministry of foreign affairs 11; political learning 69, 72, 74, 151, 162; transition 57–60, 68, 72; unilateral exhumations 107, 113
restorative justice 6, 71
retributive justice 4, 5, 72, 145

silence 1, 8, 10, 12, 15, 68, 70, 74, 149, 154; breaking of 59, 104, 150, 152, 162; construction of 11, 16, 67–9, 148, 150, 160, 161; in Cyprus 46, 47, 55, 57, 59, 63; in Greece 14, 130, 133–45; in Spain 1, 13, 23, 27, 33, 36, 38, 42n13, 81–5, 100–4; selective 59, 63, 68, 133, 145, 149

Slav-Macedonians 127, 128, 137–44, 146n3, 157; citizenship of 139, 144; securitization 140, 156
Spanish Civil war: atrocities 21, 22, 25; disappeared 1, 12, 13, 22–4, 27, 32–4, 41n8, 75, 83, 87, 89,, 92, 93, 97, 99, 100, 103; mass graves 42n15, 81, 82, 88, 156; memory of 24, 25, 28, 30, 33, 38, 41n7, 82, 87, 93; silence *see* silence in Spain; reconciliation *see* reconciliation in Spain
Spanish Communist Party (PCE) 29, 39, 68
Spanish Socialist Workers' Party (PSOE) 13, 24, 25, 38–41, 68, 83, 92–103, 135

Taksim 2
Talat Mehmet Ali 46, 120, 124, 167
transitional justice 3, 4, 6–10, 17n7, 46, 67, 71–6, 107, 108, 148; in Cyprus 47, 48, 63; in Greece 14, 136; in Spain 130
trials 2–7, 10, 17n8, 32, 70, 72, 82, 130, 150, 159n1, 161, 164

truth commissions 3–10, 70, 73, 75, 154, 155, 159n1, 164
truth recovery 7, 8; critique of 6, 7; narrow truth 7, 17n8, 24, 34, 36; broader truth 149; right to truth 103, 147n19
truth seekers 14, 15, 26, 38, 69, 70, 105, 148, 150, 163
Turkey: missing in Turkey 130; stance on missing in Cyprus 45, 48, 54, 108, 112, 114, 117–20
Tzionis 112, 114, 117

UN Working Group on Enforced or Involuntary Disappearances (WGEID) 89, 144, 152, 153, 159n3

valley of the fallen 22, 81, 98
victimhood 122; cultures of 2, 5, 9, 52, 66n38, 67, 68, 74, 149, 158; in Cyprus 15, 52, 53, 60, 63, 75, 76